THE RUSSIAN REVOLUTION

THE RUSSIAN REVOLUTION

JOHN BRADLEY

Bison Books

Page 1: Soldiers in Petrograd demonstrate their support for the February Revolution.

Page 2-3: Lenin discusses the plan for the electrification of Russia.

Below: The smashed statue of Czar Alexander III in Moscow.

Published by
Bison Books Ltd
Kimbolton House
117A Fulham Road
London SW3 6RL
England

Copyright © 1988 Bison Books Ltd.

ISBN 0-86124-454-0

Printed in Hong Kong

Reprinted 1989

CONTENTS

Introduction	6	War on all Fronts	126
Romanovs and Revolutionaries	8	Trotsky's Red Army	144
Russia at War	22	Lenin Triumphant	164
The February Revolution	40	Stalin and the State	178
Provisional Government	52		
The October Revolution	68	Revolutionary Parties	188
Soviets and Strikes	88	Index	190
Assault from the East	104	Acknowledgments	192

INTRODUCTION

The Bolshevik Revolution of 1917 and the subsequent protracted civil war which ended in 1922 saw the emergence, against all the odds, of the first modern communist state based, at least in principle, on economic and political collectivism. The core of Marxist philosophy, the intellectual force behind the thinking of the Bolshevik Party and its charismatic leader, Vladimir Ilyich Ulyanov (Lenin), was the overthrow of the existing order. When applied to Russia, this meant the destruction of the czarist regime, its power structure and its servants. The old system was to be replaced by common ownership and a political apparatus based on committees of workers (Soviets). The process of change was to be brought about by violent revolution controlled and directed by a close-knit group of politically-inspired intellectuals – the powerhouse of the revolution. The politicized industrial working class would provide the revolutionary 'muscle.'

The process of modernization was nothing new in Russia. Previous rulers, notably Peter the Great in the eighteenth century, had made attempts to carry out reforms by importing outside ideas and technologies. These so-called 'revolutions from above' did not include sweeping social and political change, however. Political power was always destined to remain firmly in the hands of the czar. The established order – both the conservative elite and the semi-literate peasantry – never fully accepted the edicts of reformist absolute monarchs like Peter. Change was never as widespread or as deep as planned, and what little progress that was achieved provoked rather than satisfied Russian society. Both the administrative class and the peasants willingly forsook change for stability and the maintenance of order.

Members of small intellectual circles, groups calling for limited political freedom, offered only weak opposition to the status quo. Many paid a high price for voicing their opposition. The Russian security forces, though corrupt and inefficient, were quite able to stifle any low-level internal dissent. Despite the power of the established order, revolution did break out in the aftermath of the disasterous Russo-Japanese War (1904-05). Popular uprisings did occur throughout Russia but these were ill-coordinated and, above all, lacked any guiding force of organized revolutionaries. The czar's armed forces remained loyal to the crown and swept the demonstrators from the streets. Yet the political situation in Russia had changed so dramatically by 1917 that the czarist regime was violently and totally overthrown in the space of a few months.

By the third year of World War I the imperial system was no longer able to contain the forces that were poised to bring about its downfall. Famine, massive losses at the front and brutal repression all played their part in the outbreak of widespread unrest. Nicholas II might still have survived were it not for the political will of Lenin. The 1917 Revolution did not run smoothly for the Bolsheviks and its final outcome remained in doubt until the end of the civil war. Assailed by czarist forces and foreign interventionary troops, the Bolshevik Red Army fought well, but without the skill of Lenin the outcome might have been very different.

Left: Soldiers and civilians celebrate May Day in Petrograd, 1917.

Right: A Bolshevik propaganda poster of 1919 shows the Mensheviks in league with czarist generals, priests and landlords.

ROMANOVS AND REVOLUTIONARIES

Some historians, both Russian and Western, detect in Russian history a specific pattern in which periods of seemingly great stability are followed by periods of chaos (*stikhiynost*). As a result of wars, internal conflicts, social upheaval or power struggles, the structure of the state suddenly and inexplicably collapses, the very fabric of Russian society disintegrates and the dreaded *stikhiynost* takes over. The Russian people have come to fear the 'time of trouble' (*smuta*) most of all. Even if they detest the state and the established regime and abhor its repressive measures, they still prefer the status quo to the chaos which seems to follow the collapse of authority. Russian regimes have exploited this popular fear to strengthen their own power, though they have also tried to avert chaos by anticipating events. The modernization drive of Nicholas II early in this century, when constitutional monarchy was introduced, was an attempt to stem the tide of dissolution. As seen with Peter I, the Russian imperial system of government was designed for strong rulers; only such rulers could use the system to defeat revolutionary change. Unfortunately, Nicholas II was not a strong ruler and his corrupt regime provoked rather than pacified Russian society.

Previous page: Russian peasants undergoing interrogation in a St Petersburg police station following the assassination attempt on Czar Alexander II in 1880.

Opposite page: A painting of Alexander II as the liberator of the Slavs from Turkish rule in 1877. The style is that of an icon, with scenes around the edge from the battles of the Russian Army (icons of saints often have scenes from the life of the saint around the edge).

Below: Lenin, leader of the Bolshevik uprising in 1917.

The ignominious collapse of the imperial regime in March 1917 can be seen as conclusive proof that the weak monarch had been unable to stop the slide into dissolution that had begun before he ascended the throne. The basic causes of the decline and fall of Russian autocracy (*samoderzhavie*) can be traced to the generations that preceded it, particularly to the reign of Nicholas's grandfather, Alexander II (1855-81). Alexander II did prove capable of stemming the tide of dissolution, which followed the defeat of his father, Nicholas I, in the Crimean War. Though he launched a modernization drive, Alexander had no intention of depriving himself or his successors of absolute power; indeed it was a necessary prerequisite to carrying out his reforms.

The most momentous of Alexander II's reforms was the emancipation of the peasants, over 80 percent of the empire's population. Alexander hoped the reforms would win the support of the overwhelming majority of his subjects. However, because of the long delay, the peasants' expectations were never fully met. Moreover the liberated peasants chose to express their dissatisfaction in unprecedented, 'revolutionary' ways. In the comparatively free days of Alexander's reign, they were able to organize revolutionary movements demanding full freedom: enough land for everyone to be prosperous and secure from famine.

From 1861 free peasants could leave their land holdings and could migrate to urban areas in search of work. Neither Alexander nor anyone else in Russia had any idea of what forces were being unleashed. On the one hand, the most intensive period of industrial development the empire had ever known was ushered in. On the other hand, a new social group was created, the industrial working class. Just like the emancipated peasants, the new industrial class started to organize bodies to put their grievances to the authorities.

In 1861 neither the landlords, who owned some 22,000,000 serfs, nor the liberated serfs were satisfied by the reforms. The former disliked them for economic reasons and sabotaged their execution to the last. The free peasants did not get as much land as they expected. Years later, they were still waiting for another 'emancipation' reform to put this injustice right. Even the freed serfs, if they wanted to work their land, had to stay in the old communities where land was allocated on the basis of family size and frequently rotated as family numbers increased or decreased. Slavophiles liked the system because it was traditional and because redemption fees for emancipation could be collected more easily from stable communities than from individual peasants. Apart from making the peasants highly dissatisfied, the communes were a hindrance to the modernization of agriculture itself. When they were given special legal status, the old-style villages became a type of ghetto.

While discontented peasants were making life dangerous in the country, their city champions, the Slavophile intelligentsia, set the towns aflame. As early as 1861 the intelligentsia and students took advantage of Alexander's

reforms and founded the first revolutionary society, Land and Liberty. Neither Alexander nor his government took 'secret' societies or their newspapers clamoring for 'freedom' seriously. The political 'revolutionaries' seemed to the government to be much more troublesome than the rebellious peasants or the restless students. These new revolutionaries consisted not only of the intelligentsia, but also of many liberal-minded nobles and state servants themselves.

From the beginning of Alexander's modernization, it was assumed by everyone, except the monarch, that political change would also be on the agenda. Ever since Peter the Great's days politics was the monopoly of the monarch and of his servant, the government. No one else could take part in such proceedings. Many Russians mistakenly thought that a constitutional monarchy would be established in which all the necessary freedoms would be granted. However, Alexander failed to think his reforms through to their logical conclusion. As early as 1856, when the Emancipation Commission started to depart from its narrow brief by suggesting the extension of political freedom, he firmly squashed such ideas. Alexander rejected all moderate proposals for constitutional reform until January 1881, but it was too late. He was assassinated on 1 March 1881 by Land and Liberty revolutionaries.

Only early and real constitutional reforms could have dampened the revolutionary spirit of non-Russian nationalities, especially the Poles. The Poles, not as patient as the Russian peasants, would not wait 100 years for their freedom. In 1863 they rose in revolt and Alexander used Russian forces to put them down. In 1866 the more impatient Russian revolutionaries attempted to assassinate Alexander but failed. These two events gave the imperial government an excuse for not only delaying any further reform, but also for ruthless retaliation against the Poles and the revolutionaries, which action alienated Russian society as a whole. Thus while writers were executed or sent into exile, an important civil servant thought that 'our most important enemies were neither the Poles nor the revolutionaries, but the lack of sincerity and good faith by the government.'

The polarization of Russian society became as extreme as the government's measures. As the government would not share power with anyone, Russians built for themselves parallel 'governmental' structures. In 1864 Alexander set up elective bodies, *zemstva*, to administer the Russian provinces. They were organs of local government responsible for roads, schools, health, famine relief and such tasks, but central government tried to direct them. They had no control over the police and the minister of the interior had to confirm their elected chairmen. Within the next 30 years they were transformed into a 'parallel' administration in which the government's authority did not apply. During World War I the *zemstva* became an indispensable part of Russia's power structure and Prince G Ye Lvov, the chairman of the All-Russian Union of *Zemstva*, became the first non-imperial prime minister in 1917.

Apart from being an alternative government, the *zemstva* were important employers of full-time propagators of liberal and anti-government ideas, the so-called 'third element.' These revolutionaries, some 70,000 by 1903, with their constant preaching of reform, widened the gap between the central government and the *zemstva* until it became unbridgeable. In addition they prepared the country for a form of revolutionary change quite distinct from that of the 'political' revolutionaries. Though subject to government harassment, these men became the only surviving activists after the long years of severe repression which followed the assassination of Alexander II.

In the autumn of 1881 Alexander III (1881-94) passed a series of 'temporary' security measures which virtually transformed his empire into a police state. These measures allowed the empire to be put under 'limited' or 'full' martial law, whatever circumstances required. With the exception of the revolutionary era between 1905 and 1906, Russia was permanently under martial law. Army courts replaced assizes and juries; their stiff sentences curbed student unrest. Special police, later called the *Okhrana*, were give sweeping powers. Without police permission, a Russian could not become a student; ice-cream shops could not be set up; individuals could not travel either abroad or within the empire; citizens could be exiled by administrative decrees and their property could be partially confiscated. All sorts of civil disqualifications were forced on suspected revolutionaries. The secret police took these powers extremely seriously and even dreamed of a perfect police state where trade unions would be run by its officers, and elected State Duma (parliament) and *zemstva* deputies would be police agents. One police chief, General Zubatov, established the first central photographic and fingerprinting files of revolutionaries. Despite his fanaticism and zeal to serve the emperor, he was dismissed when disgruntled employers complained that he was organizing strikes of their workers. These excessive police powers failed to restrain the revolutionaries who transferred their central commands abroad to be out

Left: A typical scene of
Russian peasant workers
in the late nineteenth
century.

Right: Leon Trotsky (1879-
1940), a leading figure in
the revolutionary
movement before 1917.
Although he had serious
disagreements with Lenin
over the period, it was
Trotsky who was mainly
responsible for the
organization of the Red
Army after the October
Revolution.

Below: Czar Alexander II
is rushed back to the
Winter Palace after being
fatally wounded by a
terrorist bomb in March
1881.

of reach. Nevertheless all the assassins of Alexander II and the plotters against Alexander III were efficiently tracked down, tried by martial courts and executed. Among the executed was a certain Alexander Ulyanov, elder brother of Vladimir Ulyanov, better known as Lenin. During the rest of the Romanov reign, however, only 1700 revolutionaries were arrested and dealt with under these draconian laws. The laws continued to be renewed until 1917.

In a sense Alexander's freeze on reforms and his police measures amounted to a seemingly successful counter-revolution but, in reality, these measures did not deter terrorist attacks. Several ministers responsible for security were shot and the Romanov family became used to living under constant terrorist threat. What these measures did achieve was the final break between the monarchy and Russian society.

On the accession of Nicholas II (1894-1917) the Russian people cheerfully assumed that a

Right: Karl Marx (1818-83), the inspiration for Lenin and the communist movement.

Below: The principal members of the last Russian royal family: Czar Nicholas II, Czarina Alexandra and the heir to the throne, Czarevich Aleksey.

new liberal reign was about to begin, and the *zemstva* petitioned the young emperor to create a constitutional monarchy. Nicholas knew of such 'senseless dreams,' and dashed them publicly. To his last days in 1917, he attempted to rule the empire as an autocrat through his personal administration: the government, army and secret police. He was a religious ruler, full of good will and generosity, but he was neither particularly intelligent nor of strong character. He never realized that, without supervisory bodies under his personal control, he would never be acquainted with the activities of his administration, army or secret police. In addition, he was easily influenced by his family and public servants which gave his character and regime a certain instability.

The first decade of Nicholas's reign was full of contradictions. The autocrat refused to grant any more 'freedoms' to his subjects, but he ended up with a liberal interior minister, Prince Sviatopolk-Mirsky, in charge of the empire. Paradoxically, the latter's repeated requests for liberal reforms were fully implemented by the emperor after the first revolutionary outbreak in 1905. Throughout these years, the *Okhrana* remained omnipotent and its head, General Zubatov, considered himself as such. Nonetheless, his organization, as well as the state administration in general, lacked the financial means to be really effective. Zubatov, together with the emperor, thought that their relatively few agents could dominate Russia by anticipating events and penetrating 'dangerous' groups. Thus, for example, he tried to turn dissatisfied workers in favor of the emperor by establishing trade unions. His agents penetrated all the revolutionary parties, especially the Bolsheviks. Nicholas eventually dismissed Zubatov but he continued in the service until he committed suicide on hearing of Nicholas's abdication. In contrast, the efficient financial policies of Count Witte brought about a period of intense, unprecedented economic development with the hope of future prosperity. Yet, despite the revolutionary movement being severely handicapped by the *Okhrana*, and the likelihood of economic improvement, revolution did break out in Russia.

Prior to 1905 there was general dissatisfaction with conditions in Russia. The upper classes had no hope of sharing power with the 'autocratic' emperor and even their patriotism had cooled. The intelligentsia were as restless as ever, committing intermittent acts of terrorism, but were scattered and politically impotent. The working class's living conditions were miserable, but the workers were not sufficiently organized and had to suffer their fate, though occasional violent strikes did happen. The 'liberated' peasants were the worst off. They were burdened with redemption debts and struck by famines in 1891 and 1901. Because of their repeated spontaneous revolts public flogging was not abolished until 1904, while their debts were only wiped out by the revolution. At the same time, these peasants were the backbone of the emperor's army. In 1904 Russia became involved in a war with Japan in the Far East. By and large Russian soldiers were unenthusiastic and ill-equipped; their officers were incompetent and unable to lead the sullen peasants. Russia suffered a series of most humiliating defeats on land and sea, and subsequent disruption served to spark off a revolution.

On 9 January 1905 Father Gapon, a police agent, led a march of workers to the Winter Palace in St Petersburg to complain to the emperor. The emperor could not have accepted Gapon's petition asking for better working conditions and some political rights, even if he had been in residence. As the procession approached the palace, the inexperienced palace guards panicked and opened fire into the crowd. Some 96 people fell dead, while 34 others died of their injuries. Rumors had it that casualties amounted to several thousands. This outrage provoked a series of revolts: workers went on unlimited strike; peasant revolts were so widespread that the army could not deal with them; and the intelligentsia, particularly the students, demonstrated in the streets and put forward their political demands. Even the national minorities, especially the Poles, demonstrated their disgust at the events in St Petersburg.

On 18 February the emperor, faced with such widespread disorder, panicked and publicly acknowledged that the massacre was his fault. Henceforth he permitted petitions concerned with public well-being to be presented to him. Immediately afterward another decree promised the establishment of a representative assembly, the State Duma. This decree was, however, not made known until August. In the meantime, revolts and disorder continued. Had these measures been taken and announced in December 1904, as Prince Sviatopolk-Mirsky had wanted, they might have forestalled the revolutionary outbreak. In October 1905 many workers observed the general strike which marked the culmination of general unrest. However, there were no revolutionary leaders capable of toppling the imperial administration and seizing power. Not even the Petersburg Soviet, a spontaneous offshoot of a strike committee, and its leader, Leon Trotsky, were capable of such action at this stage. The emperor recovered his wits and, seeing that the army remained loyal to him, was gradually able to eliminate the threat to his power.

On 17 October the czar published a manifesto in which he promised to dismantle the police state and replace it with a constitutional monarchy. Citizens would henceforth enjoy all freedoms and the emperor's government would be 'supervised' by the elected Duma which would also be allowed to pass laws. The electoral franchise for this Duma was wider than in

Below: A painting of the early period of unrest by N Nikonov depicting a revolutionary throwing a bomb into a group of Cossacks during the 1905 Revolution.

previous proposals. The emperor granted these
considerable political concessions under duress,
but wanted to give them a good chance to work,
provided the turmoil ceased. Because of the
delays in granting reforms, disorders continued
but the revolutionary fire had burnt itself out.
In December a general strike in St Petersburg,
called by the soviet, was easily suppressed. On 3
December Trotsky and others with him were
arrested, tried and deported to Siberia. There
was another insurrection in Moscow, but loyal
troops mastered it. The revolution had spent
itself, though sporadic and spontaneous out-
breaks of violence, punctuated by terrorist
action, continued for two more years. On the
whole the Russians were more eager to try out
the new system of sharing power with the emperor rather than to destroy it, although there
was a certain skepticism about the experiment.

The emperor was still rather reluctant to give
up his absolute power. After the re-establishment of public order, he tried to minimize power
sharing and did modify, for example, the electoral franchise. But he wanted the system to
work to some extent because he hoped to attract
as much Russian support as possible. His efforts
were fully backed by the extreme right-wing
members of the Union of the Russian People.
From the left, particularly the divided socialists, he found no support; the leftists did not
accept the difference between an autocratic and
a constitutional monarchy and Lenin ordered a
boycott of the 1906 election. Later he acknowledged his mistake and subsequently the Bol-

sheviks, and socialists in general, participated
in the constitutional system, exploiting the
election campaigns and Duma sessions for their
own propaganda purposes. The success of the
new power sharing mainly depended on the
smooth co-operation between two liberal-conservative groupings, the Constitutional Democrats (Kadets) and the Union of 17 October
(Octobrists).

On 23 April 1906 the emperor published the
fundamental laws on which his new system
would be based. The document provided for an
elective State Duma and half-elected State
Council (the other half was appointed by the
emperor). However, the constitutional arrangements turned out to be more complicated than
was first thought. For example, the government
was to be appointed by the emperor and was responsible to him personally and not to the Duma.
The latter could not initiate laws, which was the
prerogative of the government. Only the three,
the emperor, the government and the Duma,
acting together could finally pass laws. The
Duma could ask questions of ministers and
block draft laws, but nothing more. Civil liberties were guaranteed but they were subject to
the existing laws, which meant that after a time
the administration had recourse to the 'limited'
martial law passed as an emergency measure in
1881. This law had been abused before the 1905
Revolution and it was abused again during the
era from 1906 to 1917. This, coupled with the
'misunderstandings' of the 1906 constitution,
soon made it clear that the old rift between the

monarchy and society, particularly the middle class, had not been healed.

In the first election the liberal Kadets gained a substantial majority of the Duma seats and immediately demonstrated to the emperor and the country that they interpreted the constitution in a different way. Their reasoning was as follows. The emperor granted the constitution to Russia to appease the middle classes, if not to lure them to his side. They now stated the price for their support. They demanded a general amnesty for political prisoners including those convicted during the recent urban and rural disturbances. Next, they called for the annulment of all emergency laws. They also wanted a government directly responsible to the Duma, and the transfer of agricultural land from Crown holdings and the landlords to the peasants. The emperor found these proposals unacceptable, while the landlords, who represented 25,000 citizens, resisted the proposals tooth and claw. The outcome of this disagreement was the dissolution of the first Duma after only two months of existence.

The second Duma also only lasted a few months. It could not form a liberal ministry because of disagreements within the liberal-conservative coalition. After it had been dissolved the emperor's prime minister, General Peter Stolypin, decided to change, quite unconstitutionally, the electoral franchise to achieve co-operation and agreement with the Duma. After this change and some ballot manipulation, the third Duma had a liberal-conservative majority and agreed, if with reluctance, to co-operate with Stolypin's government. This Duma ran its full term. In 1912 the last Duma before the revolution in 1917 was elected on the basis of the same restricted franchise. After the emperor's abdication it took over power by forming a Provisional Government, a final Pyr-

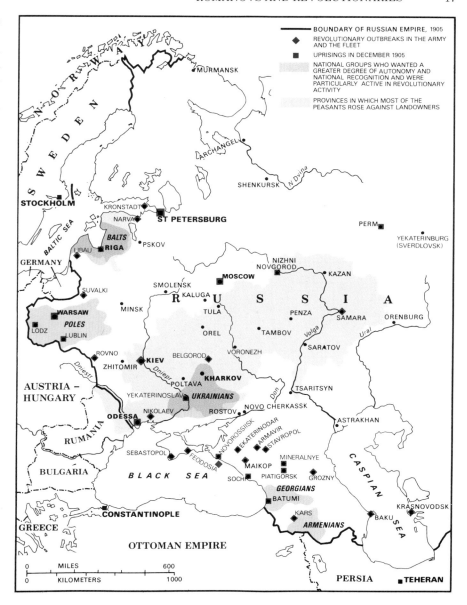

Above: The 1905 Revolution.

Left: Members of a trade union organized in St Petersburg by the political police. In the center are Father Gapon, who led the march on the Winter Palace in 1905, and Police General Fullon.

Above: The Czar's cavalry attack striking workers from the Putilov Works in January 1905.

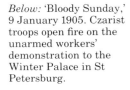

Below: 'Bloody Sunday,' 9 January 1905. Czarist troops open fire on the unarmed workers' demonstration to the Winter Palace in St Petersburg.

rhic victory for the Russian middle class, who proved unhappy and restless throughout the constitutional era.

Stolypin, after controlling the Duma, decided to rule the empire with an iron hand. He needed peace and quiet to re-establish the empire politically, economically and militarily. He was convinced that police repression was sufficient to rid him of the revolutionaries. He had just 'won' the co-operation of the middle class, now he set out to win over the peasantry.

The lost war with Japan and the subsequent political turmoil had caused severe economic damage. The strikes and disturbances produced a loss amounting to 29,000,000 roubles. Once the troubles were contained, Stolypin, urged on by the emperor, was determined to re-establish the internal strength and external prestige of Imperial Russia. Quite mistakenly, he immediately made use of the old emergency powers to 'hammer the revolutionaries,' but his senseless

repression irritated even the Russian liberal-conservatives. In marked contrast, and quite rightly, he tried to carry out the long overdue and indispensable agricultural reforms. He wanted to attract the support of Russian peasantry; to put right the various inequities left in the countryside after 1861; to encourage peasants to leave the old villages and set up individual land holdings; and grant peasants state aid so that they could emigrate from over-populated Russia to rich Siberia. Stolypin won a measure of co-operation from the Duma's middle-class supporters, but failed with other social groups. Workers were implacably hostile, while peasants opposed him, particularly in his attempts to break up the communes. Gradually Stolypin became unpopular even with the emperor. It was obvious that Nicholas failed to comprehend the rationale behind Stolypin's efforts. To cut the ground from under the Socialist Revolutionaries (SRs), he aimed to make agriculture prosperous by making peasants private holders of land and thus transform the restless and rebellious peasants into pillars of the 1906 establishment. Before Nicholas could dismiss him, Stolypin was assassinated by a Socialist Revolutionary, who was also a police agent. Stolypin's death illustrated the ambivalence that people in the emperor's service had to face. If properly understood, Stolypin might have saved the emperor from the fate that overtook him in 1917.

The consequences of Stolypin's partially successful agrarian reforms were beneficial all round. Surplus agricultural labor was released for industry which in the period 1900-13 expanded by 74 percent. With relative agrarian prosperity came an expanded internal market for the goods produced by the expanding industries. By 1913, Imperial Russia was fourth in the

world league of industrialized countries in the production of the four basic industrial commodities. The empire even drew benefits from the ravages of 1906. In that year Russia finally snapped out of economic depression; the expansion of the railways and foreign investments began to yield benefits. After the shock of 1905-06, the government decided to spend an extra 2,500,000,000 roubles to provide an additional stimulus to internal consumption. The increased government revenues, between 1900 and 1914 they almost doubled, reflected a general upturn in living standards. Had peace lasted, Russia was possibly on the eve of real and general prosperity. Three long-term weaknesses prevented the empire from enjoying immediate prosperity: mass illiteracy, poor urban housing, and the non-enforcement of the promised freedoms.

Although it is generally accepted that World War I was the final straw which broke the back of the imperial system, the men who took over the succession caused a surprise. It was generally expected that the middle classes, who by sharing power had some experience of it, would emerge as successors. Instead it was the 'wild,' idealistic revolutionaries. Their success seemed impossible to all rational Russians. They were penetrated by the imperial police to a large extent; they were deeply divided among themselves; and they were often unreasonably doctrinaire and highly unrealistic in their addiction to individual terrorism. These weaknesses applied as much to the leaders as to the rank and file. There was one exception to these assessments of the Russian revolutionaries: Vladimir Ilyich Ulyanov, known as Lenin.

Lenin was born on 10 April 1870 at Simbirsk (now Ulyanovsk) on the Volga River, where his father was a school headmaster. On his father's side there were innumerable generations of peasants or small merchants, though his father gained hereditary nobility as a teacher. On his mother's side there was a line of German surgeons, ennobled and endowed with an estate (*pomestie*). Lenin was brilliant at school, and terribly shocked when his elder brother was hanged 'for plotting the assassination of the emperor' in 1887. It was a typical police accusation thrown at all sorts of Russian revolutionaries with the same fatal result. The secret 'terrorist' organization to which Alexander belonged was probably a small discussion circle, inspired by the kind of socialist-populist ideology then in fashion in Russia and possibly harmless. Lenin's interest in the secret organization followed the trauma of his brother's execution. He had joined one group at the University of Kazan, and after they had organized a small-scale riot, he was arrested and expelled. He then had to reside at Kokushkino on his maternal grandfather's estate. He read Russian radical writers and was most impressed by Chernyshevsky's pamphlet *What is to be done?* He learned from it that the Russian system could not be reformed, but had to be destroyed by violent revolution. He also learned that dedicated revolutionaries had to perform this task and that liberals and other like-minded opposition could not be trusted.

Later, in Samara, he studied Marxism and reached the conclusion that the revolution could only be successful if a well-organized revolutionary party carried it out.

Marxists existed both in Russia and in exile, but Lenin was acquiring revolutionary theory and experience in his own way. In time, he rejected revolutionary populism, or at least its ideological principle that the revolution could be carried out by or on behalf of the Russian peasantry. By 1894 he believed that capitalism was established even in the Russian countryside, and that a socialist revolution, if it came, would have to not only destroy the autocracy, but also the capitalist economic order. In Samara and St Petersburg, where he concluded his legal studies, he came in contact with practicing 'social democrats,' who worked politically among the workers. He then advocated the struggle for workers' political rights in conjunction with other opponents of the autocracy; he thought that such a struggle would inevitably result in the revolutionary destruction of the latter. In the next stage of struggle, this revolutionary alliance would be broken off and the leadership would 'complete' the revolution by the pursuit of working-class interests on its own.

In 1895 Lenin's political ideology was almost

Above: Vladimir Ilyich Lenin (1870-1924), leader of the Bolshevik Revolution of 1917. The photograph bears two signatures – first in his real name, Ulyanov, then as Lenin in brackets.

Above: The consecration of the last Duma in 1912 by the Metropolitan of St Petersburg.

fully formed. He left Russia to study in Western Europe and talk with Russian émigré Marxists. Lenin was most impressed by Plekhanov, Akselrod and others, even if the former chided him for his rejection of a liberal alliance. He acknowledged their theoretical superiority and was pleased that they were prepared to 'legitimize' his own brand of Marxism. They, in turn, admired this young revolutionary, so serious, modest and realistic. Revolutionary strategy in Russia would be his recognized monopoly. Lenin returned home fully satisfied with his research. In Western Europe he also met numerous social democrats, and these meetings gave him added political self-confidence, already evident after Plekhanov's endorsement of him. However, shortly after his return to Russia he was arrested and exiled to Siberia.

Though certainly unpleasant, his Siberian exile did confer some advantages. Firstly he had time to reflect and he wrote *The Development of Capitalism in Russia*. He also drafted the Social Democratic Party program in 1896, and Akselrod warmly approved it. In 1898 it was approved by the foundation congress of the Russian Social Democratic Party, but that was as far as this brilliant program ever went. Immediately after the meeting all the nine participants in the congress were arrested by the secret police and sent into exile. Lenin had time to repudiate the views of some moderate Russian Marxists who

believed that under an autocracy the Russian working class should struggle for economic gains alone and leave the political struggle to the bourgeoisie (the hated Liberals). He insisted on a two-stage revolution: the working class would carry out the revolution jointly with the liberals, but turn against them; then a socialist revolution would destroy capitalism. Shortly afterward, on his release from Siberian exile, he left Russia for exile in Western Europe to further refine his strategy and wage his war on the autocracy from abroad.

During his Siberian exile Lenin became convinced that the Russian working class needed a theoretical journal which would teach it how to struggle against autocracy. In December 1900 he founded *Iskra* whose board included Plekhanov, Akselrod, Martov, Vera Zasulich and Potresov. From the beginning *Iskra* made it clear that, apart from teaching the Russian working class, it was also going to combat Marxist views within Russia which were not in harmony with its own. This struggle went on during the years 1901-02, while the preparations for the Second Congress were in progress. Lenin, aided by Martov and his own wife-secretary, Krupskaya, attempted to make all of the Social Democratic committees in Russia adhere to the *Iskra* group, and their efforts were largely successful. The *Iskra* group became the only really organized 'faction.' At this time Lenin also published a pamphlet, *What is to be*

Done?, in which he imitated his teacher, Chernyshevsky, and told everyone what he was actually doing.

He argued that the revolutionary party of the proletariat should be a tightly organized body, staffed by dedicated professional revolutionaries who 'should lead the working class and not be dragged by it.' Lenin had noticed that the émigré Marxists were nothing but 'twaddlers,' whose theoretical ideas only brought about disunity. As early as 1902 he staked his claim to the seizure of power and offered the Marxists a historical shortcut to victory: 'Give us an organization of revolutionaries and we shall overturn the whole of Russia.' When his views became known everyone seemed to disagree with him. At the Second Congress in 1903, first in Brussels and then in London, the Social Democratic Party split into several factions, so strong was the controversy provoked by Lenin's views.

As in the preceding years Lenin proved himself a determined and skillful manipulator, and emerged from the Second Congress as leader of the major (Bolshevik) faction (the Bolsheviks were part of the Social Democratic Party until 1918). He also controlled *Iskra* and a large section of the underground committees within Russia. The 'minority' (Menshevik) faction was of nuisance value. Its leaders, Plekhanov, Martov, Akselrod, Zasulich, Potresov and Trotsky, could not lead. The very idea of their leadership 'would make a chicken laugh,' declared Lenin. In any case, he was determined to keep them out of practical politic making, and the Menshevik faction out of party life. He was even more determined to make his own revolutionary strategy prevail within the whole of the Social Democratic Party. However, the factional split became permanent not because of ideological or tactical disagreement, but because of Lenin's success with the organization of his Bolshevik faction and his influence in Russia. Seeing his disciple's triumph, Plekhanov quickly changed sides and deprived Lenin of *Iskra*; the other leaders simply refused to acknowledge him as a board member. Frustrated, Lenin spelled out his tactics in even more extreme terms: he rejected the 1905 Revolution as inept and semi-anarchic, and declared that the next 'democratic' revolution had to be followed by a 'democratic dictatorship of the proletariat and the peasants.' This 'democratic dictatorship' would immediately improve workers' conditions and modify the land-tenure system in favor of the peasants. Last but not least, this 'democratic revolution' had to be carried out worldwide.

From 1900 until 3 April 1917, when he returned to Petrograd from Switzerland, Lenin conducted the revolutionary struggle, chiefly against fellow Social Democrats, in exile. Though he outclassed them in all respects, the bitterness of these disputes caused him several nervous breakdowns; it also confirmed him on his 'lonely' path. His opponents tried and failed to have him expelled from the Second Socialist International, while he, at the Prague conference in 1912, expelled them from the Bolshevik faction as 'liquidators.' In 1914 Lenin perversely welcomed the war, which he thought would

soon be turned into a civil war between the officers (imperialists) and the men (proletarians). He felt sure that revolution would result from the imperialistic war, but was rather unsure about its timing. He spelled out his tactics for the revolution to come in 1915, and applied them almost literally in 1917. In a democratic revolution it would not be sufficient to ask for a constituent assembly, the vital question would be who was in power during the election. If soviets arose as in 1905 he would treat them as the insurrectionist vanguard against the bourgeoisie. The Bolsheviks could not participate in a provisional government alongside 'social chauvinists' (other socialists, including the Russian Socialist Revolutionaries). If 'social chauvinists' found themselves in power, he and the Bolsheviks would not support them in an imperialist war or in an international revolution if they attempted to launch one. His enemies accused him of hysterical ranting and closed their ranks against him. He was then a penniless émigré living in Zurich, theoretically in charge of a minute revolutionary faction whose greater membership was outside Russia. Friends and foes either despised him or underestimated him. Lenin was going to prove them all wrong.

Above: Georgiy Plekhanov (1856-1918), 'the father of Russian Marxism.' Although Lenin was highly critical of Plekhanov, he continued to acknowledge the work he had done for the movement in the late nineteenth and early twentieth centuries.

Below: Peter Stolypin, a leading minister in the Russian government from 1906 until his assassination in the Kiev Opera House in 1911.

RUSSIA AT WAR

The historical consensus on World War I as one of the root causes of the Russian Revolution in 1917 is well known. The reverse hypothesis is that Imperial Russia would have survived, as it then was, without the war. However important, these theoretical questions only add to the confusion. Let us instead answer the question of why and how the last Russian emperor came to join Republican and Liberal France, and declare war on the two conservative monarchies, Austria-Hungary and Germany, in 1914.

From 1894, and even after the constitutional changes of 1906, Nicholas II was solely in charge of Russian foreign policy and the country's armed forces. For the conduct of foreign affairs he had a ministry whose role was strictly advisory and executive. The armed forces, particularly the navy, existed to give teeth to his foreign policies. He controlled them tightly through the monopoly of appointments of ministers of war and senior general officers. Until 1905 the armed forces were administered by the war ministry which had no influence in foreign affairs. However, the armed forces were not the greatest military machine in the world as the defeat in the war against Japan had clearly demonstrated. Nicholas did not feel directly responsible for the weaknesses of his foreign policy or of his armed forces; they were simply his inheritance and he was determined to hand them over to his successor in better shape.

In fact the foundations of both foreign and military policy were laid before Nicholas ascended the throne in 1894. In 1891 Germany permitted its Reinsurance Treaty with Russia to lapse, and Alexander III signed a political agreement with France in the same year. At the time, this agreement seemed the best arrangement for the maintenance of the balance of power in Europe and it had the added advan-

tage, from the Russian viewpoint, of financial credits. In 1887, Germany had refused to grant credits, now France readily offered them. It was no surprise that in 1892 the two allies agreed to give the political alliance a military dimension: in 1914 both signed a defensive military convention.

On becoming emperor, Nicholas automatically accepted his father's alliance treaty with France, together with the military convention. He was still inexperienced in diplomacy, but was determined to make his mark in world affairs. First, he dismissed his father's foreign minister, N K Giers, and appointed his own. As early as April 1895, acting on his own initiative, he combined with France and Germany to force Japan to abandon the Liaotung Peninsula. Russian interests in the Far East were in no way threatened by Japan, and Russia would pay dearly for this gratuitous action in 1904. The young emperor had acted on the advice of his foreign and war ministers, and felt perfectly justified in doing what he did. This was perhaps an error of judgment by a young emperor but, even if it was an error, it showed that the emperor considered it his right to dabble in foreign affairs. It also demonstrated his determination to act. Nonetheless, from the beginning of his reign Nicholas acquired an uncertain and unpredictable reputation in both Germany and France. Belatedly, Germany concluded a commercial treaty with Russia which served to increase French uncertainty about its Russian ally.

In 1897 Nicholas made diplomatic initiatives in another unexpected direction. Emperor Franz Joseph of Austria-Hungary paid him a visit and they came to an agreement over the Balkans. In many ways this diplomatic agreement was surprising: in the past the two powers had been rivals and had even clashed over their

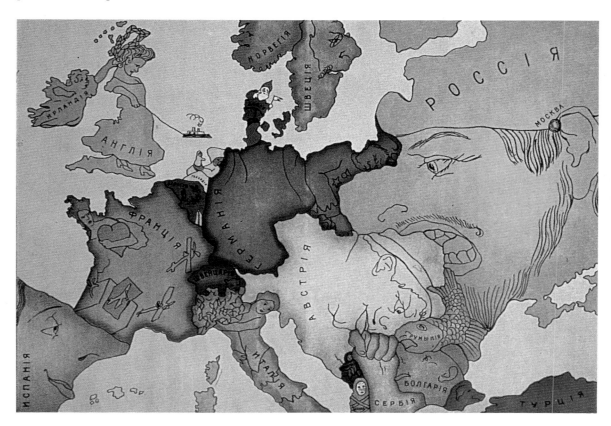

Previous page: Russian infantry parade before the czar in 1914.

Right: A Russian cartoon depicting Europe in faces at the start of the World War I.

conflicting interests in the region. Now they agreed to wait for the collapse of Turkey before undertaking any further action. They promised to consult each other in future and postponed their quarrels until such time as the two empires came into direct conflict. At this time Russia's real interest, the Dardanelles, lay beyond Austria-Hungary's grasp, and the Balkans were experiencing a period of stability. Both factors made this surprising entente between the two powers possible.

The unpredictable Nicholas acted much more curiously in 1904 and again in 1905, when Germany's Emperor William II postponed an alliance directed against Britain. Russia had been brought close to war with Britain in October 1904. The German emperor thought that France could be 'forced' to join such an alliance by Russia. He must have convinced Nicholas, who signed the Treaty of Bjorkoe in July 1905 without consulting anyone. Unfortunately for Germany, the treaty was never ratified. On his return, Nicholas's foreign minister, Lambsdorff, finance minister, Witte, and Grand Duke Nicholas Nikolayevich persuaded the impetuous emperor that the Bjorkoe Treaty was not really compatible with Russian interests and, above all, that it was wholly incompatible with the Russo-French alliance. Nicholas's reputation for unpredictability was confirmed.

Though Nicholas was able to make initiatives in foreign affairs as he pleased, even in complete isolation, he also had to withdraw them when they misfired. As long as he limited himself to paper diplomacy, all was well, except for the damage to his reputation. However, his miscalculation over Liaotung backfired on Russia. The Russian Empire had certain security obligations in Asia, but they were not considered important enough to be defended by arms. Notwithstanding this lack of regional 'muscle,' Nicholas became involved in the political intrigues and ambitions of his subjects in Manchuria and the Chinese Far East. The Russians were opposed by the rising Asiatic power, Japan. Since its rebuff in 1895, Japan had insured itself against Western interference by concluding a treaty with Britain in 1902. In February 1904 Japan unexpectedly attacked Russia in the Far East. To Nicholas's, and everybody else's, surprise, Russia lost the war. The Japanese defeated the Russian Army in the field, took the fortress Port Arthur and destroyed the Russian Pacific and Baltic fleets. The Russian armed forces were shown to be antiquated, disorganized and badly led. Japan had treated Russia as a second-class power by attacking her without warning and proved to the world that she was a paper tiger.

Above: A drawing showing the Japanese Navy smashing a Russian fleet at Port Arthur in 1904.

Left: General of Cavalry V A Sukhomlinov, minister of war between 1909 and 1915.

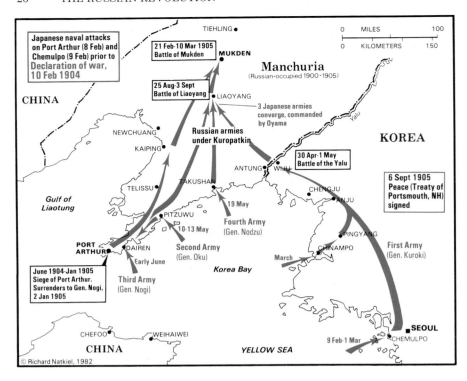

Japanese naval attacks
on Port Arthur (8 Feb) and
Chemulpo (9 Feb) prior to
Declaration of war,
10 Feb 1904

21 Feb-10 Mar 1905
Battle of Mukden

TIEHLING

MUKDEN

Manchuria
(Russian-occupied 1900-1905)

CHINA

25 Aug-3 Sept
Battle of Liaoyang

LIAOYANG

3 Japanese armies
converge, commanded
by Oyama

NEWCHUANG

KAIPING

Russian armies
under Kuropatkin

KOREA

Yalu

30 Apr-1 May
Battle of the Yalu

ANTUNG   WIJU

6 Sept 1905
Peace (Treaty of
Portsmouth, NH)
signed

TELISSU

TAKUSHAN

Gulf of
Liaotung

CHENGJU

ANJU

19 May

PITZUWU

10-13 May   Fourth Army
(Gen. Nodzu)

PINGYANG

First Army
(Gen. Kuroki)

PORT
ARTHUR   DAIREN   Second Army
(Gen. Oku)

CHINAMPO

March

Early June

Korea Bay

June 1904-Jan 1905
Siege of Port Arthur.
Surrenders to Gen. Nogi,
2 Jan 1905

Third Army
(Gen. Nogi)

CHEFOO   WEIHAIWEI

CHINA

SEOUL

9 Feb-1 Mar   CHEMULPO

YELLOW SEA

© Richard Natkiel, 1982

MILES   100
KILOMETERS   150

Above: The course of the Russo-Japanese War of 1904-05.

There were two main consequences of the terrible defeat in the Far East: the Russian armed forces had to be reorganized and the navy entirely rebuilt before another war could even be contemplated; and, realizing how vulnerable his interests were in the Far East, the emperor transferred his attention to Europe and the Balkans. The shock of the defeat in the Far East, coupled with the revolutionary turmoil at home, made Nicholas much more circumspect in his foreign adventures, particularly in the Balkans, but his new-found caution did not spare him from further humiliations. His entente with Austria-Hungary was reaffirmed in 1903 and 1904, and for almost four years, while Russia was engaged in internal reconstruction, all was well in the Balkans. Then in January 1908 the Austrian foreign minister, Aehrenthal, announced Austria's plans to build a railway in the Sandjak of Novi Bazar. It was evident that the Austrians intended to expand their zone of influence and upset the status quo. Immediately, the Russian foreign minister, Izvolsky, engaged in negotiations with Aehrenthal to restore harmony between the two powers. At Nicholas's request and without the knowledge of the Council of Ministers, Izvolsky concluded an ambiguous deal with Austria which was broken almost before it was signed. Austria annexed Bosnia and Herzegovina. The crisis dragged on while Russia attempted to marshal international opposition to the annexation, but neither France nor Britain was willing to back Russia against Austria in the Balkans. In the end Germany issued an ultimatum on behalf of its Austrian ally which forced Russia to accept the *fait accompli*, especially since Turkey, on the payment of financial compensation, also agreed to it. Nicholas asked his minister of war, General Rödiger, if the forces were ready to support his policy with arms, but was told that they were not. Nicholas felt profoundly humiliated by this 'surrender' to the empire of the Habsburgs.

The crisis of 1908-09 increased Nicholas's determination not to be caught 'unprepared' ever again. He dismissed Izvolsky and appointed Sazonov as foreign minister. He also

Right: The arrest of Gavrilo Princip after he had assassinated the Archduke Franz Ferdinand and his wife on 28 June 1914.

sacked Rödiger and replaced him with Sukhomlinov, whose brief was to create a modernized army and navy able to deal with the next crisis. With the Young Turk revolution raging, Nicholas believed that the next crisis would be over Russia's vital interests in the Dardanelles. To this end, he had a bill passed in the Duma for the construction of a squadron of battleships in the Black Sea. In October 1911 Ambassador Charykov even started negotiations with the Turks for the opening of the Dardanelles to the Black Sea Fleet.

In 1912, however, events in the Balkans took an unexpected turn. Everyone was waiting for the final collapse of the Turkish Empire, and everyone was waiting to seize their share of Turkish territory. Even the Balkan mini-states entertained hopes of gaining independence. In 1912 they combined to accelerate the final demise of their erstwhile master, Turkey. In March of that year Serbia and Bulgaria formed an alliance to this end and Greece joined them late in May. In October this group, the Balkan League, defeated Turkey and forced it to accept territorial concessions. Both Austria and Russia desired to further their own interests, but the success of the Balkan League had taken them unawares. They both made military preparations for an intervention, but in the following year both abandoned their plans as the situation in the region swiftly changed. The Balkan League fell apart and the members started fighting among themselves. Bulgaria was badly mauled by its former allies. Austria and Russia had no time to intervene on behalf of their clients or to further their own ambitions. In November 1913 Russia was informed of the appointment of a German general to command the Turkish Army. This military move was seen as direct German involvement in the Balkans-

Russia was again treated as a second-class power, this time by Germany. Russia's response was the launching of its 'Great Military Programme' in early 1914 which would make her armies fit to face the combined Austrian and German armed forces by 1917. Then, unexpectedly, another crisis arose in the Balkans in July 1914. Russia would not accept another humiliation at the hand of Austria or Germany. This time the emperor's decision would be to go to war.

From the very beginning of his reign Nicholas needed a strong army and navy to conduct his foreign policy, by force if necessary. The armed forces he inherited seemed impressive enough but, as he soon found out, they were impressive only on paper. However, they were sufficient for service in Asia and the Near East. Throughout the nineteenth century, Russian armies had fought well against several Asiatic enemies, such as Turkey and Central Asian Muslims. They also proved perfectly capable of defeating rebellious Poles, Transcaucasian insurgents or Chinese adversaries. It was, therefore, a terrible shock when they lost the war against Japan. Russia's 14 capital ships were sunk and the navy practically ceased to exist after the Battle of Tsushima in May 1905. Port Arthur was shot to pieces by heavy Japanese artillery and fell after a lengthy siege. The army, badly supplied, with each arm fighting separately, was decisively beaten in Manchuria. Even Nicholas was convinced by this defeat that his military establishment had to be fundamentally rebuilt and modernized before he could make use of it again.

The military establishment was, as everything in Russia, a huge bureaucratic machine which creaked with incompetence and corruption. A war minister headed the establishment,

Above: General Kuropatkin and his staff being received by the Chinese authorities in Mukden during the Russo-Japanese War.

Above: In the first few months of World War I there was great popular support in Russia for the conflict. Here a group of civilians in Petrograd (a wartime change of name for German-sounding St Petersburg) demonstrates in favor of the czar, the Russian Army and Russia itself. The banner on the right proclaims: 'Victory to Russia and Slavdom.'

responsible directly to the emperor. Before 1905 there existed in the army the so-called Main Staff (*Glavny Shtab*), but this was just another department of the war ministry alongside infantry, cavalry, fortress, engineering, supply and artillery staffs, and was chiefly responsible for promotions. Inside the military machine itself, bureaucrats, who never saw active service, were little more than self-serving, bungling administrators. No efforts were made to initiate or advance policies. An additional reason for this state of affairs was the lack of professional staff officers. While military academies produced officer-commanders, the small General Staff Academy produced few staff specialists. However, these staff specialists often reverted to command because of the shortage of trained field officers. Under these conditions it was obvious that rebuilding the armed forces would be a long process.

The lost war, followed by revolutionary unrest, did not make the task of rebuilding any easier. To make matters worse, the badly trained Russian generals drew all the wrong conclusions from the Russo-Japanese War. General Kuropatkin, noticing how effectively Japanese infantry, armed with repeating rifles, had dealt with Cossack cavalry, came to the conclusion that their charges were not pressed with sufficient determination and courage. To put matters right, he recommended the withdrawal of their rifles, allowing them the use of lances only. Even worse, fortress generals, instead of demanding their demolition since they proved so vulnerable to heavy artillery fire, wanted to rebuild and strengthen their fortifications. Field artillery batteries, with their eight guns per battery, were found cumbersome, but could not be halved in imitation of the French because it meant interfering with the command structure. The old batteries were

commanded by colonels, while the new ones were led by captains. The potential impact on the salaries and pensions of the redundant officers proved too much for both the reformers and bureaucrats. Only the navy needed outright rebuilding. However, the Russian Empire was close to financial ruin and simply could not afford massive reconstruction.

Russia's ally France provided the loans for reconstruction, believing that it would also have a decisive say in the reform of the Russian Army. The French suggested that, as the defeat in the war against Japan had been caused by the lack of a senior co-ordinating body in the armed forces, the Russians should establish a general staff. The suggestion was readily accepted by the Russians who thought that further French loans would follow after the acceptance of their idea. In 1905 the emperor set up the General Staff and the Council of State Defense, a body which did not figure on the list of French suggestions. The former, commanded by General Palitsyn, was given the task of reconstructing the land forces. The latter, presided over by Grand Duke Nicholas, was in charge of overall reconstruction. The Russians could not reconstruct their armed forces without a bureaucracy and Nicholas, preoccupied with problems elsewhere, let the military establishment get on with the business of restructuring. Unfortunately for the emperor, the military establishment was simply incapable of putting its own house in order, and Franco-Russian military relations suffered as a result. This incapacity to carry through change was almost entirely due to the composition of the high command of the armed forces.

The Officer Corps of Nicholas II was an amalgam of serving nobles, meritocratic peasants and foreigners. Whenever this curious balance was upset, emperors had difficulties with the

Right: Russian military uniforms of World War I: (L to R) a general; an infantry officer of the Czar's Own Guards Semenov Regiment; a Guards infantry soldier; an NCO scout of the Czar's Own Guards Kexholm Regiment; a soldier of the Czar's Own Guards Lithuanian Regiment.

Below: General A A Brusilov (1853-1926) led the Russian Eighth Army at the start of World War I and became commander of the South Western Front in 1916. He became the army's supreme commander for a time in 1917 but joined the Red Army in 1920.

army. In 1825 Nicholas I clashed with serving army officers, the Decembrists, who demanded political reforms. By the days of Nicholas II, the traditional composition of the Officer Corps was a certain prescription for trouble. Serving officers had lost interest in politics long ago but, because of the cultural differences and social incoherence of the Officers Corps, the armed forces found it virtually impossible to agree on anything. Moreover, officers of foreign origin tended to be favored by the emperor but, on the whole, they did not merit his patronage. General Rödiger, Nicholas's war minister, was a limited pedant who busied himself with routine administrative matters. Tradition mattered to Nicholas, and he continued to elevate empty-headed officers with foreign names because of it. In 1914 only five of the 16 generals commanding the emperor's forces had Russian names. Serving Russian nobles tended to join the cavalry and artillery or serve in Guards regiments, and proved even more clannish than the 'foreigners.' Over two-fifths of officers between the ranks of subaltern and colonel were of peasant or other humble origins. They had to maneuver between these mutually hostile groups. Although often promoted on merit or because of their expert knowledge, they still needed the support of one or another of the power groups to make use of their skills. Furthermore, all three groups served in the army for different reasons. The 'foreigners' formed what amounted to the emperor's personal legion; the serving nobles, particularly those from the traditional military families, served for patriotic reasons; while the officers of peasant origins (Denikins, Kornilovs, Alexeyevs) joined for patriotic and social reasons – without the army they had no place in Russian society. They were all badly paid, their social status was not greatly enhanced and, in any

case, none of these sub-castes could abide each other. To top it all, 'civilian' grand dukes were made Inspectors-General of all the arms. In such conditions even modest reforms proved impossible to realize.

After two years of squabbling and wrangling, a statute governing the relationship between infantry and artillery was finally produced, but it was so ambiguously worded that no one knew how to implement its recommendations. The Council for State Defense became aware of this and hastened to discredit the General Staff in the eyes of the war minister and emperor. The emperor took the claim seriously and sacked the chief of the General Staff. Instead of improving, matters got worse: the military began to wrangle with the naval authorities. In 1908 Nicholas dissolved the Council for State Defense, downgraded the General Staff and again made the war minister the most important figure in the military establishment. He failed to perceive that without dissolving the Officer Corps, the military situation would not improve. In any case, he could not purge it, as that was against existing laws, just reshuffle it. When, in 1909, General Rödiger made it clear to him that the armed forces were still unfit to be used as a backup to his foreign policy in the Balkans, Ni-

cholas dismissed him and appointed General V A Sukhomlinov.

Sukhomlinov did achieve a measure of success during his term of office. In fact he 'survived' in the hot seat of war minister until 1915 when he was arrested for incompetence and corruption. He was not incompetent, but he was certainly corrupt. However, who was not corrupt in Russia? There was no rational system of remuneration in the empire, only pompous titles and grandiose uniforms. In 1908 Sukhomlinov complained to the French Chief of the General Staff that in terms of remuneration he was worse off as the Chief of the General Staff than a general commanding a military district, his previous appointment. The war minister had to maintain his social standing and, since the costs were disproportionately high, he decided to solve his problems the only way he could. Thus, for example, he farmed out the sales monopoly of mineral water in the armed forces to the general commanding the palace troops, Voyeykov. He also collected a large commission from Prince Andronnikov, whom he tipped off about land the army was going to buy. Without doubt, he also made handsome profits from insider dealings on the stock exchange. Nonetheless, despite the corruption which was,

in a sense, forced on him by the Russian social system, he turned out to be an effective reformer because of his unrivaled knowledge of the system and his incredible ability to manipulate it.

In 1910 Sukhomlinov presented Nicholas with a list of reforms which the armed services badly needed, and they were almost all implemented by 1914. They mainly concerned cavalry, artillery, reserve formations, fortresses and, above all, operational planning. In army matters he employed low-born specialists with some effect. He did not win all the battles, however. For example, Grand Duke Constantine Mikhaylovich preserved the fortresses which Sukhomlinov wanted to raze, and distorted Sukhomlinov's artillery reforms. The fortresses swallowed up heavy guns which were missed in the field artillery. All the same, the Russian armed forces were modernized by him more than by any other war minister. His success was largely due to his skillful exploitation of the promotion system. He was able to place his own men in all the important positions and defeat his opponents. As a result, the Russian armed forces were in a considerably better shape in 1914 than when he took over in 1909. On the other hand, they were irreconcilably

Above: The outbreak of revolution.

Above left: A squadron of Russian Cossacks on parade.

Left: A Russian officer kisses a cross held by an Orthodox priest before leaving for the front in late 1914.

Right: Grand Duke Nicholas was the supreme commander of the Russian Army at the start of the war, but took over command of the Caucasian Front in 1915.

split into the pro- and anti-Sukhomlinov factions who refused to co-operate with each other even during the war. Sukhomlinov's greatest achievement was in the sphere of operational planning.

In 1873 General Miliutin drew up the first set of plans for a war against Germany and Austria. They were strengthened in 1880 by General Obruchev. Because of geographical conditions and an inefficient mobilization system, both planners thought that Russia had to begin a war on the defensive and counter-attack later, particularly against Austria. In 1894 the Russians promised the French to field 800,000 soldiers against Germany and in 1900-02 offered to launch an offensive against both Germany and Austria in the first month of any war. The basic conditions must have improved considerably in the past 30 years. After 1905 Russian military planning, quite understandably, became more defense-orientated, but six years later Sukhomlinov, with the help of General Danilov, who was responsible for the drawing up of the army's operation plans, restored the idea of a Russian offensive against Germany within the first month of a war. Finally in 1912, under pressure from the anti-Austrian lobby, the army's offensive deployment and operational plans were again modified. According to Plan A, which was actually used in 1914, offensive operations against East Prussia by two Russian armies were devised to tie down as many German troops as possible. The main offensive by four Russian armies was, however, directed against

the Austrians, east of the Carpathian Mountains. This final plan was a compromise, but it was Sukhomlinov's crowning military achievement.

In June 1914 the Austrian heir apparent was assassinated in Sarajevo, the Bosnian capital. Austria decided to 'punish' Serbia whom it blamed for the assassination. Traditionally, Russia was Serbia's 'protector' and decided to intervene against Austria. All the European powers thought that the alliance system would act as a deterrent and that the crisis would be resolved peacefully. But it soon became obvious that all of them, for different and often complicated reasons, were bent on war. The Russian emperor asked the advice of his foreign and war ministers: was Russia in a state to 'protect' Serbia, even if it meant war against Germany and Austria simultaneously? Sazanov answered that Russia should protect Serbia. Sukhomlinov also answered the emperor's question positively, provided the war could be won in three to six months. On 25 July the Russian Council of Ministers endorsed the decision of its two 'experts' and the emperor confirmed it. Three days later Austria declared war on Serbia and, after a day of hesitation, Nicholas ordered a general mobilization. After the mobilization order, events ran their own course: Germany declared war on Russia on 1 August and on France two days later; on 4 August, Britain declared war on Germany. World War I had begun. Before its end, the Russian Empire would have collapsed and disappeared forever.

World War I began in accordance with the plans laid down by various military leaders some considerable time before the conflict opened. Despite certain transport difficulties in Russia due to the unfinished strategic railways, the army's mobilization was a great success. Officers and men were rapidly shifted in great numbers from rear military districts to the western borders to execute Plan A. According to this plan, the First and Second Russian Armies were to invade East Prussia and the Third, Fourth, Fifth, Eighth and Ninth Armies were to attack Austria-Hungary by 15 August. There was some enthusiasm for the war among Russia's 'educated' and urban population, but the emperor was impressed by this half-hearted show of patriotism: it confirmed him in the belief that he had made the right decision. However, the mass of soldiers and the peasants were less enthusiastic, in fact rather sullen, but this was considered relatively unimportant as the outcome of the war would be decided they hoped within six weeks. Sukhomlinov, who as war minister had the automatic right to become commander in chief of the armed forces, refused the honor. He foresaw certain setbacks in the short conflict and offered the glory of leading the Russian Army to victory to the emperor. The emperor, equally cautious, passed the honor to his uncle, Grand Duke Nicholas. The latter could not refuse the offer of his sovereign and therefore set up a general field headquarters (*Stavka*) in railway coaches at Baranovichi. However, this was his first, and last, resolute act. Nothing else went right for the Russian military establishment. All the problems of unfinished reforms, factional conflicts, incompetence and bad leadership blew up in the face of *Stavka*.

From the declaration of war, *Stavka* was supposed to command and co-ordinate the Russian forces in the field, but the hapless grand duke was not a military man. After appointing his brothers and other aristocratic companions as adjutants, he concentrated on receiving visiting foreign military leaders, good living, and putting his signature to all the military papers that were submitted to him, but avoided the tasks of command and co-ordination. *Stavka* was supposed to be the powerhouse of the armed forces. It administered a war zone which comprised a great part of European Russia with Poland thrown in. The grand duke, however, was interested in other matters. His appointments, acclaimed in the name of efficiency, were really intended to erase Sukhomlinov's influence in the armed forces. The chief of staff appointed by Sukhomlinov, General Yanushkevich, was little more than a clerk. He was, therefore, kept by the grand duke. In any case he quickly joined his new master's faction. General Kondzerovsky, who was the secretary of the Attestation Commission responsible for general officers' appointments and an anti-Sukhomlinovite, became part of the grand duke's staff. He did not know what to do at *Stavka*, so he set up a restaurant service and then amused himself with intrigues and making senior appointments. Due to factional differences, defeated corps commanders were promoted to army commands,

while Sukhomlinov made sure that 'his' sacked men were promoted to posts in the rear areas where he still held sway. Only the Operation Department ran by General Danilov, supposedly the quartermaster general, was reasonably well established. However, because of its distance from the field armies and its relative isolation in the middle of Byelorussian countryside, *Stavka* was severely hampered in its functioning. The means of communication were inadequate and front commanders could not be contacted. It was not until October that a telegraph cable was laid to link *Stavka* with field headquarters. The atmosphere at *Stavka* changed when it was realized that the war was going to last more than six weeks. At first, *Stavka* officers had to do without drink and their wives, and religious services were held daily. By December vodka was being served illegally in the mess. Yanushkevich apparently developed a taste for pornography, while the grand duke asked the chaplain to make his choir perform arias rather than masses. Even though some technical aspects of command improved, *Stavka* never became the military nerve center that its equivalents were in Germany or France.

It fell to the individual front, army, corps and divisional commanders to conduct war in the field. They worked under the same conditions as the *Stavka* generals. In addition, their difficulties were aggravated by personality clashes. The North Western Front under the command of General Zhilinsky (a Sukhomlinovite) failed

Below: Russian troops man a trench on the Eastern Front.

to co-ordinate the moves of the First and Second Armies. General Rennenkampf, an anti-Sukhomlinovite, refused to communicate with his superior, General Samsonov. On the other hand he did communicate with Samsonov's chief of staff. Samsonov was a Sukhomlinovite and his chief of staff was not.

No one knew what to do with the cavalry forces which had previously clogged up many troop trains, the only detected hitches during the mobilization. Wandering aimlessly around the Prussian countryside in search of an enemy to attack, the cavalrymen and their horses strained the supply services to breaking point. When they finally found the enemy, their commanders were left behind. The aristocratic, but ancient, Khan of Nakhichevan was found alone in a tent bewildered and unable to say where his cavalrymen had galloped off to. Under such conditions it would have taken several major miracles to win a victory. The opening battle in East Prussia ended in disaster.

In the south, however, Russian forces did score several significant successes, possibly because the Austrians' military machine suffered from even graver defects. The Austrians sent troops intended for Galicia to fight in Ser-

bia and only switched them to their right destination when it was too late. This was the real reason for the Russian victory in Galicia. As elsewhere, *Stavka* co-ordinated nothing, and front commanders quarreled and contradicted each other for no good military reason. However, they failed to defeat the Austrians decisively which they should have done given their numerical superiority and favorable geographical conditions. As in East Prussia, generals were dismissed only to be promoted, or were transferred to new jobs in the rear. After September, when the more or less planned military movements came to a stop and the fronts stabilized, the full weakness of the Russian Army was revealed. The forces were suddenly short of field artillery, because the useless fortresses received and kept most of the guns produced prior to 1914. The cavalry, magnificently equipped and led by the cream of the aristocratic officers, had nothing to do in trench warfare. The badly trained soldiers could only charge the enemy or beat an orderly retreat. Unco-ordinated operations, planned at lower levels, invariably ended in failure and utter confusion.

In 1915 the Russian Army began to suffer

anarchy and arbitrariness.' According to him even children were imprisoned in Warsaw for anti-state activities; during the retreat Cossacks dragged off refugee women with their *nagaykas* (whips); refugees marching on foot along railway lines were overtaken by express trains loaded with officers' furniture, bird cages and other chattels. The minister did not want this happening in Russia proper.

The excesses committed by the retreating Russian forces were even greater than the minister of the interior knew about. It was said that General Alexeyev's supply officer reserved a whole train for the evacuation of his mistress and her possessions. As over a million refugees moved eastward, a British observer saw a Russian officer charging them a toll to cross a bridge. The scorched-earth policy was selective, but the treatment of the Jews appalled even the most hardened anti-Semites. The octogenarian General Smirnov threatened the families of men who surrendered to the enemy with reprisals and with courts-martial. Russian casualties were estimated at something in the order of over two million. According to enemy sources, the Austrians and Germans captured over a million Russian soldiers. General Grigoriev, aged almost 70, commanding the fortress at Kovno, panicked and fled at the unexpected approach of the enemy. Arrested later by the field gendarmerie he was sentenced to 15 years' imprisonment.

The fate of the old general was significant, for it indicated the type of remedy used to put right the great retreat of 1915. Sukhomlinov was dismissed, arrested and investigated. But his

Below: Czar Nicholas II visiting the Russian Army in 1915. On the far right is Grand Duke Nicholas.

from crippling material shortages: there was a real shortage of shells and rifles. However, it was the blundering of the generals, coupled with the shortage of officers, that led to the increasing restiveness of the Russian soldiers, and were the decisive factors behind the great defeat suffered in that year. The winter battles in Masuria and Galicia proved inconclusive but the Austro-Hungarian Army showed that it also could stand and fight, particularly when stiffened with German officers and troops. In May 1915, the breakthrough at Gorlice and the Austro-German triple offensive completely disrupted the Russian fronts; the retreating Russians abandoned Poland. By the end of September their defense line was deep in western Byelorussia and the Ukraine, running roughly from Chernovtsy in the south to Riga in the north. As Baranovichi was in the war zone, *Stavka* had to move to Mogilëv. While the Germans were full of admiration for the 'brilliant conduct' of the Russian retreat, the Russian Council of Ministers was less so. The minister of the interior, Prince Shcherbatov, was appalled when *Stavka* asked for the war zone to be extended deep into Russia itself: 'the picture of military rear areas is one of sickening outrages,

Above: Russian soldiers cheering the Czar at the front in 1915.

Right: The Brusilov Offensive (June-August 1916) saw the Russian Army advance on the South Western Front by up to 100 miles but the attack cost more than half a million Russian dead and wounded.

Top right: Russian soldiers attempting to break through German obstacles.

replacement, General Polivanov, was an incompetent intriguer, dismissed by the emperor in 1912 for exactly the same reasons. Polivanov was used for the business of dismissing others. The first task the emperor conferred on Polivanov was to purge *Stavka*. The emperor wanted to assume supreme command himself and make a clean sweep of *Stavka*, which he rightly blamed for the recent defeats. Polivanov went to Mogilëv in person. He did not call on Yanushkevich, the chief of staff, but used the *Stavka* Rolls-Royce to visit the commander of the new Western Front, General Alexeyev. Subsequently, the emperor appointed the grand duke as Viceroy of the Caucasus and Alexeyev as his chief of staff. He also promised that the Russian armed forces were going to be thoroughly reorganized.

The emperor's takeover of supreme command was purely symbolic, even if he had good reasons for his actions. The removal of the grand duke was calculated to calm the Duma's criticism of the conduct of the war. He supposed that the Duma would not dare to criticize him. Furthermore, he was going to appoint apolitical technocrats to run the war properly on his behalf. In any case, he was busy with home affairs and knew very little of army matters. Though he was useless as a supreme commander, he made good choices in his new appointments. Polivanov was quickly replaced by a supply expert, General Shuvayev; Alexeyev was rapidly transforming *Stavka* into a nerve center and the defeated army into a fighting force. Although Alexeyev was of humble origin, he was a conscientious general officer, transparently honest (he even paid his mess

charges) and purely interested in the good of Russia. His inability to decentralize and delegate made him work too hard and soon made him ill. He immediately dismissed grand ducal and Sukhomlinov appointees, and replaced them by men of his own stamp. General Pustovoytenko was of equally humble origin, but an excellent quartermaster. Alexeyev's personal assistant, V Borisov, was once dismissed by Grand Duke Andrey Vladimirovich as a 'proletarian,' but these three now formed the working nucleus of *Stavka* which was also greatly expanded to take in seven general officers and 30 senior officers. *Stavka* now numbered 86 people spread over 14 departments. Most of the aristocratic aides had left, but the emperor brought in some of his own staff so that there were still some idlers about. *Stavka* was much more hardworking than before when business closed at 2100 hours. Nightly film shows continued to be shown, though wine was served in the mess instead of vodka.

It seems remarkable that even these timid measures produced such great military achievements in 1916. In January Alexeyev told the French that he had 1,693,000 officers and men at the front: 1,243,000 with rifles. A few weeks later he claimed that he had over two million men, almost all with rifles. Artillery shells had also arrived as well as such essential supplies as aircraft, radios, gas masks, barbed wire and bandages. It was time to plan an offen-

Above: Polish refugees flee from Russian Poland during a lull in the fighting.

sive. Because of French pressure the first in a series of attacks was staged by the Western Front in the area of Lake Naroch in March 1916. General Evert, who was in command, was pugnacious in words, but otherwise useless. Of advanced age, he was probably downright senile. His army, though superior in numbers, failed to achieve its objective because it was not sufficiently supported by the armies on its flanks. One was commanded by the ancient Kuropatkin and the other by the equally aged Smirnov. The generals in command of the artillery, Zakutovsky and Prince Masalsky, quarreled and, in consequence, their 1000 guns with plentiful munitions failed to pulverize the German lines. Of the 350,000 men engaged 100,000 were casualties. This unsuccessful battle spelled the end of the old, pre-Alexeyev army. Later offensive actions would be staged by 'new' armies of General Brusilov's command during the hot summer of 1916.

The preparations started in March 1916, when the aged General Ivanov left the South Western Front command. Brusilov, who took over the front, was himself a serving noble but kept out of factional quarrels. He immediately appointed his own men and they all studied the winter battles and defeats in Bessarabia, the area where their offensives were to take place. They stopped blaming the shortage of shells for their defeats. In their analysis, it was vital to disrupt the enemy's front and local reserves before effecting a breakthrough. The attacking forces had to avoid counterattacks by fresh troops which would have slowed them down

intolerably. They decided that the offensive's objectives could only be achieved by means of surprise which excluded the employment of extensive artillery fire. Though approving the plans Alexeyev did insist on a two-pronged offensive. Thus, he more or less forced General Evert to launch his drive on Kovno with the newly formed Guard Army. General Bezobrazov obtained command of the new army on the emperor's personal intervention. The Guard Army was to attack in the 'old' way, after a heavy artillery barrage, on a narrow front. On 4 June the Russian forces went over to the offensive, subsequently named after Brusilov. Ultimately it was only successful on the South Western Front. Bezobrazov's guards hardly dented the German front line and were bled white. Their generals were discredited, though not yet in the eyes of the emperor. Brusilov's men smashed their way through the Austrian lines, seizing huge chunks of Austrian-occupied territory. However, Brusilov's casualties were also high: 5000 officers lost, 60,000 men killed, 370,000 wounded and 60,000 missing. The 'new' methods had been proved right, though Brusilov's drive also drew to a halt when he ran out of reserves. By the end of that fateful summer the Germans, who stiffened the Austrian forces, retook the lost territories and conquered Romania which had rashly declared war on Germany. In reality, the Russian victories proved to be illusory, though no one guessed it at the time. As the winter of 1916 brought the fighting to a halt, Russian generals felt most optimistic about the prospects in the coming year. Early in 1917 they told an Allied conference at Chantilly in France that the year would be decisive for the outcome of the war. They repeated these views to the Allied politicians who came to another conference in Petrograd. Little did they suspect that they themselves had reached a decisive point in their careers. The last Russian offensive in July 1917 was going to be fought by a completely different set of officers elected by 'liberated' men under a new revolutionary government.

While the army was fighting its bloody battles, the rest of Russia suffered as well. Millions of refugees fled the fighting, retreating into overcrowded cities. The endless stream of war casualties had a great impact on civilian morale. By 1915 the shortage of shells provoked an acute political crisis. After its demonstration of enthusiastic patriotism in 1914, the Duma became increasingly critical of the conduct of the war, especially since it felt left out of the decision-making process. After attacking Sukhomlinov as corrupt and incompetent, the Duma brought about his downfall. The immediate pretext for this was the affair in which one of his officers, Colonel Myasoyedov, was accused of being a German spy: Myasoyedov was found guilty and executed. Apart from Sukhomlinov's resignation, the Duma achieved little else. The 'patriotic but dissatisfied' Duma members formed a majority 'Progressive Bloc' and demanded reform in spite of the war. They wanted a cabinet government appointed by and answerable to the Duma and the emperor's powers curtailed or downright abolished. To this end, they also plotted with army generals, Grand Duke Nicholas and Allied diplomats to put pressure on the emperor. In 1915 the emperor easily outwitted them though he granted them two important concessions. However, he thought they would discredit themselves in the eyes of the Russian public by acting imprudently. The concessions gave the *zemstva* powers and state subsidies to look after minor army supplies and most of the hospital services; the War Industries Committees were invited to resolve the shell crisis as well as other material shortages. The Industrialist Union, a collection of factory owners and bankers, was keen to become more closely involved in the war effort – for its own benefit.

In time the Progressive Bloc established itself as a 'parallel' administration which quickly overshadowed the moribund imperial administration. However, instead of addressing the war effort, they chased after political goals. The case of an Urals industrialist, Solodovnikov, demonstrates the peculiar brand of patriotism that animated Russian capitalists. He took large state advances for armament contracts, but could not use them properly. Instead, he speculated in sugar, grain and other commodities in short supply. When asked about the contracts by Sukhomlinov, he quickly granted equal wages to men and women workers in his arms plants and used the resulting strike as an excuse for non-delivery. Industrialists were always prepared to extort the maximum prices for their shells and armaments from the state, but were quite unwilling to pay their workers

wages in line with inflation. Such sharp and unpatriotic practices incited workers to abandon the war industries and seek better pay elsewhere. Labor unrest was particularly acute in 1916 and 1917. The *zemstva*'s contribution to the war effort turned out to be not only inefficient, but also unreasonably expensive. They could not produce enough army uniforms to satisfy demand, and ordered them from the United States without notifying the ministry of finance. Their army blankets were five times more expensive than those from ordinary suppliers. They took huge advances for contracts (242 million roubles) and had honored only a fraction of them (80 million) by January 1917. With hospital services they were a little more successful. These were run better than those staffed by well-meaning aristocratic and 'common' Russian women. In spite of these shortcomings, both 'parallel administrations' succeeded in creating the legend that their efficient and patriotic war effort was thwarted by the undemocratic and corrupt imperial administration. This type of propaganda went down well in Allied countries, though not in Germany: the Germans accused the industrialists and *zemstva* of being the greatest talkers in the world who never achieved anything practical. Both the Allied and German opinions of the two Russian alternative administrations were wide of the mark. They did achieve concrete results. The *zemstva* administration produced the first non-imperial prime minister. The Industrialist Union, perhaps without knowing it, left 18 million shells for the Bolsheviks.

Above: As the war dragged on the Russian Army was forced to draft ever younger recruits to replace its losses.

THE FEBRUARY REVOLUTION

Historians, communists and others, agree that the two most important factors affecting the revolutionary collapse of Imperial Russia in March 1917 were the dissolution of central authority (the emperor's abdication and the government's 'resignation') and the army's mutiny in face of popular demonstrations in Petrograd, the capital. Communist historians concentrate on the political aspects of the revolutionary struggle, while others tend to over-emphasize other factors: the destruction of the army and police in World War I; the general 'betrayal' of the Russian monarchy; the German conspiracy with Russian revolutionaries; the Russian Army conspiracy; and the Russian freemasons' conspiracy.

The political factor is indeed the foremost historical cause. In 1915 many Russians, friends and foes alike, objected to the assumption of supreme military command by the emperor. Very few realized how important his presence in Petrograd was for the central government;

Previous page: Fighting on the streets of Petrograd in the early days of the February Revolution of 1917.

Below: As disillusionment with the czar spread, satirical cartoons began to appear. This one, entitled 'The Russian Royal House,' shows a simple-looking Nicholas and a devious Alexandra being completely dominated by the monk Rasputin.

even though his wife Alexandra tried to act as his substitute she could not fullfil this role. When, in July 1914, he decided, because of the war emergency, to suspend the constitution and rule 'dictatorially' for the duration, he had few illusions about the extent of his power. Generals and armies would do the ruling. The only illusion he retained was that autocracy was a sacred inheritance to be passed on to his heir; his wife firmly supported him in this view. In a sense the emperor reclaimed his power when he assumed supreme command. In addition, as was mentioned previously, he had many other military and political reasons for going to Mogilëv. However, his wife had no reason to think that she could replace him in Petrograd. Therein lies the tragedy of that fatal decision: he was irreplaceable. As it turned out he was useless at *Stavka* as he was pre-occupied with internal problems which should have been dealt with from Petrograd. Alexandra's actions were interpreted as interference and further complicated current problems. After all, she was a German princess and, during a war against the country of her origin, she should have kept in the background.

Furthermore the emperor, who was appointing numerous government ministers from afar, was blamed for their wrongdoings. On the advice of his wife, he was particularly unlucky in appointing a whole string of increasingly incompetent prime ministers: Stürmer's appointment was the most unfortunate not only because of his German name, but also because of his inexperience. He was a simple courtier, devoid of any political and administrative ability. Rasputin, the monk who was appreciated by the imperial family because of his powers to stop their haemophiliac son's bleeding, was usually blamed for such political blunders. Rasputin, though an adventurer whose lifestyle was a public scandal, was politically cautious. Nonetheless, rumors concerning his supposed influence over the imperial couple were much more damaging to the monarchy than his actual influence. In the end Rasputin provoked such hatred that he was assassinated by a grand duke, Prince Yusupov, and a right-wing politician, Purishkevich, 'so that the Monarchy can be saved.' The emperor continued to appoint inept servants to high office. The last prime minister, Prince N D Golitsyn, a friend of the empress, was completely incapable. Because of his advanced age, he regularly dozed off during the deliberations of the Council of Ministers. In March 1917 he simply walked out of office, uttering that he had had enough. In the imperfect constitutional monarchy, strong ministers of the interior were of utmost importance. From autumn 1916 the emperor had the most inept minister of the interior ever. Protopopov was not only corrupt but a scatterbrain as well. He was appointed because of his friendship with Rasputin, and after Rasputin's death this powerful minister asked the spirit of the dead monk for instructions through the intermediary of a spiritualist.

Central power, weakened by this division of authority and the scandal attached to it, was on the verge of collapse, battered by the political assaults from the Duma. In August 1915 a large majority of Duma deputies and substantial numbers of the State Council formed the Progressive Bloc which, apart from criticizing the government, also launched an exaggerated propaganda campaign vilifying the monarchy. It is true that the emperor's absence from Petrograd and his intransigence had provoked the Duma. As if there was no war on, the Duma drew up a list of demands: a general amnesty for political prisoners; strict legality; the limitation of military power; trade union reform; broad legislation in favor of the peasants and *zemstva*. It was equally true that rumors of the empress's high treason emanating from the Duma were extremely mischievous and quite false. The unfair action of the bitterly disappointed Duma showed its complete frustration at being left out of the war effort. During the spring session in 1917, the Duma discussed again the extreme demands raised previously. At the end of the debate, it issued a quasi-ultimatum to the emperor on the subject of the appointment of a 'responsible government' suggested by and responsible to the Duma. The emperor would not have yielded to it even in peacetime; in wartime, he had a perfect excuse. With the benefit of hindsight, this desperate struggle proved suicidal to both the monarchy and the Duma-

Left: Boris Stürmer was appointed premier in early 1916 thanks to Rasputin's influence.

Below: A meeting of the fourth and final Duma.

Above: President Mikhail Rodzianko led the final Duma from 1912.

spending money lavishly, particularly on war contracts. By 1916 industrial profits from war deliveries hit the sky: the stock exchange boomed and banking business was greatly extended – the number of state savings banks doubled to 15,000 in the period 1914-17. A similar explosion affected the workers. In January 1917 registered employment amounted to 3,643,000 (only a small proportion of the labor force was registered), 1,000,000 more than in 1914. But the numbers might have been greater as wartime statistics were unreliable. Unregistered numbers of state-employed workers also increased from 120,000 in 1914 to 400,000 in 1917, one third located in Petrograd. Railway employment increased by 500,000 to reach 1,200,000, though the system was much reduced. Mines doubled their employment to 800,000; oil-extraction workers rose to over 500,000; even the building industry expanded, rather unusually for wartime, its working force rising by one third to 1,500,000. All this labor came from the countryside. It was the industrial boom that depopulated the country and not conscription, as was thought. Some 4,500,000 peasants moved to the towns between 1914 and 1917, and the social impact was never properly assessed. Incredibly overcrowded, Petrograd was at the root of the imperial collapse.

More immediately, the emperor beat off the Duma's challenge: he simply ended the session. Duma debates generated a lot of public excitement, but its closure upset no one except the deputies, who refused to disperse. Early in February 1917 rumors circulated round the country of impending change, either violent or peaceful. The emperor, who was in Petrograd for the Inter-Allied conference, seemed to be ignorant of them. He headed for Mogilëv, leaving behind a capital peaceful only on the surface. In his absence the destruction of the imperial system had begun.

It was not fully realized that during the war years the Russian Empire was in the throes of another industrial revolution. This cycle of industrial development was immensely accelerated by the war. Economic and social chaos can safely be ascribed to it, and not to such bogus reasons as relative economic backwardness or wartime disruption, though they all contributed to the final collapse. Russian economic chaos was produced by the undetected economic explosion brought about by intensified industrial changes aggravated by the war: much greater commercial activity, much greater labor mobility and much more investment. For the first time the imperial government was

As always, the Russian state invested exclusively in heavy industry to obtain armaments. These investments distorted the economy and, since taxation was not raised to cover state investments, the government had to borrow and print money. In 1917 US printers had to do the work, as the Russian ones refused. They were being paid with the money they printed. Inevitably, this process triggered off inflation. In 1914 there were 2,400,000,000 roubles in circulation, in 1917 there were 11,200,000,000 roubles, a rise of nearly 500 percent. In the same period prices rose by over 700 percent. Attempts to check inflation by price fixing worsened the problem instead of remedying it. They produced flourishing black markets and shortages. In such conditions peasants kept their grain in the hope of making real profits out of late sales. The government did not seem to know about this situation. In any case, it lacked any economic imagination and had recourse to standard remedies: raising the exchange value of the rouble and blaming speculators. By 1915 workers were demanding wage increases to keep up with inflation; by 1917 industrial production was halved because of strikes. The government abandoned its responsibilities and, in the end, striking workers were one of the immediate causes of the imperial collapse.

The principal problem was that wages could not be readily translated into food. Agriculture did not profit from the pre-1916 boom as much as industry. Though the harvests were on the whole higher than in 1914, the peasants, who held some 60 percent of the market, were not making sufficient profits. These were made by various intermediaries and, above all, by speculators. By 1916 they were beginning to hoard their harvest for better times. Moreover, all the available grain had to be transferred from the countryside to the cities and this was the task of the railway system. Up to the end of 1916, the railways seemed capable of tackling their tasks with considerable success. Between 1914 and 1916, passenger traffic increased from 235,000,000 to 348,000,000 and freight carried in 1916 amounted to 17,228,000,000 pounds as compared to 13,826,000,000 pounds in 1913. After November 1916, however, food deliveries slowed down. By the following March, Petrograd had only a few days of grain reserves, and bread riots were one of the immediate causes of the imperial demise. Widespread famine was prevalent throughout Russia.

However, the most immediate cause of the collapse was an army mutiny in Petrograd. By the spring of 1917, peasant soldiers were disgruntled with the conditions under which they

Below: A queue for sugar in February 1917. Shortages of basic necessities were common during the war.

had to fight, if not with the war itself. Casualties were disquietingly high: 2,000,000 to 5,500,000 prisoners and the rest killed or wounded. Reliable estimates put the number of dead at 1,850,000. In 1916 they amounted to 3,000,000. By spring 1917, the men were beginning to blame their officers for the casualties. They had questioned their authority from the beginning in 1914. Discipline was enforced by public beating; men had to call their officers by high-flying titles, which clearly demonstrated the cultural gap between the two groups. Peasant recruits were largely illiterate and their behavior was often uncivilized. One divisional headquarters noticed repeated breakdowns of its telephone lines every afternoon. On investigation, it was discovered that soldiers guarding the lines were chopping up telephone posts to brew their tea. The men, however, were

treated like savages by their officers: 'They look on us as soulless lumps, without any feeling at all. Beatings are savage; sometimes old men with long beards are beaten. We throw our rifles away and give up, because things are dreadful in our army, and so are the officers.' At least army censors could see the gravity of the conflict between men and officers. Officers seemed to suspect nothing. They were genuinely puzzled, when leading a company of fresh recruits to the line, that after a burst of shellfire the company should start crying. General Dragomirov thought the lack of NCOs, the intermediary link between men and officers, was responsible for these tensions and low morale.

The *Stavka* chief of staff, General Yanushkevich, was much nearer to explaining the soldiers' lack of motivation. As the war dragged on, with defeats and deteriorating conditions all

Right: Soldiers join the revolution behind a banner proclaiming 'Long Live Free Russia.'

Below: A demonstration by women on Nevsky Prospekt in Petrograd during March 1917. The banner makes the appeal, 'Comrade Workers and Soldiers, Support Our Demands.'

round, he thought that the men's fading patriotism should be reinvigorated. He proposed to the Council of Ministers that peasant soldiers who fought well should be guaranteed 25 acres of land. The proposal was met with derision, and Yanushkevich failed to become the man who saved the Russian monarchy. Between 1914 and 1916, while supplies of food and clothing in the armies were abundant, men were prepared to put up with officers' brutality and inefficiency, and with the war in general. However, by 1917 soldiers were receiving poor rations at irregular intervals, and sometimes none at all. Instead, they were given paper money to buy their meals, but they could find nothing in the army and civilian stores, and could not afford the black-market prices. Army life became intolerable. From the declaration of hostilities in 1914 army morale steadily declined. The first signs of it were the careless attitude of the men, their malingering, passive resistance, dumb insolence, and overstaying their leaves. During the Brusilov Offensive in 1916, men were shooting themselves in the finger and were carried away by other men, indicating a more serious decline in morale. Desertions were on the increase and surrenders frequent enough to worry the command, which promptly formed a field gendarmerie to stop them. By 1917, men living on rotten herring under the influence of drink from illicit stills were openly mutinous, attacking and sometimes killing their officers. Demoralization stared the army authorities in the face, at the front and in the rear. It was worst in the large garrisons, particularly in Petrograd.

By 1916 some 16,400,000 men were in uniform, a large part of them in reserve. After the great retreat in 1915, both casualties and reserves were billeted in the large cities in pre-war barracks. *Stavka* already had an idea of what could happen to demoralized garrison troops. During the great retreat, discipline completely disintegrated and Warsaw was sacked in the most dreadful fashion by mutinous mobs before they ran away in panic. This outburst of armed anarchy was considered exceptional. As long as the turnover of troops on reserve duties in barracks in the Russian rear was sufficiently regular and rapid it was believed that discipline could be maintained. But by the autumn of 1916,

the transfers of reserves to the front slowed down and then practically stopped. At the same time casualties from the 1916 offensives poured in. After hearing the stories of the wounded, the morale of the garrisons reached rock bottom. The situation in the capital was perhaps more dangerous for the troops than anywhere else as they were constantly under the threat of being sent on active duty to the nearby Northern Front. Consequently, desertions were rife and the number of 'incidents,' with officers provoked by garrison troops, disquieting. The majority of the garrison soldiers were over 40 years of age and their young officers were mostly recent recruits – only some 10 percent were regulars – incapable of enforcing discipline. Early in 1917 widespread civil disorders suddenly broke out in the capital. Given the morale of the garrison troops they could not be expected to suppress them. It seemed inevitable that these disorders would entail a complete breakdown in public order and army discipline, and turn into a similar situation to that in Warsaw. Still the high command seemed blissfully unaware of these dangers.

In the middle of February 1917 the reserves of flour and foodstuff in general were dangerously low in Petrograd. Rumors spread that hunger would overwhelm the population if nothing was done and new supplies of food were not brought into the city. Nothing could be expected from the government, since it was not directly responsible for supplies. The Duma politicians, strident in their criticism of bureaucracy, were on the whole ignorant of the real situation. But the police reports to the governor, General Khabalov, predicted a hunger riot. Given the scale of industrial strikes, often politically motivated, and the restlessness of the Petrograd garrison, the anticipated riot was going to be too large for the police forces to handle alone. The governor, apart from filing these reports, took no other measures.

In the city itself the responsibility for security and public order rested with a number of officials whose records were particularly unimpressive. The minister of the interior, A D Protopopov, was responsible for the police forces. This friend of Rasputin could not be relied on to do anything decisive in a real emergency. Similarly nothing could be expected from General M A Belyayev, the minister of war, who was an army bureaucrat without service experience. General S S Khabalov, in command of the city garrison, was, like his minister, without service experience. Both owed their appointments to the political influence of Rasputin, but were typical Russian officers. They quarreled with General Ruzsky, commanding the Northern Front, and used their political influence to have the Petrograd Military District excluded from his command. Consequently, contingency plans for the city's security did not include troop reinforcements from the Northern Front in case of a serious breakdown in discipline. Apart from the garrison of up to 450,000 troops, there were 3500 police and 3200 Cossacks, experienced in crowd handling with *nagaykas* (whips), in the city. According to the plans, troops, if employed at all against rioting mobs, were to use firearms only in the last resort. On paper at least, security in the capital seemed assured.

From the beginning of 1917 popular excitement in the capital rose. On 9 January, to commemorate 'Bloody Sunday,' some 300,000 workers went on strike. Strikes, a traditional way of commemorating the terrible event, were widespread throughout the country, particularly in Moscow. At the same time in Petrograd, after the postponement of the scheduled Duma session was announced on 14 February, workers organizations took up the Duma's demand for a 'responsible government' and proposed a demonstration in its support. On 24 January the first serious appeal to demonstrate in support of the Duma was issued by the workers group of the War Industry Committee. It stated that 'the autocratic system was incapable of pursuing the war to its successful conclusion; it should be replaced by a Provisional Government based on a democratic principle.' In response to these 'subversive' calls the government ordered the arrests of the workers group who were mainly Mensheviks. In the end there was no mass demonstration and only some 10,000

workers went on strike. In fact the relatively small demonstration in support of the Duma which did take place consisted of students. However, the arrests deprived the strikes and demonstrations of the moderate Menshevik leadership and opened the way for the more radical Socialists, Bolsheviks and Socialist Revolutionaries (SRs). The Bolsheviks were at this stage of no significance. A Shlyapnikov aided by V Molotov and P Zalutsky ran a central committee which, without Lenin, could not even control the local Petrograd committee. Socialist Revolutionaries had no organization, but had prominent members placed in all the existing organizations. The best known of them was A Kerensky, a member of the Duma. In the Duma and the State Council excited calls for a government of national confidence were repeated, but this 'parliamentary furore' was confined to the palaces in which the two chambers sat.

On 19 February and again on the 21st, food riots finally broke out. The government, in order to do something about the crisis, fixed the prices of bread, but Petrograd bakers, who were Bolshevik sympathizers, started selling off their bread at irregular intervals, often keeping back some of the supply. Customers who had to queue for a long time to obtain bread knew of this practice and, during these two days, they would sometimes rush the bakeries or vent their frustration on other shops. Looting was widespread. The police were able to handle these predicted and traditional riots perfectly well. On the other hand, when women workers, mainly from the textile factories in the Vyborg district, went on strike on 24 February and others then joined them, the police had problems dealing with this unexpected situation. The pretext of these riots was the celebration of the International Women's Day and the rallying cry was 'Bread!' Moreover, the strikers forced non-striking workers to stop work, another unprecedented feature. Contrary to the established ritual, they spilled out of their plants into the streets and marched through the Vyborg and neighboring districts.

Right: Rebel soldiers and students fire on policemen who have taken refuge in several attics. Petrograd, February 1917.

Left: Revolutionaries murder a policeman in Petrograd. Attacks on state officials were common during the takeover.

The resulting large-scale rioting and widespread looting could not be checked. The small police forces found it impossible to handle such large numbers, while the mounted Cossacks, with their whips, seemed reluctant to charge the crowd of women rioters to disperse them.

In contrast to preceding events, the rioting on the 25th was better 'organized.' Local Bolshevik committees showed interest and urged their followers to participate in them. Later, it was alleged that German agents also contributed to the organization of this riot, though there is no conclusive proof of their participation. Nonetheless, the demonstration was the largest since the outbreak of the war: between 158,000 to 197,000 people took part and, apart from cries for 'Bread,' political slogans against the war and the autocracy made their appearance. The crowds penetrated into the center of the capital, but the mounted police managed to disperse them. The Cossacks proved as reluctant as before to use force against the crowds. The mysterious death of a mounted police captain was attributed to them. Some Cossacks apparently fired on the mounted police. What remained unknown to the police was a Bolshevik decision to involve garrison soldiers in the demonstrations.

On the 26th, a 200,000-strong crowd of striking workers brought the entire city to a standstill. General Khabalov continued to issue misleading statements claiming that bread was in plentiful supply. In his reports, particularly to *Stavka*, he claimed that the situation was under control. Bolshevik workers were so excited by the turn of events that they asked the garrison soldiers for arms, but were refused. Their propaganda aimed at involving them in street demonstrations had little effect. Shlyapnikov argued against arming the workers; he considered they should wait for the garrison to go over to them voluntarily and then fight alongside them. Disorders, however, were on such a scale that the police sounded the alarm. The emperor at Mogilëv at long last heard about the disturbances in Petrograd from his wife who was at Tsarskoye Selo (now Krasnoe Selo), just outside the city. The same evening he sent an order to General Khabalov 'to put an end, as from tomorrow, to all disturbances in the streets of the capital.' Khabalov executed the order by plastering notices all over the city, forbidding further demonstrations. He threatened to order the troops to open fire at demonstrators who disobeyed his call, and that strikers would be called up into the army. This latter threat was

Above: Artillerymen supporting the February Revolution man a barricade on Liteiny Prospekt in Petrograd.

with arms and persuaded to join in. Over the next few days, the situation in the capital deteriorated. Demonstrators were joined by armed soldiers, who returned fire annihilating the police. Many police were lynched and looting was widespread. Excited demonstrators broke into the arsenal and seized arms. Prisons were stormed and all prisoners released; criminals joined in the orgy of looting and rape most readily. Tax offices and courts were burning. All of Petrograd lived in the streets. There were no leaders of the insurrection, no plan for further action, just mass hatred and destruction of property.

Four days after the events in Petrograd, the emperor put the formal seal on the dissolution of his empire. General Khabalov, according to eye-witnesses, resigned as governor on 27 February, panic-stricken, since he could not accomplish the emperor's mission. The Imperial Government, fearing mob violence, had resigned earlier. Before abandoning his office, Prince Golitsyn suggested the formation of a temporary dictatorship under the regency of Nicholas's brother, Grand Duke Michael. The emperor was confused by contradictory reports, rumors and evident signs of collapse. But he was only really worried about the fate of his family at Tsarskoye Selo. Earlier, despite General Ruzsky's entreaties for the appointment of a 'government of confidence,' he had sent the aged General Ivanov and a battalion of men decorated with the St George's Cross, the Russian equivalent of the Victoria Cross, to Petrograd to 're-establish public order.' He also hoped that Ivanov would assure the security of his family at Tsarskoye Selo. Since then there had been no news. In fact, the general had had great difficulties accomplishing the task. He and his battalion were often shunted off the main track and progressed very slowly. The general could only rage and cry; even such elite troops as the Cavaliers of St George's Cross were not taught to run trains. Still without news, the emperor decided to leave Mogilëv for Tsarskoye Selo on 28 February to be with his family, whom he knew were ill. It was to be a long journey home.

Duma commissioner Bublikov slowed down the imperial train so much that by 1 March it had only reached Pskov, where General Ruzsky had his Northern Front headquarters. In the meantime, Duma President Rodzianko and Professor Milyukov each devised a plan for the resolution of the crisis. The former favored an appointment of a 'government of confidence,' while the latter wanted the abdication of the emperor in favor of his son and the appointment of Grand Duke Michael as regent. Simultaneously, *Stavka* generals, informed about the true situation in Petrograd by the Duma, began to take steps to resolve the crisis on the spot. General Alexeyev told Ruzsky to inform the emperor that if he appointed a 'government of confidence' the army would support it. After a meeting with Ruzsky, who finally told the emperor about the chaos in Petrograd, the latter issued a manifesto agreeing to the appointment of a responsible government. General Ivanov, who by now had reached Tsar-

so ridiculous that it could not be taken seriously. With hindsight, this was the final straw that broke the imperial regime: a nonsensical order by an impotent autocrat to his equally impotent subordinate who had no idea of the real situation in the city.

On Sunday 26 February, the police arrested 100 known revolutionaries, patrolled the streets and posted guards at all the strategic points in the capital. Despite the governor's proclamation, people collected in large crowds, marching and countermarching in the city center. Troops from the Guards regiments stationed in the center were called out to disperse demonstrators. They belonged to the training battalion for NCOs. In four separate incidents, they fired into the crowds when ordered by their officers, causing heavy casualties. The fury of the mobs was terrifying but the high command was convinced that the riot had been quelled. In the Pavlovski regimental barrack there was a mutiny when a group of soldiers marched out to 'punish the training battalion.' Almost immediately, most of the mutineers were disarmed and imprisoned. However, 20 of them escaped with their arms. Later that day they probably murdered their commanding officer when he left the barracks. General Khabalov failed to mention the Pavlovski Regiment mutiny in his report to the emperor. Nevertheless, diehard revolutionaries thought that the revolutionary insurrection had suffered a serious setback.

On 27 February both sides were proved wrong in their assessments of the situation. Garrison troops, some involved in firing on the crowds and some that were not, finally realized what they had done the day before. Feverish discussions on the subject went on all night and in the morning the Volynski Guards Regiment suddenly mutinied. Soldiers under the command of two NCOs killed the commanding officer, an unpopular Pole, and then spilled out into the streets with arms. Many approached neighboring barracks asking the soldiers to join them. Many refused but gradually, after murdering their own officers, they also joined the mutiny. In the end, only the Bicycle Battalion under the command of their colonel had to be subdued

skoye Selo, was ordered to abandon his mission to Petrograd. All seemed set for a smooth constitutional change. However, in the early morning of 2 March Rodzianko changed his mind about the responsible government; he telegraphed Ruzsky to convince the emperor to abdicate. Ruzsky in turn consulted Alexeyev, presenting him with the latest idea of Rodzianko. When all five front commanders and the navy commanders concurred, Ruzsky went to see the emperor, whose train was still immobile at Pskov.

The final denouement was pathetic. The emperor, seeing himself betrayed by almost all his servants, first abdicated in favor of his son and his brother's regency. Then, seeing that he would have to live separated from his son, he abdicated on his behalf, in favor of his brother who would never accept the succession. The Romanov dynasty had been 'elected' to the Russian throne in the seventeenth century after a period of chaos. Now it was leaving the throne in confusion, leaving the Russian people to face alone another period of great instability.

Above: Distribution of newspapers and leaflets on the streets of Moscow in 1917.

Left: Czar Nicholas II hands the notice of his abdication to a messenger from the Duma in his railway carriage near Pskov.

PROVISIONAL GOVERNMENT

On 27 February 1917 two committees came into existence: the Provisional Committee of the Duma and the Petrograd Soviet. The politicians of the Progressive Bloc in the Duma were dismayed by the turn of events. Though they were severe critics of the imperial regime, they had no wish to see it collapse, particularly during the war. The President of the Duma, M Rodzianko, still hoped that he could save Russia from political chaos. To this end, he sent several telegrams to the emperor at Mogilëv, urging him to appoint 'a government of confidence.' The emperor thought him a panic-stricken troublemaker, especially after he spoke of the 'mortal danger to the dynasty and the war arising out of the events in Petrograd,' in his last telegram. Confronted by the turmoil in Petrograd, the president and the Progressive Bloc leaders could not decide how to take over power from the former imperial regime and give their actions a semblance of legitimacy.

On the 27th they agreed to meet unofficially and, after long and agonizing discussions, they formed the Provisional Committee of the Duma, presided over by Rodzianko. This body was to act as a caretaker government. Early on the following morning, the committee issued two proclamations: one appealed for the restoration of public order; the other explained the committee's formation and its assumption of responsibilities. Later that day commissioners were sent to various imperial ministries to take them over on behalf of the committee. Without authorization, A Bublikov, the commissioner in charge of the ministry of state railways, sent a telegram to all the railway stations informing them that 'the State Duma has formed a new government.' Although not strictly speaking true, it was, nonetheless, the first announcement of a post-imperial regime. Rodzianko informed senior army commanders of the formation of his committee at the same time. However, official, unofficial and provisional announcements appeared as confused as the situation outside the Tauride Palace. Next day another leader, Professor Milyukov, 'assumed' power in place of the 'uncertain' and contradictory Rodzianko.

It was soon obvious that the assumption of power by various Duma leaders was illusory. All these leaders seemed capable of dealing with the constitutional problems left by the imperial regime, but taking real control was a different matter. Milyukov's solution to the abdication and succession crisis was even more confusing than the one enacted at Pskov; moreover it was constitutionally unsound. In the end Grand Duke Michael refused the throne, spelling the end of the Romanov dynasty. Next, the Duma's Provisional Committee had to deal with another *ad hoc* body, forming in another wing of the Tauride Palace, the Petrograd Soviet. The subsequent agreement between the Provisional Committee and the soviet to form a provisional government was a public but temporary marriage of convenience. In real terms, the agreement stated that there were two committees in the same palace and that they had assumed power. Although the empire was without an emperor, it had a Provisional Government – at least on paper. It was a coalition government consisting mainly of Pro-

Previous page: The May Day demonstration on the streets of Petrograd in 1917.

Below: Members of the Provisional Government, including prime minister Georgiy Lvov (second from left), Russian Army commander General Alexeyev (center) and Alexander Kerensky (second from right), minister for war. At the end of August 1917 Kerensky took over as supreme commander of the army.

gressive Bloc leaders, though the prime minister, Prince G Ye Lvov, was a non-party man
who had been the chairman of the All-Russian
Union of the *Zemstva* (local government movement). Milyukov (Kadet) was the foreign minister and Guchkov (Octobrist) the war minister.
Significantly, a lone Socialist Revolutionary, A
Kerensky, joined the government as justice
minister against the wishes of the Petrograd
Soviet, of whose executive committee he was a
member. The Provisional Committee of the
Duma claimed that it had acted constitutionally in creating the Provisional Government
and also announced the new government's
eight-point program which would serve as a
guide to its future actions.

The fear of conspiracies haunted the emperor
throughout the war years right up to his abdication. Curiously enough, the formation of the
Provisional Government was probably the
result of a conspiracy. It is now known that all
the members of the Provisional Government,
except Milyukov, were members of a secretive
masonic lodge founded in St Petersburg in 1905
or 1906. In addition to the members of the Provisional Government, numerous social republicans and all sorts of radicals, including many
Bolsheviks, belonged to this lodge. Their aim
was the destruction of Russian autocracy and
they were almost all republicans. It can be said
that the Russian masons seized power in a con-
spiratorial way and clung to it until they were
deposed by the Bolsheviks. In the meantime,
the masons soon ousted the outsider Milyukov
and Guchkov, who though a mason was unpopular in the lodge.

The Petrograd Soviet, which was formed at
the same time as the Provisional Government,
was a revolutionary organization, created to
take advantage of and channel revolutionary
fervor. The majority of the soviet's founding

Above: Those connected
with the deposed royal
family were made to pay
by the forces of the
Provisional Government.
This was some of the mess
caused in the palace of
Mathilde Ksheshinskaya, a
one-time mistress of the
czar who later married one
of his cousins.

Left: Kerensky and
Kornilov arrive with their
guard at Tsarskoye Selo to
arrest the czarina.

members were Mensheviks or Socialist Revolutionaries, but their position was as ambivalent as that of the Provisional Government. At first, the soviet members thought of themselves as a purely 'consultative' body which had nothing to do with the government. The chairman of the soviet, N S Chkheidze (Menshevik), declined an offer to join the Provisional Government, and Kerensky's membership was never officially approved, although the public announcement of his appointment was greeted with rapturous applause. The soviet did not directly participate in any of the government's political initiatives though its objections to certain policies were taken into account from the very beginning. The soviet objected to Grand Duke Nicholas's reappointment as the army's supreme commander and its demands for his immediate dismissal were fulfilled. The soviet also objected to Prince Lvov's appointment as

Below: Aksenov's depiction of Lenin's return to Russia in April 1917. Having arrived at the Finland Station in Petrograd, he then addressed his supporters from the top of an armored car.

prime minister, but its objections were not heeded in this case.

The soviet and the Provisional Government, although coexisting, would never act in harmony, both preferring to follow separate roads in the pursuit of different objectives. Both bodies held what in reality was only a semblance of power. In any case the soviet, after initial confusion, opted to appeal to an entirely different section of the people: it would represent popular forces, which meant the mass of mutinous soldiers. In the military there was a clear division between officers and men, and the soviet came out in support of the latter. First of all, however, the soviet had to gain the soldiers' support and this was done by the simple act of legitimizing their mutiny. The Provisional Government was left to seek support among the army's officer class.

The executive committee of the Petrograd

Soviet was formed by those Menskevik workers' representatives released from prison by mutinous troops. It was to be an organ of workers' and soldiers' self-government and, as such, the committee appealed to them to elect their deputies (one per 1000 workers and one per company). Some 40 of these delegates as well as a crowd of unelected people sanctioned the election of the executive committee. The three socialist Duma members, Chkheidze, Skobelev and Kerensky were elected chairman and vice-chairmen respectively. A Military Commission was set up to sort out the problems of the mutinous garrison and restore public order. This proved most difficult to achieve. The peasant soldiers, who had made great sacrifices for the revolution (there were 2000 casualties, including 960 deaths), were asked to 'calm down,' give up their arms and return to their barracks in return for immunity. To the soldiers, such an appeal sounded like a betrayal of the revolution. They obeyed the soviet's appeals with great reluctance. If anything they desired an end to the war and a return to their villages, where they hoped to receive land taken from the large landlords. On the other hand, they were

Above: A meeting of the 'Freedom Loan' organization on Nevsky Prospekt in May 1917. The Provisional Government tried to persuade workers to subscribe five percent of their earnings to help reduce the country's massive debt which was growing with each month of the war. Despite the time for receiving subscriptions being extended twice, the scheme was not a success.

Left: General Alexeyev, the supreme commander of the Russian Army under the Provisional Government, later became a military adviser.

Left: With the spread of greater disillusionment, discipline problems in the Russian Army increased. Here, a soldier threatens two potential deserters.

Below: As with any war, however, all was not total gloom and despondency on the Eastern Front. German and Russian soldiers often fraternized in No Man's Land – much to the disgust of senior officers.

determined to defend their revolution with their lives, because it was the only guarantee of their immunity from the consequences of the mutiny.

During the excitement of continuous government sessions which discussed these problems, a Bolshevik soldier-representative, N D Sokolov, drafted a document which was to pave the way for the pacification of the Petrograd insurgents. The document, later known as Order No 1, contained many points: committees were to be elected by soldiers and naval personnel; each company was to elect a delegate to the Petrograd Soviet; the armed forces in Petrograd would only obey the soviet; the orders of the Military Commission would only be carried out if they were approved by the soviet; all arms were to remain under the control of company and battalion committees; weapons should not be handed over to officers; while on duty, soldiers were subject to military discipline but off duty they were to be treated as private citizens; officers' titles (Excellency) were to be abolished; the maltreatment of men by officers was outlawed; and men were to have the right of appeal if abused. Order No 1 was approved by the soviet and took immediate effect, although it was intended for the Petrograd garrison alone. Subsequently, the order appeared in the soviet's newspaper, *Izvestiya*, and numerous pamphlets, and, therefore, applied to the armed forces as a whole. Its short-term effect was the immediate restoration of public order in Petrograd, giving the impression that the soviet, not the Provisional Government, was the real power. It also seemed that the soldiers transferred their allegiance from the emperor to the soviet's committees. In the long-term, however, it undermined discipline in the armies, thus hastening the end of the war.

The Provisional Government was in no position to countermand Order No 1. In fact, not even the soviet was in any way aware of its far-reaching consequences. The two bodies were both busily hammering out a political agreement on the new government's program. The agreement consisted of the following points: a complete amnesty for all political prisoners; freedom of speech, publication and strike; the creation of a republic; the convocation of a constituent assembly; the establishment of a people's militia to replace the police; the setting up of democratic local administration; the abolition of class, national and religious discrimination; the election of army officers; and no disarming or transfer of the Petrograd garrison. After the announcement of this agreement the two bodies went their separate ways.

The government, initially representing moderate liberal and conservative forces (with the exception of Kerensky), had to face four major crises during its existence from March to November 1917. The Allied governments had recognized the Provisional Government on 4 March on condition that it assumed the obligations of its imperial predecessor, and on 18 April, Foreign Minister Milyukov sent them the prime minister's statement on the war. This was, in fact, a compromise formulated after the soviet's objection to Milyukov's initial draft. Milyukov added a personal note to the statement in which he spoke of continuing the war to the 'decisive victory' in direct conflict with the prime minister's wish for a 'war without conquest and indemnities.' Of course, Milyukov affirmed that, while he was foreign minister, Russia would remain a loyal ally to the end of the war. It is still uncertain who leaked the note to the Russian press, whether it was a masonic or Bolshevik plot. During 20-21 April armed demonstrations for and against Milyukov's note took place in Petrograd; casualties were registered on both sides. As a result, Milyukov resigned from his post. Shortly afterward, possibly as a result of the same demonstrations, War Minister Guchkov resigned, claiming that the government could not govern and that it was under constant pressure from the soviet. In the subsequent government reshuffle Lvov remained premier, but Milyukov was replaced by M Tereshchenko (a mason), Guchkov by Kerensky, and another Socialist Revolutionary, V Chernov, became minister of agriculture.

The next crisis, in June, was in fact the result of a struggle within the soviet. Throughout March the government carried out its promises. In the general euphoria felt after the revolution, it was thought that the Russian people would create social cohesion and self-discipline without needing the many state constraints of the past. It was argued that it was a question of commonsense. Surely a civilized, orderly life was preferable to chaos? However, it soon became clear that such arguments lacked strength. While the government was granting the Russians all the liberties they had clamored for, together with a general amnesty for prisoners and abolition of the death penalty, it was completing the destruction of the old state. It also dissolved local government offices (*zemstva*) replacing them with soviets, and

replaced the police with a people's militia. Thus, even Lenin admitted that Russia was the freest country in the world at this stage. The Bolsheviks were only interested in making use of the new freedom.

After Lenin's return on 4 April, the Bolsheviks, who had installed themselves in ballerina Ksheshinskaya's palace, began to plan a revolutionary demonstration as a prelude to the overthrow of the Provisional Government. Lenin retained a firm belief in his tactics which stated that after the first phase of the revolution the proletariat would turn against the bourgeois government and take power from it. In the present circumstances the pretext for the takeover would be the defense of the Anarchists who, in spite of the proclaimed freedoms, were, it was claimed, unjustifiably persecuted by the government. The Bolsheviks, therefore, meticulously planned a mass demonstration for 10 June, to coincide with the All-Russian Congress of the Soviets. When Bolshevik intentions became known, congress prohibited all demonstrations (some military units even threatened to come to Petrograd to deal with the Bolsheviks) and, instead, organized its own, peaceful march for the 18th. With hindsight, this con-

gress-sponsored demonstration was a tactical mistake. The soviet representatives were still unacquainted with Lenin and the Bolsheviks, and could not believe that their prohibition would not be observed. The Bolsheviks decided to exploit this golden opportunity for their own ends. At first the demonstration was orderly, though crowds of socialist supporters shouted various slogans like 'Down with the 10 Capitalist Ministers,' making allusion to the threatened resignation of 10 liberal ministers, and 'All Power to the Soviets,' which was a Bolshevik-inspired slogan. The Anarchists, who kept their weapons, made sure that the demonstration turned ugly. The demonstrators stormed a prison, and released fellow Anarchists arrested a few days before the march. In turn, they were attacked by government forces rushed there to save prison guards from being lynched, and one of their leaders was killed. Subsequently, congress passed a resolution prohibiting any street demonstration without prior soviet approval.

Though the government emerged from this crisis strengthened, it was only for a short time, for neither the Bolsheviks nor the Anarchists were intimidated by this show of strength. They immediately started planning the next demonstration. Coinciding with the unrest in Petrograd, the armies in the field launched their last offensive against the German and Austrian forces. Initially successful, the offensive proved to be the last blow to the army's morale. The

government would no longer have disciplined and controlled military forces at its disposal.

In July, the most dangerous crisis of them all was provoked by the Bolsheviks. Previously the Georgian Social Democrat, Tsereteli, had argued that the Bolsheviks should not be given another chance to threaten the government. However, the All-Russian Congress of the Soviets did not heed his warning and passed the ambiguous resolution on soviet control of demonstrations, a resolution it could not enforce. Three weeks later Tsereteli was proved right. Encouraged by their limited success on 18 June, the Bolshevik Military Committee began to plan another attempt to seize power. This attempt would be led by Bolshevik soldiers, especially the soldiers of the 1st Machine Gun Regiment. The pretext was the resignation of several liberal ministers on 2 July in protest at government policy toward the autonomy of the Ukraine. While the Bolshevik soldiers led by Podvoysky felt strong enough to topple the government, Lenin was more cautious and ordered Podvoysky to 'scuttle the coup.' Despite this Bolshevik decision, some 100,000 soldiers and sailors, together with 30,000 Putilov munition workers, massed round the Tauride Palace, as if to storm it, early on 3 July. Apart from Bolshevik 'conspirators,' the Putilov workers were there demanding higher wages; the soldiers to avoid being sent to the front since the foolhardy offensive was turning into a rout; and the

Above: Russian troops surrendering after heavy fighting in Galicia in 1917.

Right: N Chkheidze, chairman of the Petrograd Soviet from February to August 1917, delivering a speech in favor of continuing the war against Germany and her allies.

sailors were protesting against the reinstatement of their officers. Despite the soviet's prohibition, the demonstration turned into a bloody riot with 400 casualties. Early on 4 July Lenin and the Bolsheviks belatedly tried to exploit the ensuing chaos by assuming leadership. Violent clashes continued and the whole of the Petrograd population seemed to be involved. Into this situation of generalized violence arrived some 20,000 Kronstadt sailors who, after being 'reviewed' by Lenin, were sent on to the Tauride Palace which was virtually besieged by hostile demonstrators. Minister Chernov, the Duma's most radical socialist member, was sent out to calm the mob; he would have been lynched had it not been for Trotsky. This was indeed the most violent turmoil that Petrograd had witnessed so far. Still without Lenin's decisive leadership, it profited no one. Even today, historians can only speculate as to why Lenin shrunk from a direct assault of the Tauride Palace. It was surely not because the executive committee of the All-Russian Soviet had voted against a seizure of power by the left; perhaps the rumors of frontline troops coming to Petrograd had a sobering effect on Lenin and the mob. When three guard regiments did march to the Tauride Palace, it became evident that the Bolshevik coup had been thwarted. An additional reason for the Bolshevik failure was the accusation, released by the minister of justice, that Lenin and the Bolsheviks were German agents.

Mobs turned against the Bolsheviks, as well as Jews with German names. Fully informed of the real situation, Lenin appealed to the soldiers and sailors to return to their barracks in a *Pravda* statement. With loyal troops continually arriving in Petrograd, the government took its revenge. A detachment wrecked the *Pravda* printing plant, though the Bolshevik headquarters was evacuated before the troops arrived there. Thousands of arrests were made; the Kronstadt sailors surrendered and were disarmed; and the Anarchists were dispersed. Many Bolshevik leaders (Kamenev and Trotsky) were imprisoned; others (Lenin and Zinoviev) escaped to Finland. Lenin, while vehemently denying the charges of being a German agent, refused to appear before a tribunal, which was taken as admission of guilt.

However, no direct connection between Lenin and the Imperial German authorities has ever been established by historians since 1917. German public archives revealed nothing conclusive when consulted after 1945. The private contacts of Lenin and the Bolsheviks were neglected. It has since been established beyond any doubt that Lenin and the Bolsheviks did obtain German financial support through the private company Siemens. Lenin's brother-in-law, Mark Yelisarov, was the Russian director of the company and throughout the war was in receipt of his salary and other sums. In the end Lenin's opponents failed to investigate the German connection properly, and after the successful Bolshevik coup in November the subject became taboo. The Bolsheviks were not dealt with sufficiently firmly because the government was faced, immediately after the abortive coup, with another crisis which ended in another reshuffle.

It was the turn of the socialist members of the Provisional Government to take political

advantage of the clear victory over the Bolsheviks. They argued that their negotiations with the Allies on ending the war were sabotaged by the liberals, their land reforms by the conservatives and their industrial measures by both. This political sabotage provoked 'popular feeling' against the government and enabled the Bolsheviks to attempt another coup. On 8 July Prince Lvov resigned and was succeeded by Kerensky, the firebrand socialist. Immediately, even before he had formed a cabinet, Kerensky publicly announced the land and industry measures which his government would take to pacify peasants and workers alike. As befitted a coalition government socialists were finally in a majority. Kerensky's measures were not radical enough to satisfy extremists, but they were far-reaching enough (for example, land could not be sold before the enactment of the agricultural reform) to alienate conservative and liberal support for Kerensky. When the collapse of the armies in the field became known, the government restored the death penalty in the army. This measure alienated even the moderate left, which formed the government's political base. The question was who was supporting the 'victorious' government? In November the Bolsheviks answered the question with surprising lucidity.

The final August crisis revealed the supposedly real enemies of the government. Up to then the threat to it came mainly from unruly mobs and the left. Now it turned out to be the extreme right and, above all, the army command. The latter was naturally blamed for the failure of the unfortunate offensive intended to 'restore the army's morale.' It was launched on 18 June, largely in response to French pressures. Throughout July, while the Bolsheviks were being dealt with in Petrograd, hordes of deserters were spreading anarchy throughout the country. Industrial production was coming to a halt and food supplies were breaking down. The economic system collapsed for it could no longer function in such chaotic conditions. On 16 July Premier Kerensky met the high command in person to hear their proposals. Most of the high command had no ideas, no proposals; some generals offered excuses.

The youthful General Denikin suggested the restoration of the old system; only General Kornilov put forward practical measures to restore morale and stop desertions. Two days later he was appointed commander in chief in place of Brusilov and the death penalty was reintroduced. Kornilov boldly proposed to work with military commissars representing the network of army committees, but only if it led to the re-establishment of order. The chief commissar, and Kornilov's close collaborator, B Savinkov, who was in Russia as an agent for the French government, was appointed vice-minister of war to be near to the war minister – Kerensky. The latter evidently hoped to cement the political unity of his government out of this military effort in which the right and left were in agreement. During the month of August, Kornilov twice went to Petrograd to seal this understanding with Kerensky with something very much more tangible.

Instead he found Kerensky increasingly difficult to deal with. As an excuse, Kerensky told the general that his cabinet might contain German agents. At the Moscow Political Forum, which was a broadly based political meeting convoked in support of the Kerensky government, right-wing forces championed the general, while the prime minister declared that he would defend the revolutionary gains against any threats coming from the left or the right. The misunderstanding between the premier and his commander in chief became increasingly evident and both harbored unreasonable suspicions of each other. Nonetheless, Kornilov was neither a conspirator nor a politician; at worst the right-wing forces wanted to make use of him. An open conflict broke out between them after a bizarre intrigue spun by N V Lvov, a namesake of the former premier, which turned their misunderstanding into outright hostility. According to Lvov's version of events, Kerensky authorized him to negotiate with the general on the establishment of a 'strong government' (dictatorship) to prevent Russia from lapsing into complete and utter chaos.

After the fall of Riga, Kornilov had made military dispositions to protect Petrograd against another German offensive. General Krymov's Third Cavalry Corps was sent to the city to protect it. It could also be used to uphold the Provisional Government, if need be. At the same time, Kornilov told Lvov that a Bolshevik coup was being organized in Petrograd. He was willing to suppress it, if the government proclaimed martial law and Kerensky withdrew to the headquarters at Mogilëv for safety. Lvov ultimately confused them so much that, on 26 August, they moved against each other instead of tackling the Bolsheviks. On 27 August Kerensky dismissed the general and proclaimed martial law in Petrograd to deal with Krymov's cavalry who were advancing on the city. Kornilov was declared a counter-revolutionary and the soviets rallied to defend the Provisional Government. By that time Krymov's troops had refused to advance farther since they had found out that instead of 'bashing the Bolsheviks' they were going to besiege the Provisional Government. After the arrests of Kornilov and other military 'conspirators,' Kerensky assumed the supreme command himself and reshuffled his government for the last time: General Verkhovsky, a man of extreme left-wing views and of great instability, became war minister. At the same time he proclaimed Russia a republic. On 14 September, when the crisis was over, Kerensky addressed the Democratic Conference, convoked by the soviets, and obtained a prolonged ovation for his speech. However, that was the limit of his achievement; he had to wait until the election of the Constituent Assembly for any major reforms. Since the Duma was dissolved, a pre-Parliament was set up to supervise his government. Kerensky and the Provisional Government emerged from this crisis considerably weakened: on the one hand the center and right forces had been alienated; on the other the left, including the Bolsheviks, were participating in democratic

Right: Some of the delegates to the First All-Russian Congress of Soviets held in Petrograd during June 1917.

Below: Petrograd, July 1917. Troops of the Kerensky government disarming soldiers of the !st Machine Gun Battalion who, along with their officers, had gone over to the Bolsheviks.

Above: A demonstration on
Nevsky Prospekt during
the attempted coup by the
Bolsheviks in July 1917 is
broken up by machine-gun
fire from government
troops.

politics. The damage wrought on the army by
the Kornilov affair could not be assessed, but it
would reveal itself in November.

As long as the armed forces existed, even in
their demoralized form, the Provisional
Government felt safe. It reasoned that the
armed forces would support it automatically.
After all, the Petrograd mutineers were amnestied thanks to the government; the command
was reinstated thanks to its intervention; and
both officers and men had sworn allegiance to it.
It was the Petrograd Soviet which had been
accused of causing the collapse of the army and
navy as a fighting force through the issue of
Order No 1, not the Provisional Government.
However, the soviet did not feel responsible for

any harm done to the armed forces by its Order
No 1. If any harm was done, it was uninten-
tional. When the soviet became aware that
Order No 1 was being applied throughout the
armed forces and not, as intended, in the Petrograd garrison alone, it decided to issue Order No
2. Order No 1 applied to the Petrograd garrison
but was declared invalid elsewhere. However,
those elections of committees and officers
already accomplished remained valid everywhere. Though the committees were paramount in public and political life, in military
matters officers had to be obeyed. Though the
Bolsheviks opposed No 2 tooth and nail, many
in the army accepted it. In the minds of peasant
soldiers, the orders were indistinguishable;

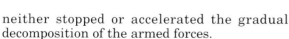

by soldiers bent on having their companions acquitted. The jury courts ceased to mete out capital punishment, the only real deterrent in wartime. All these ministerial measures, coupled with Orders No 1 and No 2, did no more than sanction the new conditions in the armed forces. When sailors of the Baltic Fleet murdered about 100 of their officers and brutally beat up hundreds more, they were not obeying any of these measures. Subsequently, they used the provision to grant themselves immunity. Similar actions occurred among both garrison and frontline troops. The unsystematic arrests of unpopular officers started in March 1917 and continued until the Bolshevik coup in November. They could not be stopped, not even by the men's elected committees. Pretexts for arrests were always found: old scores to settle with unpopular officers; counter-revolutionary 'tendencies' of outspoken officers – the most favored pretext; and sometimes a foreign name (very frequent among officers) was sufficient. The soviets themselves wanted to win the war and were, therefore, interested in maintaining discipline in the armed forces but, on the other hand, the committees were reluctant to publicly condemn men's maltreatment of

Below: General Kornilov, leader of an attempted military coup, addressing his troops.

neither stopped or accelerated the gradual decomposition of the armed forces.

However, it is simply untrue that the damage to the army was done solely by Orders No 1 and No 2. The war minister, Guchkov, also contributed to it by acting in a 'revolutionary manner.' Thus, for example, he extended the abolition of disciplinary restrictions to the frontline troops. In addition, he set up a commission under the former war minister, Polivanov, whose task was to revise the laws of military service. As if this was not enough, the Provisional Government abolished the death penalty on 12 March which meant that army court martials were replaced at the front by jury courts. These new tribunals could easily be pressurized

РАЙОННЫМЪ
Совѣтамъ Рабочихъ Депутатовъ
Фабрично-Заводскимъ Комитетамъ

ПРИКАЗЪ.

Корниловскія банды Керенскаго угро-
жаютъ подступамъ къ столицѣ. Отданы
всѣ необходимыя распоряженія для того,
чтобы безпощадно раздавить контръ-ре-
волюціонное покушеніе противъ народа
и его завоеваній.

Армія и Красная Гвардія революціи нуждаются въ не-
медленной поддержкѣ рабочихъ.

Приказываемъ районнымъ Совѣтамъ и Фабр.-Зав. Комитетамъ:

1) выдвинуть наибольшее количество рабочихъ для рытья окоповъ,
воздвиганія баррикадъ и укрѣпленія проволочныхъ загражденій;
2) гдѣ для этого потребуется прекращеніе работъ на
фабрикахъ и заводахъ, немедленно исполнить;
3) собрать всю имѣющуюся въ запасѣ колючую и простую про-
волоку, а равно всѣ орудія, необходимыя для рытья окоповъ и возведенія баррикадъ;
4) все имѣющееся оружіе имѣть при себѣ;
5) соблюдать строжайшую дисциплину и быть готовыми поддержать
армію революціи всѣми средствами.

Предсѣдатель Петроградскаго Совѣта Раб. и Солд. Депутатовъ
Народный Комиссаръ ЛЕВЪ ТРОЦКІЙ.

Предсѣдатель Военно-Революціоннаго Комитета
Главнокомандующій ПОДВОЙСКІЙ.

120

TO THE DISTRICT
SOVIETS OF WORKER'S DEPUTIES AND
SHOP-FACTORY COMMITTEES

ORDER

THE KORNILOV BANDS OF KERENSKY ARE
THREATENING THE OUTSKIRTS OF OUR CAP
ITAL. ALL NECESSARY ORDERS HAVE BEEN
GIVEN TO CRUSH MERCILESSLY EVERY
COUNTER-REVOLUTIONARY ATTEMPT
AGAINST THE PEOPLE AND ITS CONQUESTS

THE ARMY AND THE RED GUARD OF THE REV
OLUTION ARE IN NEED OF IMMEDIATE SUPPORT OF
THE WORKERS.

THE DISTRICT SOVIETS AND SHOP-FACTORY
COMMITTEES ARE ORDERED:

1) To bring forward the largest possible number of workers to dig trenches,
erect barricades and set up wire defenses;
2) Wherever necessary for this purpose to SUSPEND WORK in shops
and factories, it must be done IMMEDIATELY.
3) To collect all available plain and barbed wire, as well as all tools FOR
DIGGING TRENCHES AND ERECTING BARRICADES;
4) ALL AVAILABLE ARMS TO BE CARRIED ON PERSONS;
5) Strictest discipline must be preserved and all must be
ready to support the Army of the Revolution to the utmost.

President of the Petrograd Soviet of Workers & Soldiers Deputies
People's Commissar LEV TROTSKY.

President of the Military-Revolutionary Committee
Chief Commander PODVOISKY.

[Reproduction in English of the Russian text on opposite page.]

121

Above: Russian and English versions of the order issued by Trotsky at the outbreak of the civil war which followed the Bolshevik seizure of power in Petrograd and Moscow.

officers, who were often considered as potential counter-revolutionaries. Last but not least, the collapse of discipline was uneven in garrison towns and at the fronts.

Some 10,000,000 officers and men were on active service along five fronts and in the rear and the breakdown of discipline among them varied. It was absolute in the Petrograd Military District. The two fronts, the Northern and Western, bordering on Petrograd and Moscow, were also badly affected by the breakdown. However, the strategically important South Western Front was hardly affected, while the Romanian and Caucasian Fronts were not at all. On 11 March 1917 the commander in chief, General Alexeyev, seeing that the movement to elect soldiers' committees was spontaneous and could not be stopped, issued orders to have them instituted everywhere, at all levels, with officers participating in them. Thus, in some units, officers served alongside their men on committees, but these were exceptions. Usually officers were represented on higher level committees which proved to be far less radical than their low-level counterparts. The higher level committees were under Menshevik and Social-ist Revolutionary influence, while many of the low-level ones came under Bolshevik influence.

In time, the radical politicization of army committees made them less interested in dis-cipline and more concerned with burning issues such as the land reform proposals before the Constituent Assembly. When the Provisional Government failed to react to the 'agricultural' demands of soldiers' soviets, Bolshevik influence was automatically extended, and was particularly noticeable on the Northern Front. By then, of course, officers were not of the same caliber as those serving at the outbreak of the war. They were no longer regulars, but mostly recruited from the peasantry and often sym-pathetic to their men's plight and the revo-lution. The few regular officers left after the spontaneous bloodletting during the first days of the revolution were purged by the war mini-ster. Guchkov dismissed 70 divisional com-manders in three weeks. It became increasingly

difficult to restore discipline and morale in the army as the revolution progressed.

Perhaps the most potent and dangerous fac-tor affecting discipline was the spontaneous fraternization with enemy troops at the front. Cases were so numerous that nothing could be done about them. At first it was thought that the German and Austrian Armies would also be affected, but when it was recognized as an one-way process, attempts were made to stop it. However, the measures proved ineffective, especially when the Bolshevik-dominated com-mittees supported the fraternization movement as a means of fighting the Provisional Govern-ment after the failure of their coup in July. Curiously, the German and Austrian com-mands also favored it, though for different reasons: they benefited by obtaining intelli-gence about the Russian forces and by recruit-ing secret agents.

Another factor affecting morale was purely psychological: the Russian peasant soldiers were not sophisticated enough to distinguish between negotiations leading to a peace with-out annexations and indemnities, as favored by the Provisional Government, and immediate peace which was what they believed the govern-ment statement to mean. They stuck to this interpretation throughout. Milyukov's unfortu-nate note to the Allies further increased their confusion, and its repudiation by the govern-ment and Milyukov's resignation strengthened their impression that an immediate peace treaty was to be negotiated. It is probably true that the emperor's abdication did not affect the men as much as the delay before the men were told of events by the command. Rumors sug-gested that the emperor had been murdered by his officers, who persisted in going on with the war. 'Men were calm,' General Alexeyev reported on 11 March, 'but extremely suspicious of their officers, who were undoubtedly up to something.' On the whole the command was rather optimistic about army morale in their reports to the government, and the new com-mander in chief declared on 14 March that the overwhelming majority of men were for a victorious conclusion to the war. However, the situation on the fronts continued to deteriorate as was reported by Duma deputies who visited the armies several times during March and April. Early in May, General Brusilov, com-mander of the South Western Front, confirmed these reports. He blamed the Bolsheviks and their agitation and supported Alexeyev's view that an offensive would cure the spreading malaise. After some Allied pressure the Provi-sional Government sanctioned an offensive. It was launched with disastrous consequences on 18 June. Some units fought bravely, other units behaved in the most cowardly fashion, retreat-ing or simply deserting.

The nationality factor also added to the army's demoralization. After the revolution, it was assumed that such nationalities as Ukrai-nians, Estonians, Latvians, and Caucasians would form separate army units. Halfhearted attempts led to the formation of Ukrainian and Latvian units. However, these soldiers were mainly peasants interested in an immediate peace and the sharing out of the landlords' land. Since the land question was ignored, these units gradually melted away after the Bolsheviks had given them 'permission' to seize land by issuing the famous land decree in November. There was one exception to the mass desertions: the Latvian Rifle Division retained its cohesion and joined the Bolsheviks, who promised them free land after the complete liberation of their motherland.

The degenerating economic situation in the country as a whole affected the army's morale considerably. As transport networks gradually broke down and supplies could not be sent to the armies in the field, soldiers became certain that the war had come to an end. Shells, clothing and horseshoes were in short supply (only 40 per cent of required deliveries reached the front) and the country was facing a famine by August. In some parts of the various fronts hunger was rife among the troops. The soldiers felt unable to help their families. During the summer of 1917, numerous bands of soldiers roved the country behind the fronts searching for food, or simply attacking food trains and taking their rations from them. Over 1,000,000 soldiers deserted on these food expeditions; another 1,000,000 were lured back home because of the autumn sowing work. Since the fronts needed soldiers to fill the gaps left by these desertions, garrison troops began to arrive to replace the deserters. However, the garrison soviets vigorously opposed such transfers, particularly in Petrograd. It is not an exaggeration to say that such transfers were the final, fatal blow to the morale of the army. These were highly politicized units, entirely against the continuation of the war and intent on desertion as soon as an opportunity arose. They undermined the morale of the troops so far unaffected and commanders quickly called for a stop to these transfers. However, the Petrograd garrison soviet successfully resisted any transfer. The transfer quarrel became the pretext for the successful Bolshevik seizure of power in the city.

Lenin made it clear that he would make a bid for power as soon as the army ceased to be a counterforce. Following Lenin's tactics, the Bolsheviks immediately formed a Military Commission under Podvoysky to co-ordinate their activities in the army. Their task was twofold: though not spectacularly successful, they tried to penetrate as many army committees as they could; and, more successfully, they waged an anti-war propaganda campaign. As it became clear that they would never win over a majority of the army committees, their tactics changed. Henceforth they supported any unreasonable demand of the soldiers if it increased demoralization. Thus they actively supported fraternization; they were solidly against the June offensive; they instigated officer witch-hunts after the collapse of the Kornilov coup; and they encouraged desertions.

Below: A mixed audience of soldiers, sailors and civilians listen to a speech by Rodzianko in the Catherine Hall of the Tauride Palace in Petrograd shortly after the October Revolution.

THE OCTOBER REVOLUTION

In September 1917, with tactical requirements in their favor, the Bolsheviks decided to make another attempt at seizing power. Curiously, although individual Bolsheviks suffered persecution after the abortive *coup de force* in July, the party itself was left untouched, retaining its cohesion and even holding the Sixth Congress (26 July-3 August). However, Lenin and Zinoviev were in hiding in Finland, while Trotsky and Stalin were in gaol. Many other Bolsheviks remained in detention until the successful coup in November. The future seemed hopeless for the party, but Lenin continued to argue with the Bolshevik Central Committee to support another coup attempt. Then, on 11 September, Trotsky was released from imprisonment. Acting independently of the Central Committee, he immediately began to plan his own coup. Yet it was only on 23 October (2 November in the Julian Calendar) that the Central Committee finally yielded to Lenin's epistolary instructions and voted overwhelmingly for an armed uprising.

Lenin learned a valuable lesson in July, when it became apparent that the counter-revolutionaries, supported by the Mensheviks and Socialist Revolutionary Party, were too strongly entrenched to agree to a peaceful transfer of power to the soviets. He therefore decided that power had to be seized by the Bolsheviks on behalf of the working class and the poor peasants. Stalin was charged with getting this idea approved by the Sixth Congress in the shape of a resolution. He found it tough to persuade many delegates to vote for it. The representatives lacked confidence – they were perfectly aware of the tiny proportion of the proletariat enrolled in the Bolshevik Party. However, Lenin and the Bolshevik intelligentsia abounded in confidence. Immediately after the abortive Kornilov coup in late August, Lenin wrote to the Central Committee. He stated that, despite the right-wing danger,

Kerensky must not be supported or Russia defended. Instead Rodzianko and Milyukov should be arrested and the Duma dispersed; land should be given to the peasants; soldiers should assault their officers; and immediate peace proposals should be made to the Germans. What the Sixth Congress called 'favorable conditions' for revolution were at hand and Lenin's resolution could be implemented.

Though Lenin's letter was unknown to the soldiers and peasants, there was unrest at the front and in the countryside, but the Central Committee proved more obdurate to his exhortations than the proletariat. Early in September, the Bolsheviks scored their first political successes: their resolutions won majority support in the Petrograd and Moscow Soviets. This made Lenin more insistent and the Central Committee had to deal with his two strongly worded letters on 15 September. Lenin justified the coup ideologically, citing Marx. He also gave them a prescription for the steps to take and the measures to put into effect: send the most reliable pro-Bolshevik regiments to occupy the St Peter and Paul fortress, and seize telephone exchanges and telegraph offices – exactly as it was to happen in November. But on 15 September there were no supporters for Lenin's coup. The committee even wanted to destroy the two letters; only a narrow majority decided to keep one copy of each for posterity. At the same time Kamenev, who participated in the conference, rejected Lenin's proposals by suggesting that a 'democratic' government be formed together with the Bolsheviks. Six days later the Central Committee voted to take part in the Pre-Parliament; two days after the decision the committee agreed to convene the All-Russian Congress of Soviets in Petrograd on 20 October. All these steps indicated that the olshevik leaders were less willing to back Lenin and his coup than participate in public affairs.

Then on 15 September, the Bolsheviksbecame

Previous page: The 1st Petrograd Partisan Detachment.

Right and far right: Kamenev and Zinoviev – two of the leading figures in the Bolshevik Revolution. Kamenev became People's Commissar for Trade, and Zinoviev was Chairman of the Comintern. Both were to become victims of Stalin's purges and were shot after show trials in 1936.

the majority party on the presidium of the Petrograd Soviet and Trotsky was elected its chairman. This seems to have been a turning point. Trotsky was already pursuing his own plans for a coup but, after gaining this important position in Petrograd, he seems to have thrown in his lot with Lenin. On 5 October the Central Committee reversed its decision to participate in the Pre-Parliament and Trotsky himself led a noisy walkout on the 7th. On the same day Lenin arrived in Petrograd to intensify his campaign for an insurrection. With the Military Sections in Petrograd and Moscow res-

ponding positively to his cries for an insurrection, Lenin went on to attend a session of the Central Committee on 10 October. It took place in the flat of Sukhanov, who was a Menshevik but not present. His wife was a secret Bolshevik. Lenin arrived disguised in a wig and clean-shaven. After six weeks of resistance, the Central Committee 'surrendered' to Lenin in person; only Kamenev and Zinoviev voted against the decision to organize the *coup d'état* to coincide with the All-Russian Congress of the Soviets. Lenin's two opponents wanted to win power through the Constituent Assembly.

Above: A workers' demonstration in Petrograd following the October Revolution marches under the slogan 'All Power to the Soviet of Workers' and Soldiers' Deputies!

Left: A meeting of soldiers at the front in October 1917.

Lenin was absolutely right to ignore the dissenters' objections. He realistically assessed the low chances of the Bolsheviks winning the assembly election and rejected Kamenev's and Zinoviev's claims as 'naive.' Moreover, he was furious with them for making their views public; he even wanted to expel them from the Bolshevik Party. As rumors of a Bolshevik uprising were already circulating in Petrograd, Lenin urged party members to launch the coup before the Provisional Government took preventative measures. He wanted the coup to coincide with the meeting of the Northern Regional Soviets and wanted the Petrograd (Bolshevik) Committee, which was more radical than the Central Committee, to carry it out.

He was overruled. Another resolution which advocated 'the creation of a Soviet government at the time of the All-Russian Congress' was passed. The Petrograd Soviet was also reluctant to act, though Trotsky was playing Lenin's game by pretending not to know about the planned insurrection. On 16 October an extended meeting of the Central Committee again endorsed Lenin's resolution for insurrection and set up a Military Revolutionary Center with five members (Stalin was one of them, but not Trotsky). However, Lenin had to wait for the All-Russian Congress of the Soviets before launching the uprising. Annoyingly, the majority socialists postponed the convention until 25 October (7 November). Though Bolsheviks as a

Below: A demonstration in Palace Square in Petrograd late in 1917.

whole did not manifest particular enthusiasm for the insurrection, Trotsky did, and it was through his Military Revolutionary Committee of the Petrograd Soviet and not Stalin's Military Revolutionary Center that the Bolshevik coup was carried out.

Late in September the Provisional Government decided to transfer some troops of the Petrograd garrison to the Northern Front. The front commander, General Cheremisov, did not really want the demoralized garrison troops but went along with the political wishes. These 'sinister' moves alarmed the garrison considerably: many soldiers did not want to quit the safe capital to face the risks at the front. On 9 October they decided to set up a committee to

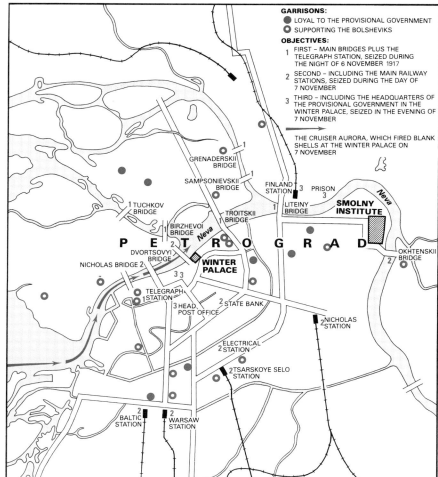

GARRISONS:
● LOYAL TO THE PROVISIONAL GOVERNMENT
○ SUPPORTING THE BOLSHEVIKS

OBJECTIVES:
1 FIRST – MAIN BRIDGES PLUS THE TELEGRAPH STATION, SEIZED DURING THE NIGHT OF 6 NOVEMBER 1917
2 SECOND – INCLUDING THE MAIN RAILWAY STATIONS, SEIZED DURING THE DAY OF 7 NOVEMBER
3 THIRD – INCLUDING THE HEADQUARTERS OF THE PROVISIONAL GOVERNMENT IN THE WINTER PALACE, SEIZED IN THE EVENING OF 7 NOVEMBER

→ THE CRUISER AURORA, WHICH FIRED BLANK SHELLS AT THE WINTER PALACE ON 7 NOVEMBER

consider 'war planning' – the transfer of troops. However, they accepted Trotsky's idea of a 'revolutionary defense committee,' which became the staff organization of the Bolshevik insurrection. Nevertheless, Trotsky had to tread carefully as the Petrograd Soviet still had a socialist majority. The chairman of the Military Revolutionary Committee (MRC) formed on 20 October was an 18-year-old, Lazimir (left-wing Socialist Revolutionary), who later joined the Bolsheviks). But the MRC was in fact led by Trotsky himself, and Stalin's Military Revolutionary Center was subordinated to him as well. There can be no doubt that Trotsky was the real driving force behind the coup.

Trotsky had convoked a conference of the Petrograd garrison to canvass its opinion: 15 out of 18 representatives of various units in the capital expressed themselves opposed to the government and desired a transfer of power to the soviets. However, they all opposed armed-

Above: The 1917 Revolution.

Below: The Sailors' Soviet at Kronstadt.

Right: A meeting at a Petrograd railway station to encourage the formation of detachments of Red Guards.

confrontation; only seven representatives declared they would use force against the government if called on by the soviet. Lenin met secretly with the MRC and was informed of the garrison's mood. Nevertheless, he persisted in urging the MRC to launch the insurrection immediately before the All-Russian Congress of the Soviets, meaning before Kerensky, could get loyal troops to the capital. While disagreeing with Lenin, the MRC was taking irreversible steps toward the coup. Bolshevik commissars were appointed and attached to all the units of the garrison, and to the capital's arsenal and ammunition stores 'to take defensive measures.' On 22 October Colonel Polkovnikov, commander of the Petrograd garrison, was told by MRC delegates that only their orders would be obeyed by the troops. In reply he threatened them with arrest, but did not do it. Instead he sent the MRC an ultimatum to rescind the order. Polkovnikov's demands were partially met due to pressure from Socialist

Revolutionaries who joined the MRC on condition that it would not attempt an insurrection. However, the committee's Bolshevik members ignored Polkovnikov's ultimatum.

On 23 October Trotsky had reports that all the recently appointed commissars were in control of their units. This meant that most of the 350,000 garrison troops were 'neutralized'; only two regiments refused outright to obey the MRC's orders. Of the 63,000 guard reserve troops, Trotsky thought that they would heed neither Bolshevik nor government orders, and was proved right. Some 25,000 infantry troops in transit, as well as 5000 women volunteers and 7000 officer-cadets were a headache. Trotsky found out that they were leaderless and became convinced that they would remain inactive once the Bolsheviks made their bid for power. He had no precise plan for the coup, but Lenin's suggestions for the seizure of the central post office and similar objectives were followed by Antonov-Ovseyenko and Podvoysky who were in charge of operational planning. Bolshevik commissars with the help of a few units would 'neutralize' the fortress of St Peter and Paul, and take over clearly marked objectives, such as railway stations, power stations and sewage plants. The bulk of the Bolshevik forces would storm the Winter Palace, the seat of the Provisional Government. In addition to the few reliable garrison troops, Trotsky had at his disposal the Red Guards (10-12,000 men) under the command of I Yurenev and 60,000 elite Baltic sailors, who were to act as the shock troops of the Bolshevik coup. All this 'might' was to move into action on 25 October.

Kamenev's and Zinoviev's rejection of Lenin's proposals for an insurrection were virtually common knowledge. Gorky's left-wing journal published the fact and even the prime minister seemed acquainted with the planned coup. Even if everyone knew of the planned insurrec-

Below: Cadets guard the Provisional Government in the Winter Palace on the eve of the Bolshevik Revolution.

tion, no one seemed willing to do anything concrete to pre-empt it. The socialist-dominated executive committee of the soviets issued a declaration in which it spoke vaguely of the 'dark forces' trying to seize power; the Pre-Parliament, which met with great pomp and circumstance, did not even put 'public order' on its agenda; while the right-wing forces limited themselves to discussing the Bolshevik plot and planned no counter-coup of their own. The left-wing war minister, General Verhkovsky, nevertheless, warned the government that the army had ceased to be an effective fighting force (with the exception of the Cossack units) and that the Bolsheviks would sooner or later exploit this situation. However, instead of counter-measures, Verkhovsky proposed a separate peace with Germany.

Given the general lack of action, it seems remarkable that the Provisional Government was not shaken in its belief that it could deal with a Bolshevik insurrection in Petrograd. In fact, Kerensky was convinced that he had enough loyal troops to crush any Bolshevik coup attempted until it was far too late. He boasted privately that he wished the Bolsheviks would attempt a coup, and put *Stavka* at ease by repeating his optimistic views to the high command. It seems that he was being misled as to the real military situation in Petrograd by Polkovnikov. The latter kept asserting that the

garrison was loyal to the government and refused to undertake any real measures to check a possible insurrection. Finally, during the night of 23-24 October, Kerensky decided to act on his own. It is not known whether he had ceased to trust Polkovnikov but, nonetheless, he sent a force of officer-cadets to close down and occupy the premises of two Bolshevik newspapers. However, the MRC sent out its own troops, who easily dislodged the cadets and subsequently printed blood-curdling proclama-

Above: Workers at the Putilov factory in Petrograd walk out in support of the revolution. Industrial workers provided the majority of the Bolsheviks' civilian 'fighters' in the capital.

Below: Cossack detachments in Palace Square, Petrograd.

Above: Red Guards outside the Smolny Institute, the Bolshevik headquarters during the revolution of October 1917.

Commissars were also sent to all the railway stations in the city and the ships moored in the Neva. On this very day Trotsky was angered by the MRC's Socialist Revolutionary members' declaration that they were a defense committee, not the revolutionary staff of the Bolshevik insurrection. There were other problems: the garrison in the St Peter and Paul fortress refused to remain neutral in the coup, yet its neutrality was a pre-condition of going into action. In the evening, however, Antonov-Ovseyenko reported to the MRC that the Petrograd Soviet had approved all the measures taken during the day. This was a considerable political success which nullified the left-wing Socialist Revolutionaries' *cri d'alarme*.

All through the following day the MRC members and Trotsky went round inspecting all the regiments in Petrograd. Several reluctant units had to be 'agitated,' the Bolshevik term for persuading the soldiers either to join the coup or remain neutral. The fortress garrison and the Bicycle Battalion proved to be the most reluctant units, and Trotsky had to deal with the fortress personally. In the morning the Bolshevik Central Committee met and charged Kamenev with political work with the wavering Socialist Revolutionaries; Bubnov was sent to take over Petrograd's railway stations and Dzerzhinsky to occupy the post and telegraph offices. The coup was managed from the Smolny Institute (Petrograd Soviet building) which was initially unprotected until barbed wire and machine guns were placed round the building. The government's intelligence and counter-intelligence services seemed to have broken down completely, since no one thought of sending a raiding party to the Institute. On the other hand, the Bolsheviks even thought of establishing a reserve headquarters at the fortress in case the government forces did act. Nonetheless, the government knew of the Institute's role and ordered its telephone lines to be disconnected. The order was executed and throughout the coup Bolshevik commands had to be trans-

tions inviting all citizens to fight the counter-revolutionaries (the Provisional Government), who had dared to close down the left-wing newspapers.

Early on 24 October (6 November) the Military District HQ decided to counteract orders issued by the MRC. It ordered the rifle regiment at Tsarskoye Selo to the city; the 1st Company of officer-cadets at Petergof was to follow. Similarly, the Pavlovsk Battery and the Women's Battalion were ordered to move to the Winter Palace. At the same time, General Bagrateni dismissed the Bolshevik commissars and declared that arms from the arsenal could only be issued on orders signed by himself. Another futile, but true, declaration was issued by the incompetent Polkovnikov on the very day the Bolsheviks went into action: 'The government has no troops at its disposal.'

As early as 22 October (4 November) the MRC had brought all the regiments in Petrograd under its control by detailing them to commissars who were mostly handpicked Bolsheviks.

Right: A group of female soldiers in 1917. Involved in the fight for control of the Petrograd bridges, they were unable to prevent the Bolsheviks from gaining the initiative in the battle for the capital.

mitted by runners, slowing down communications considerably. Several warships with pro-Bolshevik crews, among them the cruiser *Aurora*, arrived from Kronstadt and immediately trained their guns on targets in the city. The war ministry issued orders bidding them to return to base, but they hesitated. At the same time three units of the officer-cadets began to carry out government orders for raising the bridges across the Neva. It was clear that Bolshevik troops, the Red Guards and sailors, would have to enter the city across them. In fact the Helsingfors sailors failed to arrive, to the despair of Trotsky and Lenin, who made his way to the Institute, heavily disguised, to take charge of political direction of the coup.

The last day before the coup could be called the 'battle of the bridges.' The Bolsheviks began to load their suburban Red Guards on requisitioned lorries to mass them round the Institute. To do so the lorries had to cross the bridges which were supposed to be lifted and guarded by pro-government officer-cadets. The Liteyny bridge was not raised by the cadets, because an unknown and unidentified unit of the garrison had arrested and disarmed them before they could accomplish their task. The Troitsky bridge was down as well. The Women's Battalion could not raise it. The Nikolayevsky bridge was raised and the Red Guards trying to cross it were disarmed, though not arrested as they were too numerous to be kept under guard by the cadet picket. The Dvortsovy bridge was also under government control, but it was not clear who controlled the rest. The battle of the bridges caused confusion on both sides, particularly to the Bolsheviks, but government bun-

gling ended the stalemate. The pro-government forces expected, after a day of service, to be relieved by other units. However, the command simply forgot. When no relief arrived, the pickets drifted away to their billets, leaving the bridges unguarded. Bolshevik units were then able to lower them and reinforcements, consisting of some 4000 Kronstadt sailors, were rushed to the Institute to prepare for action the next day. The Bicycle Battalion guarding the Winter Palace left its post and went into billets. The cadets stationed outside Petrograd refused to obey government orders to come to the city; the Pavlovsk Battery acted likewise.

At 1700 hours Commissar Pestkovsky, who tried to take over the telephone exchange, frightened the operators so much that instead of having the Institute reconnected, the whole Petrograd network was disrupted. Trotsky, attending a meeting of the Petrograd Soviet, repeated publicly that no coup was prepared, only the defense of the city against the Germans and the counter-revolution. Simultaneously Bolshevik commissars held meetings with all the units of the Petrograd garrison calling on the men to protect the Petrograd Soviet and the Second Congress against unspecified 'reactionaries.' They had already performed that duty before the meetings: one unit turned back a police detachment which arrived at the Bolshevik *Rabochyi Put* printing plant to close it down again; another unit disarmed officer-cadets sent to close down the Petrograd Soviet newspaper. Since no rigid plans for the coup were laid down and communications with the Institute were difficult, some commissars jumped the gun: Commissar Stark with a few Kronstadt sailors

Above: A painting of the scene outside the Smolny Institute on the night of the revolution.

Right: Red Guards on sentry duty outside Lenin's office in the Smolny Institute in October 1917.

took over the telegraph exchange, while commissar Katz did likewise with the Baltic railway terminal. By late evening all was reported ready for the launching of the coup.

At midnight the Red Guards were ordered out first. They were to patrol the streets of the city and take over from government police (militia) and troops. Shortly afterward units of the Sappers Battalion led by their commissar seized the last tactically important railway terminal, Nikolayevsky. Commissar Feirman (not a Bolshevik, but a left-wing Socialist Revolutionary) led his men to the central power station with the intention of cutting off power from the government buildings. He failed as the electricity engineers refused to co-operate. The same happened at the central telephone exchange, where the lines of the Winter Palace and the government's military headquarters remained open. What was obvious, however, was that the Socialist Revolutionary commissars had been completely deceived by the Bolsheviks. Feirman and others protested loudly against the Bolshevik coup, but too late.

Below: A Bolshevik commander reads orders to his men – a mixture of civilians and former soldiers – in the days after the successful coup in Petrograd.

The deception also caught some members of the government unawares. At 1500 hours Minister Kartashev and the chief of the Provisional Government counter-espionage service, Colonel Surin, were arrested by Bolshevik patrols while traveling by car. Neither had the slightest idea of the coup; the patrol did not know what to do with a minister and counter-espionage chief. They were taken to the Institute where Commissar Dzenis detained them for a while and then let them go free. These were the only arrests of the coup, if the arrests of the Provisional Government ministers are not counted. They occurred a day after the victorious conclusion of the coup which Lenin always claimed was over on 7 November.

The saga of the Nikolayevsky bridge finally ended. No one was able to lower this unguarded bridge until the sailors of the *Aurora*, who had refused the order to sail back to Kronstadt, saw to it. They landed a party and lowered the bridge, only to find themselves facing a crack unit sent there by the government to lift it. In the end the government soldiers were persuaded to go back to their barracks and leave the bridge down. Some 200 Red Guards then surged forward to hold the lowered bridge; they could not be dislodged without bloodshed and neither side wanted that. The Bolshevik occupation of Petrograd's railway terminals also began to bear fruit: the cadets of Petergof, who were the only ones to respond to the government's call, found the railway lines blocked. Trotsky's tactical appreciation that the government would not find troops to counter the coup was proved right. The Bolsheviks were able to gain the upper hand in Petrograd.

It was at this stage, early in the morning of the coup, that Kerensky finally decided to act in person. He knew that the 1st, 4th and 14th Don Cossack Cavalry Regiments were stationed in the city. These were elite formations but the government was so frightened of them that it had forbidden a public procession, a religious Cross march, through the city a few days before the coup. Now the same government wanted these Cossacks to come to its aid. Kerensky forced General Bagrateni and Commissar Malevsky to issue orders to these regiments, summoning them to the Winter Palace. Quite bluntly, the Cossacks refused to obey the order and Kerensky became frantic. He telegraphed General Cheremisov of the Northern Front to send some of his units to Petrograd to protect him and suppress the Bolshevik coup. Nothing seemed to happen. Whether this was due to the Bolshevik occupation of the telegraph exchange will never be proven. The Bicycle Battalion failed to report for duty at the Winter Palace and the Oranienbaum cadets found the railway lines blocked, hence they also failed to arrive. At the same time, Bolshevik-controlled troops took over the National Bank, another telephone exchange (the government and military command had secret lines, independent of the exchange) and the Warsaw railway terminal, though no forces from either side were expected there.

Clearly both sides were bungling, though the government more so than the Bolsheviks. By

Left: The seizure of the telephone exchange in Petrograd was one of the Bolsheviks' first tasks in the revolution.

1100 hours Commissar Kislyakov-Uralov had occupied all the printing plants in Petrograd which gave the Bolsheviks the monopoly of public information. The MRC moved out of the Institute and established a field headquarters, while Antonov-Ovseyenko, Bubnov, Podvoysky and Chudnovsky went to take over command in person. At 1000 hours, Lenin, who had spent the night at the Institute, issued his first political statement which was plastered all over the city: 'To All Russian Citizens . . . the Provisional Government is no more and power has passed to the Soviets.' Lenin knew that the statement was not true, for it was Antonov-Ovseyenko's mission to capture the government. However, it was true in a sense that the Provisional Government, or at least its prime minister, was on his way out of Petrograd.

All this time Kerensky was telephoning and telegraphing all round. He forced Polkovnikov to request troop reinforcements from Cheremisov and *Stavka*, where the acting Commander in Chief, General Dukhonin, was most sympathetic. However, he had no troops to dispatch urgently to Petrograd. At 1100 hours, after all these disappointments, Kerensky made up his mind. He would go in person to the Northern Front and return with loyal troops to suppress the Bolshevik uprising. He requisitioned two American embassy cars and left the Winter Palace with the United States flag flying. Although cheered by some who recognized him, most people thought that he was deserting his post. Indeed, after his departure, no one tried to oppose the Bolshevik coup. Everyone waited passively to the end. Whether he knew it or not, Kerensky was leaving Russia for exile.

Though the Bolsheviks did not know about

Below: Members of the Women's Battalion on Palace Square. On 24 October the battalion was sent to the square – supposedly for a parade. However, when it was learned that the real aim of the move was the defense of the Provisional Government all but one company returned to their barracks at Levashovo.

Kerensky's departure, Lenin was anxious to hear of the capture of the Provisional Government; he wanted to announce this triumph to the Second Congress of the Soviets in person. However, he had to wait more than a day to make the announcement. It proved relatively easy for the Bolshevik sailors and patrols from the Lithuanian and Cuxholm Regiments to dissolve the Pre-Parliament which was acting in place of the Duma, and the Council of State had been dissolved a few days before. There were only a few members of the Pre-Parliament gathered in the Mariinsky Palace and they left peacefully after making their protests. Similarly, the Admiralty building was taken over by the Bolsheviks, simply because it had been abandoned by their opponents. However, to take the Winter Palace, where the headless government was holding a session, was a different matter. The palace was a whole block of buildings, surrounded with open squares. Only at 1400 hours did the Bolsheviks succeed in encircling the palace block, and then Antonov-Ovseyenko assumed command to lead the assault. He had the elements from the Pavlovsky and Keksgolm Regiments and the Kronstadt sailors; with them was a crowd of the Petrograd, Vasilyevsky, Ostrov and Vyborg Red Guards. Still he thought that he had insufficient forces to storm the palace, and therefore postponed the assault until darkness at 2100 hours.

While the storming of the palace was being organized, Trotsky presided over a session of the Petrograd Soviet to which Lenin was invited. The former announced the birth of the soviet government, while the latter made an ambiguous short statement and was applauded by the small number of members who had bothered to attend the session. A few Mensheviks present walked out in protest against this 'conspiracy.' While Lenin agonized all day about the fate of the Provisional Government, life in Petrograd went on much as normal despite the coup. Crowds of curious spectators, particularly children, watched the Bolshevik takeover throughout the day. In the evening,

Opposite page, top: Red Guards in Petrograd after the revolution.

Left: Lenin proclaims victory in a painting by V Serov.

well-dressed people thronged the restaurants and theaters. The striking feature of the *coup d'état* was its ease and the lack of resistance. In contrast to the March Revolution, there were hardly any casualties. The few that did occur were around the Winter Palace.

Curiously enough, the 14th Don Cossacks did go to the Winter Palace, though only after Kerensky's departure. The local officer-cadets and the Women's Battalion also reported for duty in the morning of the 25th (7 November). Encouraged by this development, the government appointed a three-man defense committee (Kishkin, Palchinsky, Gutenberg) and Colonel Anayev became commanding officer of all the collected forces. Some desperate telephoning followed. Commissar Stankievich again asked

Opposite page, bottom: Red Guards with rifles turn an open truck into an armed, if not armored, car.

Left: 'Picking up the Banner,' a painting celebrating the workers' part in the fight for Petrograd.

Above: A scene from a filmed reconstruction of the storming of the Winter Palace. The event itself was much less dramatic.

General Dukhonin for some troops, but was told bluntly to help himself. 'What happened to the Bicycle Battalion?' asked the general most pertinently. No one could answer him, for no one knew what had happened to the elite formation. By this time the Bolsheviks had taken over the ministry of war which was the block next to the Winter Palace. Antonov-Ovseyenko was so excited by the conquest that he issued an ultimatum to the government in the Winter Palace to surrender. He was not at all pleased when the ultimatum was rejected. Darkness fell early and both sides lapsed into confusion.

Many good soldiers expected to be relieved of duty in the evening. Commissar Akashev of the artillery cadets ordered his boys back to their billets with their four guns as soon as it got dark. The unit left, considerably weakening the defense of the palace. Paradoxically the commissar and several other officers were intercepted before leaving and put under arrest for

sabotage. The Cossacks also became restive. They were offended by being drawn up next to the women, and did not see any point waiting outside in the dark and cold. The rest of the cadets wanted to follow their artillery comrades, but were detained in the palace by their officers. The palace commander, General Palchinsky, had very little to co-ordinate: his men were out in the dark, and the officers in the palace were hopelessly drunk. In fact, the palace was held by the old czarist commissioners who controlled the gates and the lights.

The government, presided over by Minister Konovalov, held a continuous session throughout the day. The session was adjourned for dinner, and after an excellent meal, the government again rejected another Bolshevik ultimatum to surrender. The new-found firmness had a demoralizing effect on the attackers. The next order of the government, to turn out the lights in the palace, caused additional confusion among the Bolshevik besiegers and the besieged alike. In the unexpected darkness, shots were fired by both sides. Four cadets were hit, probably by their own fire. Seeing their comrades slightly wounded, the Constantine Academy cadets, profiting from the darkness, left for their barracks without telling anyone. Both sides found out about this desertion: Lenin, almost hysterically demanded that the palace be stormed; government ministers went through a bout of frantic telephoning. After a while they were in touch with the Petrograd Duma (Municipal Council) and drew much solace from this quarter. The Duma was apparently also being besieged, but it had beaten off the Bolshevik forces. Negotiations would start immediately to relieve the government. A Duma delegation left for the Institute, but its 'mediation' was rejected out of hand. The delegates were told to go to the Winter Palace instead and ask the government to surrender as its position was hopeless. All these talks and

moves ignored the reality of the government's hopeless position. However, neither side knew the full truth. When the *Aurora* sailors as well as the fortress garrison refused to receive the Duma negotiating team, it was decided to organize a march from the Petrograd municipal building to the Winter Palace. Some 300 unarmed civilians joined the mayor in the march. They were halted several times, and when the marchers reached the palace perimeter, they were dispersed by armed sailors. Inside the palace the government knew nothing of their brave but futile gesture.

Just before the Bolshevik assault the government had received a communication from *Stavka* at Mogilëv: the Bicycle Battalion had been located and, together with three other regiments, was being sent to Petrograd. These vital troops never arrived. In the prevailing confusion General Cheremisov stopped all train movements toward the capital. Whatever hope the *Stavka* message might have raised was

Above: Anatoly Zheleznyakov, a sailor of the Baltic Fleet, took part in the storming of the Winter Palace and went on to fight heroically in the civil war. He was killed in 1919 during the battles around Verkhovtsevo.

Left: Revolutionaries gather around an armored car named in honor of Lieutenant Schmidt, an anti-government supporter shot during the 1905 Revolution.

Left: Demonstrators heading for the square in front of the Finland Station in Petrograd.

Right: 'The Storming of the Winter Palace.'

Below: Bolsheviks address soldiers and workers in Palace Square after the seizure of power and sell them copies of *Pravda.*

dashed when the *Aurora* opened fire on the palace at 2130 hours. It was not the accuracy of the shots that mattered – most missed the palace and no one was injured – but their psychological effect. The 300-strong Cossacks instantly negotiated a free passage through the Bolshevik lines to their billets. They marched off with their colonel firmly in charge, and failed to inform the palace command of their departure. When this desertion became known and after another salvo from the *Aurora*, the Women's Battalion tried a sortie. When, in turn, the Bolshevik forces opened fire (probably in the air) the battalion surrendered and was disarmed. By this time all the palace's defense forces had melted away and only a few cadets and their officers were left in the building. Nonetheless Antonov-Ovseyenko was still reluctant to give orders for the final assault as he was as much in the dark as the besieged. Instead he tried to negotiate, only to be rebuffed. Then the agitators, the subversive arm of the Bolsheviks, were sent in to demoralize the palace forces. However, they were easily arrested in the palace's dark corridors and locked in various rooms for detention, though they began to outnumber the defense force. Around 2300 hours Chudnovsky, who had been to the palace several times as a negotiator, finally realized that there were no defenders left and ordered the final assault. Crowds of sailors, soldiers and Red Guards broke down the gates and marched slowly through the maze of dark corridors in search of the Provisional Government. Only at 0150 hours on 26 October (8 November) did a group of disciplined troops headed by Antonov-Ovseyenko enter the Malachite Room where the government was waiting

for them. The huge crowd which followed this small group wanted to lynch the ministers, when it found that Kerensky was not among them. In the end Antonov-Ovseyenko managed to keep the ministers out of their reach, taking them to the safety of the fortress. He had already sent a runner to Lenin to tell him of the government's arrest.

The Second All-Russian Congress of the Soviets had opened at 1040 hours on 25 October. It was not a very representative gathering. Peasant soviets had refused to send their delegates to Petrograd as early as 27 September. But even the soldiers who did attend were chosen unconstitutionally or were simply representing themselves. This was perfectly acceptable to the Bolsheviks, provided such delegates belonged to their party. Local soviets did not elect delegates for this congress at all, because they were too busy organizing the forthcoming election to the Constituent Assembly. Most wanted the congress to take place after the Constituent Assembly's election, but Bolshevik determination to hold it and make it coincide with their coup was unshakable. Despite the widespread reluctance and electoral confusion, the Bolsheviks controlled a majority of the delegates – but only with the support of the Socialist Revolutionaries. Out of 670 delegates 300 were Bolsheviks, 193 were Socialist Revolutionaries, 68 were Mensheviks and 14 were Menshevik Internationalists. The rest represented small groups or were non-party delegates. Knowing this Chairman Dan (a Menshevik) tried to delay the opening of the congress. However, he was brushed aside by Lenin, who demanded the assembled delegates (515) elect a congress presidium: 14 Bolsheviks, seven Left SR, three

Mensheviks and one Menshevik-Internationalist were elected. The presidium canvassed the delegates on their views on handing over 'all power to the soviets,' and an overwhelming majority approved this Bolshevik proposal. In turn the socialist delegates demanded the formation of a coalition soviet government, and both Lenin and Trotsky accepted the demand. Then, suddenly and unexpectedly, the socialists changed their mind: the SR and Menshevik parties announced that they were unwilling to associate themselves with an armed conspiracy (of the Bolsheviks) and walked out of the congress. After this walkout renewed calls for a socialist coalition government, previously unanimously accepted, were rejected by Trotsky. He did not want to be associated with the 'miserable bankrupts intended for the dung heap of history.'

Lenin adjourned the congress in order to draft new resolutions and prepare a new agenda; above all he was waiting for the news of the Provisional Government. When he received it, he

convoked another session for 0300 hours and announced the real fall of the Provisional Government amid a wild ovation. Only two delegates of the truncated congress voted against the assumption of power and 12 abstained. At 0500 hours the congress approved Lenin's resolution that the soviet government should propose 'a democratic peace' and 'transfer without compensation all available land to the peasant committees.' Military measures were also voted: military revolutionary committees were to be set up at the Northern Front and in all army and navy units. The session reconvened at 2130 hours. Lenin as Chairman of the Council of People's Commissars had a government list ready. It was not a coalition, but a purely Bolshevik body. Trotsky was minister of foreign and Left SR affairs and Stalin in charge of nationalities. After a final vote putting their official seal on the Bolshevik *coup d'état*, the congress delegates dispersed, leaving Lenin and the Bolsheviks firmly in power – at least in Petrograd. Elsewhere, the outcome of the revolution was far from decided.

Left: Armed Red Guards mass in Palace Square on the morning after the Bolshevik coup.

Bottom left: Meeting in the Grenadier barracks, Petrograd, November 1917.

Right: The staff of the Red Guards in Odessa in 1917. Their banner declares that the Red Workers' Guards are fighting for a democratic republic.

Below: A political education lesson for the guards of the Tauride Palace. They are listening to a reading from the newspaper *Izvestiya*.

SOVIETS AND STRIKES

The few days following the Bolshevik triumph in Petrograd and at the Second Congress were rather uncertain. A simultaneous uprising planned in Moscow was far from peaceful. The Municipal Council and the garrison officers together with officer-cadets put up a spirited resistance. Desultory fighting went on for several days until the Bolsheviks, stiffened with Kronstadt sailors, brought up artillery and shelled their opponents into submission on 3 November. In several other cities Bolshevik takeovers came to nothing. Only distant Krasnoyarsk declared itself Bolshevik, with the aid of German PoWs, on 30 October and Krasnovodsk followed, without any aid, on the following day. By then plenty of blood had been shed, and many Bolsheviks became convinced that to stay in power a civil war would have to be fought. They were unenthusiastic about such prospects, but their leader, Lenin, was determined to face any military eventuality with iron resolution.

In 1917 Russia found in Lenin an exceptional individual who singlemindedly led his minute socialist (Bolshevik) faction in seizing and retaining power in Russia. He was a man with a sense of mission which was not based on the love of others, but the hatred of the existing order and its injustice. His strategy was doctrinaire and formulated long before the successful coup: the Russian proletariat, as represented by himself and the Bolsheviks, in alliance with poor peasants, would transform the unjust system into a just one though a socialist revolution. He was a skillful opportunist; all situations were exploited by him and used to strengthen his socialist revolution. He probably hated the German 'imperialists' even more than the Western ones; nonetheless he was ready for peace with them as soon as he was in power. He needed 'peace' and, in any case, the overwhelming majority desired it. Subsequently, despite the civil war with its Allied participation, he was ready for a compromise with the Western (French, British and American) imperialists, because he needed it to consolidate his power at home. Similarly, he sanctioned land expropria-

tion and distribution as soon as he was in power, because he needed to 'neutralize' the peasantry. All this time, while even his closest collaborators wavered, Lenin remained firm, pursuing his strategy with implacable determination.

Lenin's tactics can be summed up as follows. The Bolsheviks had to seize power in the capital to control the central government, and then they had to form a police force, their own, the *Cheka*. The Bolsheviks also had to destroy the old army, which was easily accomplished through the armistice and separate peace, and create their own Red Army, which they did after March 1918. They had to penetrate the soviet movement, take it over and put soviets in place of local government. They had to impose control on the mobs which roamed throughout Russia and eliminate terrorists. They had to legalize desertions and land acquisition, which were done at a stroke of a pen. Finally, they had to win the civil war, which appeared inevitable as soon as their foes and their allies discerned the true Bolshevik designs. In order to achieve these objectives Lenin was ready to take any opportunist or even demagogic measure. He immediately instituted an eight-hour working day, though it was pure nonsense in the chaotic economic conditions. The proclamation of national self-determination was also pure demagogy as was seen later, particularly in the case of Georgia. The abolition of religious privileges was another opportunistic move aimed against all religions. Only the suppression of hostile newspapers was a lucid power act which, forced on Lenin by circumstances, has remained with the Russians to this day.

The task of enforcing public order, first in the capital, and then all over the country, fell to the MRC. For the rest of its existence (more than two months) the MRC, which had grown to 82 members (53 Bolsheviks), proved to be a rather imperfect instrument of control, despite its membership, which consisted of the most outstanding Bolsheviks: Trotsky, Stalin, Sverdlov, Dzerzhinsky, Gusev, Uritsky, Krylenko, Latsis, Chubar, Molotov and others. In Petrograd, for example, armed bands looted the abandoned

Previous page: A crowd demonstrates in support of the short-lived Constituent Assembly in the aftermath of the revolution.

Below: Lenin, Sverdlov and the rest of the Presidium of the First All-Russian Congress on Land and Poverty in the Hall of Columns of the House of the Unions in Moscow, 11 December 1918.

palaces, starting with the Winter Palace. The looted objects were chiefly alcoholic beverages, consumed on the spot. Thus the Winter Palace, after the arrest of ministers, became the scene of unbridled alcoholic orgy. The crowds that accompanied Antonov-Ovseyenko raided the imperial cellar which contained wine and spirit reserves to cover imperial consumption for the next 50 years. Soon the mob was literally dead drunk. So many new people kept arriving to get drunk that on the following day the Bolsheviks felt compelled to send some Red Guards to evict the drunks. The Red Guards proved unequal to the task; instead they joined the orgy. Garrison soldiers were sent next, the same day, but with the same results. Similarly the fire brigade, sent to flood the cellar, failed. Only a detachment of Kronstadt sailors resisted the ancient Russian urge and walled up the cellar. However, the cellar remained the center of constant public attraction and was broken into as long as there were any wines left. The Bolshe-

viks sold some of its contents to Sweden, but most of it had to be pumped out into the Petrograd drainage system to the utter despair of passers-by. The MRC also proved incapable of preventing outbursts of lynching, pillage and public violence from taking place, though it did try hard. It scored one political success, however, when it discovered a right-wing conspiracy against the Bolsheviks led by one of Rasputin's assassins, Puririshkevich. Among the conspirators were several members of the Petrograd Officer-Cadet Academies. As the MRC was still a coalition committee, the Bolsheviks also attempted to make use of it politically. However, it soon became clear that this was impracticable. Thus the MRC succeeded in persuading the Bolsheviks to release the arrested socialist ministers, though the liberal ones stayed in prison. This tiny 'concession' to the Left SR members divided the Bolsheviks and was ultimately the reason for the dissolution of the MRC.

Not unexpectedly the first political challenge to the Bolsheviks came from the trade unions: the railway workers and civil servants. The former threatened strike action against them. Such a strike would have been potentially very damaging. It would have isolated the Bolsheviks in the capital and the few other towns under their control, and would have stopped their moves to gain control of the army in the field. They sent some 300 commissars to the army during the last few weeks of November. Alternatively, the railwaymen might have let troop trains through to Petrograd to suppress the Bolshevik takeover. Above all, it would have disrupted much-needed food trains. The Central Committee responded to the Railway Union's ultimatum by detailing Sokolnikov and Kamenev to negotiate with their leaders. Both sides were conscious of the railwaymen's strength. The strikers demanded an immediate cessation of inter-socialist hostilities and the formation of a coalition government without Lenin. The Bolshevik delegates accepted these demands without consulting Lenin, who was busy suppressing the right-wing cadet uprising and checking General Krasnov's advancing Cossack cavalry. *In extremis* Lenin was willing to broaden his government, but he was most unwilling to resign as premier. In response, Lenin persuaded the Central Committee that Kamenev, Sokolnikov, Ryazanov and others who wanted to accept the railwaymen's demands were 'capitulators' and, as such, they

were forced to resign from the offices they held. In turn, the Bolsheviks issued an ultimatum to the railway workers rejecting any sort of a socialist coalition until such time that the strike threat was lifted. The strike never took place and on 26 November (9 December) eight Left SRs joined Lenin's government – if only for three months.

The civil servants went on strike in protest against the Bolshevik coup of 26 October. Bolshevik ministers found out about it as they arrived to claim their ministries; Trotsky en-

Above: Red Guards participating in the Moscow uprising.

Right: On 28 October detachments of pro-government cadets succeeded in seizing the Kremlin in Moscow but they surrendered at dawn on 3 November.

Below: A Red Guard detachment on the streets of Moscow.

tered the ministry of foreign affairs with a group of sailors and found the building deserted. Eventually, a lonely councillor, Tatishchev, was apprehended and forced to hand over the keys to the ministry's archives and code department. Four days later Menzhinsky had to face a similar situation in the ministry of finance. However, he acted more resolutely than Trotsky: he placed senior civil servants under arrest and then forced them to start work. There was endless trouble about money releases in the State Bank, where civil servants refused to co-operate. Such political actions could only delay, but not revert, the Bolshevik takeover. On 14 November all the members of the strikers' committees were arrested, and the strikers drafted into the army and immediately sent to the front. However, as late as 26 November there was another strike in the ministry of trade, while passive resistance continued well into 1918. The Bolsheviks had to rebuild the government administration from scratch. Only a few strike-breakers were rehired, and wives and other relations of the minister-commissars were employed in the new Bolshevik administration. Thus, Krupskaya (Lenin's official wife) worked for the Commissariat of Education (Bolsheviks called it Enlightenment) and Trotsky employed his nephews. At this stage, Lenin's main priority lay in the military sphere and the central administration was for a time neglected.

The MRC took the first steps towards the neutralization of the armies by sending out hundreds of Bolshevik commissars to establish MRCs in all of them. The nearest war zone to

Petrograd, the Northern Front, was strategically vital as its troops could threaten the very existence of the newly installed Bolshevik regime. The MRC was well mobilized at Pskov, the front's GHQ, and took over control at the same time as Petrograd. The Pskov Soviet went Bolshevik after an improvised election, in which freshly released prisoners took part. Jointly, they stopped all railway movement, but there was some desultory fighting at the railway station. General Cheremisov, who was suspected of being involved in 'German conspiracies,' but was cleared by Kerensky himself, also stopped train movements. Despite this, elements of General Krasnov's Cavalry Corps got through Pskov and continued toward Petrograd to 'suppress Bolshevik trouble.' Front Commissar Voytinsky, a Socialist Revolutionary, also joined Krasnov and, later on, Kerensky also jumped on the bandwagon. They were both rather unpopular with Krasnov's Cossacks who, when the railway proved unworkable, continued their advance on horseback. They took Gatchina easily but met stiffer opposition at the gates to the capital, along the Pulkovo Heights. Here the Bolsheviks concentrated all their forces: Kronstadt sailors, Red Guards and garrison units, all under the command of a leftist Socialist Revolutionary, Colonel Muravëv. Muravëv's men also succeeded in placing several field guns on the heights which decided the ensuing engagement. Krasnov sent his horsemen four times against the Bolshevik line but each time the attack was beaten off. He then withdrew to Gatchina to await reinforcements. In a sense this was the decisive moment of the

Bolshevik coup. If Krasnov had broken through, he could have taken Petrograd and helped re-establish the Provisional Government and Kerensky, who was with him. Neither of them, however, had any inkling of the stakes involved; instead they were preoccupied with their personal problems. General Niessel, the head of the French Military Mission, who was at Gatchina, asked them both about their plans; both said they had none. In the meantime, two Bolshevik negotiators, Dybenko and Trushin, arrived at Gatchina and were permitted to speak with Krasnov's Cossacks. The result was an armistice and a plan for handing over Kerensky to the Bolsheviks. In exchange Trotsky was to be handed over to the Cossacks. Lenin's exclusion from the government figured among the conditions of the armistice. As Kerensky had disappeared and could not be handed over, the Cossacks gave the Bolsheviks Krasnov. Subsequently they were persuaded to go home to the Don region, and the Bolsheviks did not have to honor any of their conditions. Krasnov was soon permitted to follow his Cossacks to the Don after pledging his word of honor not to fight the Bolsheviks again. He did not keep his word either. (The hapless general was hanged by Stalin in 1947, after the British handed him over to the Red Army in Austria.) In this rather comic way ended the first really dangerous counter-coup against the Bolsheviks. Henceforth it was going to be a remarkably easy rise

Right: Sverdlov, one of Lenin's closest supporters and one of the leaders of the revolution, in Petrograd during 1917.

Below: Uritsky pictured shortly before his death at the hands of Socialist Revolutionaries in 1918. Though he only joined the Bolsheviks in early 1917, he played an active part in the October Revolution and the early days of the Bolshevik takeover.

to power all over the country until the outbreak of the real civil war in May 1918.

The Northern Front consisted of three armies which were all highly demoralized, with both officers and men divided politically. The First Army refused to help the Provisonal Government even before the Bolshevik coup, while the commander of the Twelfth Army, General Yuzefovich, was powerless to prevent the Latvian Rifles from deserting to the Bolsheviks *en masse*. The Latvians helped to neutralize the neighboring Fifth Army whose commanding general, Boldyrev, tried to send his armored units to Petrograd. The Latvians were then called to Petrograd to be used as security troops. Later, they guarded Smolny and the Kremlin in Moscow. Their leader, Colonel Vatsetis, became, for a time, Trotsky's commander in chief. The secret of the Bolsheviks' success was that they always had loyal soldiers in the right places, spoiling for a fight, while their romantic opponents tended to work against each other. The Bolsheviks were able to match this military maneuvering with acute political skills. Improvised elections and by-elections invariably favored them, and both their military and political takeovers were achieved in record time. Conversely, the anti-Bolshevik Committees for the Salvation of the Motherland and the Revolution, a Socialist Revolutionary-inspired movement, never got off the ground.

Similar procedures were followed on the other fronts, all ending in Bolshevik victory. On the Western Front the command, which remained loyal to the Provisional Government, initially beat off the MRC challenge at Minsk, which was occupied by Cossack forces. The

Menshevik front commissar, Kolotukhin, formed a Committee for the Salvation and then waited. In the meantime the Bolsheviks agitated to win the support of the three armies which formed the front and gained control peacefully through rigged ballot boxes. On 19 November they had an armored train, with which they retook Minsk and the front HQ, arresting General Balyev. Pro-Bolsheviks at Orsha, a key railway junction which controlled movements toward Moscow, blocked trains carrying reinforcements to the ancient capital. Subsequently, sympathetic units were sent to *Stavka* at Mogilëv to take it over for the opposing Bolsheviks.

Stavka remained loyal to the Provisional Government after Lenin's coup. General Dukhonin, temporarily in charge, kept sending units and trains to Petrograd and Moscow but without noticeable success. He also rejected Lenin's order to start armistice negotiations with the Germans. For this refusal he was dismissed and Ensign Krylenko, a lawyer but practically the only Bolshevik officer, was appointed his replacement. Krylenko collected a force of sailors in Petrograd and ordered the Second Army of the Western Front under R I Berzin to take Mogilëv. The two forces converged on *Stavka* and took it on 1 December. The pro-Bolshevik leaders could not control their excited troops and General Dukhonin and several other officers were lynched. Krylenko immediately sent a peace delegation to the German command to negotiate the terms of an armistice.

On the South Western Front the takeover was complicated by Ukrainian nationalist opposition. To the Ukrainians the new Bolshevik government (*Sovnarkom*) was essentially Russian and they did not want to recognize it as their government. Army committees firmly rejected Bolshevik proposals to recognize *Sovnarkom* as the legitimate successor of the Provisional Government. Ukrainians then formed an Ukrainian Government (*Rada*) in Kiev. Only at Vinnitsa did the Bolsheviks gain control with armed force, but they were soon suppressed by nationalist troops. Curiously *Rada* was recognized by Ukrainian Bolsheviks up to 10 November. Suddenly *Rada* forces turned on the local Bolsheviks and expelled them from all offices. Thus rejected, Ukrainian Bolsheviks moved to Kharkov where, with the aid of the Russian Bolsheviks, they set up a rival government headed by a Bulgarian revolutionary, Rakovsky. The front senior officers hung uneasily between the Bolshevik *Sovnarkom* and the Ukrainian *Rada*, while the Russian armies gradually melted away. Unfortunately for *Rada*, Ukrainian units followed the Russian example and when, on 17 December, Lenin sent *Rada* an ultimatum, either to submit voluntarily or by force, there were no real forces to oppose a Bolshevik onslaught. Colonel Muravëv of the Pulkovo Heights led a scratch force which took Odessa on 31 January 1918. Eight days later he was in Kiev where he was joined by the Bolshevik Ukrainian Government from Kharkov. In the meantime, *Rada* had moved to Brest-Litovsk where peace negotiations opened between the German, Austrian and Bolshevik governments. They appealed to the German high command to 'liberate' their country from the Bolsheviks. The German Army obliged. Both Muravëv and

Above: Petrograd citizens reading the first decrees of the Bolshevik authorities.

Above: 'All Power to the Soviets!' In this poster the Bolshevik Revolution of 1917 bursts upon a panic-stricken crowd of capitalists, military officers and priests while imperialist financiers let loose internecine strife in the background.

but ran into Moldavian nationalist forces and had to fight bitterly for control of the Moldavian capital. It was a wasted effort. On 19 January 1918, the Romanian Army, seeing Russia in turmoil, invaded Moldavia and chased out both the Bolsheviks and their opponents. Shcherbachëv was given permission to join émigré diplomats.

With the armies either on their side or neutralized the Bolsheviks could concentrate on the political takeover of the immense country. On 27 October 1917 the Petrograd Bolshevik Committee sent out telegrams to some 41 *guberniya* (provincial) committees to 'agitate' their provinces into joining the Bolshevik side. They also sent out 644 'agitators' to help them. As usual, Bolshevik words were matched by military deeds: the Petrograd Military Committee seconded 106 commissars, 61 instructors and 600 'agitators' to back the takeovers with force. On 1 November Lenin appealed to the provincial Bolsheviks in person, bidding them to supplant their 'bankrupt opponents' all over the country. In addition he sent out experienced communists to help inexperienced provincials. Ordjonikidze went to the Ukraine and the south; Chudovsky to the ostensibly anti-Bolshevik South Western Front; S G Roshal left for the dangerous Romanian Front and A S Bubnov for

the Kharkov Government beat an undignified retreat from Kiev to await better days.

The Romanian Front took the Bolsheviks the longest to win over, though in the end it went exactly the same way as the South Western Front. The front was possibly the least demoralized, though the soviet at Kishinev, the town where the front's HQ was based, recognized *Sovnarkom.* On the one hand, army committees protested against the Bolshevik uprising in Petrograd but, on the other, they accepted the armistice proposed by the Bolsheviks. General Shcherbachëv, a prewar professor of the General Staff Academy, kept the armies reasonably happy and dissolved units which showed 'signs of Bolshevism'; officers acted with vigor and were more or less obeyed. The general, however, suffered from a lack of political authority to pledge his allegiance. He rejected both the Bolshevik *Sovnarkom* and the Ukrainian *Rada*, and thus had only the regional Don Cossack Union to turn to. His troops did not care for any of these authorities and decided to go home at the first opportunity offered to them. Ultimately, the Bolsheviks succeeded in moving the front Congress of Soviets to Odessa and the newly elected presidium voted to recognize their authority. They set out for Kishinev to take over the front peacefully,

the even more dangerous Don. Voroshilov was helping the Donets basin to go Bolshevik and Volodarsky was doing the same in the Ukraine, Bessarabia and the Black Sea region. Skrypnyk and Kotsubinsky were reinforcing the Ukraine and Slutsky the Crimea. Bolshevik shock units followed these emissaries.

In the three weeks following the coup, Petrograd MRC sent 200 sailors to such places as Mogilëv, Syzran, Penza, Kaluga, Gomel, Rybinsk and elsewhere. In Moscow the arrival of 500 sailors finally tilted the balance in favor of the Bolsheviks. Moscow leader, Nogin, felt most confident about the Bolshevik chances. He telephoned Petrograd on the eve of the coup to ask for permission to proceed likewise. He then persuaded the Moscow Soviet to approve the rising and an MRC was immediately formed. The city mayor, Rudnev, appealed to Colonel Ryabtsev and his officer-cadets to maintain public order. Though the colonel was reluctant to clash with the garrison troops which obeyed the soviet, he nevertheless succeeded in occupying strategic points in the city together with the Kremlin, which was the HQ of the Military District. Ryabtsev was still negotiating with the Bolsheviks when they launched an attack on his forces and besieged him in the Kremlin.

After the Bolsheviks had brought up artillery and began to shell their adversaries and reinforcements from the Western Front failed to arrive, Ryabtsev surrendered the city. In Moscow province, Poldolsk, Koloma, Serpukhov and Bogorodsk were in Bolshevik hands before the coup; during the fighting in the city they sent Red Guards to help out. At Ivanovo-Voznesensk the soviet organized a strike in favor of the Petrograd coup which was followed by a peaceful takeover. At the Shua railway junction, M V Frunze, the future Bolshevik commander and war minister, formed an MRC and Shua came under Bolshevik control. In the neighboring provinces of Vladimir and Yaroslavl, the takeovers ran smoothly.

In many other provincial capitals the Bolsheviks skillfully exploited the political confusion caused by the coup to gain control. In Smolensk the Bolshevik MRC took over peacefully, only to be opposed a few days later by the City Council (Duma), which scratched together of few Cossack soldiers and formed a Committee for the Salvation a few days later. However, the MRC forces defeated the demoralized Cossacks, dispersed the committee, and the Bolsheviks took charge on 13 November. Similar maneuvers were employed in Pskov and Tver (now Kali-

Below: Two weeks after the revolution began, soldiers were encouraging workers to return to their workplaces.

nin), where a force fighting on behalf of the
Liberal Party was disarmed. At Nizhny Nov-
gorod (now Gorkyt) the anti-Bolshevik majority
refused to recognize *Sovnarkom* until I P Romanov improvised an election. The consequent
Bolshevik majority accepted the Bolsheviks
peacefully. In Kazan the liberal majority at first
decided to fight but then suddenly surrendered.
At Samara (now Kuybyshev), where Kuybyshev and Shvernik were in charge, the
takeover was achieved by vote; the Bolsheviks
had a fragile majority of one. Tsaritsyn (now
Volgograd, previously Stalingrad) became Bolshevik peacefully, but Satatov's Duma called in
the 2nd Orenburg (Cossack) Division and the
takeover was delayed until 11 November, when
the Cossacks decided to go home.

Political confusion was such that the Bolsheviks achieved power remarkably easily.
However, there were provinces where not even
the local Bolshevik leaders fully appreciated
the consequences of the Petrograd coup. At Ekaterinburg (now Sverdlovsk) I M Malyshev
headed a power-sharing coalition composed of
SRs and Mensheviks. Though he also had a
Central Committee emissary, P D Khokhryakov, to consult, the MRC that was formed was
again a coalition one. Only on 5 December did
the city and the Urals province became exclusively Bolshevik, after vigorous intervention
from Petrograd. Similar political difficulties
cropped up in Tula and Kursk, and the takeovers were delayed. The same was true of Archangel, Viatka, Olonets and Vologda, where

takeovers were only effected early in 1918. The
farther from Petrograd and Moscow, the more
difficult the takeovers became. At Astrakhan,
though the 156th Regiment stationed there
went Bolshevik after the coup, fighting for
power lasted for four months. The Don Cossack
Territory was conquered by force in February
1918; the Kuban and Terek Cossack Territories
submitted in March. In the Caucasus the Bolsheviks were strong only in Baku, but the provinces of Georgia and Armenia came under the
control of local nationalists.

The huge area of Soviet Central Asia failed to
recognize *Sovnarkom*, particularly after its
only stronghold, Tashkent, fell to General
Korovichenko's officer-cadets. Since there were
Russian troops in the city, the Bolsheviks
gained their allegiance and retook it after
heavy fighting. On 28 November the Bolsheviks
organized the Third Turkestan Congress of the
Soviets, gained a majority and formed a coalition government with the Left Socialist Revolutionaries who finally recognized *Sovnarkom*.
As a result Samarkand, Ashkabad and Skobelev went Bolshevik; the Transcaspian Government did the same and Fergana followed soon
afterward. However, Bolshevik power was
established rather thinly in this huge territory.
In December 1917 General Dzhunkovsky persuaded the returning Cossacks to help him take
Samarkand; then, as suddenly as they
appeared, the Cossacks surrendered to the Bolsheviks. The Kikand National Government was
in power and beat off the Bolshevik forces sent

Below: Summer 1918.
Scuffles in the street
between Socialist
Revolutionaries and
Bolsheviks.

Ко всѣмъ рабочимъ
ПЕТРОГРАДА!

Товарищи! Революція побѣждаетъ—революція побѣдила. Вся власть перешла къ нашимъ Совѣтамъ. Первыя недѣли самыя трудныя. Надо раздавить до конца сломленную уже реакцію, надо обезпечить полное торжество нашимъ стремленіямъ. Рабочій классъ долженъ, обязанъ проявить въ эти дни

величайшую выдержку и выносливость,

чтобы облегчить Новому Народному Правительству Совѣтовъ выполненіе всѣхъ задачъ. На этихъ же дняхъ будутъ изданы новые законы по рабочему вопросу и въ томъ числѣ одинъ изъ самыхъ первыхъ законъ о рабочемъ контролѣ надъ производствомъ и объ регулированіи промышленности.

Забастовки и выступленіи рабочихъ массъ въ Петроградѣ теперь только вредятъ.

Мы просимъ васъ немедленно прекратить всѣ экономическія и политическія забастовки, всѣмъ стать на работу и производить ее въ полномъ порядкѣ. Работа на заводахъ и во всѣхъ предпріятіяхъ необходима новому правительству Совѣтовъ, потому что всякое разстройство работъ создаетъ для насъ новыя затрудненія, которыхъ и безъ того довольно. Всѣ къ своему мѣсту.

Лучшее средство поддержать новое правительство Совѣтовъ въ эти дни—исполнять свое дѣло.

Да здравствуетъ твердыя выдержки пролетаріата! Да здравствуетъ революція!

Петроградскій Совѣтъ Р. и С. Д.
Петроградскій Совѣтъ Профессіональныхъ Союзовъ.
Центральный Совѣтъ Фабрично-Заводскихъ Комитетовъ.

302

TO ALL WORKERS
OF PETROGRAD!

Comrades! The Revolution is winning, the Revolution has won. All the power has passed over to our Soviets. The first weeks are the most difficult ones. The broken reaction must be finally crushed, a full triumph must be secured for our endeavors. The working-class ought to —must—show in these days

THE GREATEST FIRMNESS AND ENDURANCE

in order to facilitate the execution of all the aims of the new People's Government of Soviets. In the next few days, decrees on the Labor question will be issued. Among the very first will be the decree on Worker's Control over the production and regulation of industry.

STRIKES AND DEMONSTRATIONS OF THE WORKER MASSES IN PETROGRAD NOW CAN ONLY DO HARM.

We ask you to stop immediately all economic and political strikes, to take up your work, and do it in perfect order. The work in factories and all industries is necessary for the new Government of Soviets, because any interruption of this work will only create new difficulties, and we have enough as it is. All to your places.

The best way to support the new Government of Soviets in these days—is by doing your job.

LONG LIVE THE IRON TENACITY OF THE PROLETARIAT!
LONG LIVE THE REVOLUTION!

Petrograd Soviet of W. & S. D.
Petrograd Council of Trade Unions.
Central Council of Factory-Shop Committees.

303

Left: Russian and English versions of an appeal to the workers of Petrograd to return to their jobs and help the revolution with their labor – a tract issued in the early days of the revolution.

from Tashkent to humble it. However, the Alashorda Government, formed in Orenburg and claiming sovereignty over Kazakhstan, never got off the ground. In January 1918 Kronstadt sailors established Bolshevik rule in Kustanay, Semipalatinsk, Akulinsk, Pavlodar, Ust-Kamengorsk and took Vërny (now Alma Ata) in March. At the Fifth Congress of the Soviets, Turkestan was proclaimed an autonomous republic with two exceptions: the khanate of Khiva and the emirate of Bokhara remained under their monarchs. In the Southern Urals the Orenburg Cossacks and their newly elected Ataman, Dutov, declared war on the Bolshe-

viks, pushing them from Troitsk, Verkhne Uralsk and Chelyabinsk. However, a Bolshevik scratch force managed to defeat Dutov, who had formed an alliance with nationalist Bashkirs and Kazakhs. Nonetheless, when Orenburg city fell, the Bolsheviks were able to re-establish contact with Turkestan, while Dutov had only the countryside under his control.

In Siberia Bolshevik progress was slow because of the distances. Three days after Petrograd, Krasnoyarsk claimed to be Bolshevik. Prisoners of war and elements of the 15th Siberian Regiment led by the Hungarian left-wing radical, Lazo, were instrumental in bringing

Below: Elections for the Constituent Assembly taking place shortly after the revolution.

about the takeover. At Omsk the Bolsheviks, again aided by prisoners (among them Josif Broz-Tito, the future Yugoslav leader), had to fight for the city, but the subsequent West Siberian Congress of the Soviets acknowledged their power most peacefully. At Tomsk the Socialist Revolutionary-dominated All-Siberian Soviet rejected Bolshevik demands for recognition: instead it formed the Siberian Autonomous Duma and Government. However, in February 1918, the Tomsk Soviet dissolved the two bodies, which ran off to Mandjuria, and acknowledged Bolshevik authority. The decision was an important boost to Bolshevik morale. Though at Irkutsk the initial Bolshevik takeover proved peaceful, a rebellion by officers and cadets was far from being so. Heavy fighting was finally decided by Lazo's scratch force which arrived from Krasnoyarsk. At Chita the Bolsheviks dispersed the National Cossack Soviet and Ataman Semenov retreated with his

Left: The meeting of the Constituent Assembly on 5 January 1918. After failing to gain majority support the Bolsheviks dispersed the assembly by force the next day.

Bottom left: After toppling a monument to Kaufman, the czar's governor general in Turkestan, Red Guards hoist the Red Flag and proclaim the revolution.

Below: The Women's Death Battalion was formed in June 1887 but was abolished at the end of November 1917.

force to Mongolia. Vladivostock and Khabarovsk provinces recognized Bolshevik power in December 1917, while the nationalist Buryat forces were expelled from Ulan Ude in February 1918. Thus, by March 1918 Lenin was prime minister of roughly the whole of Imperial Russia.

As the political-military takeover of Imperial Russia was proceeding, the Bolsheviks had to beat off several challenges to their central authority. As could be expected the first political initiative came from the numerically superior Socialist Revolutionary Party, though only from its right wing. In response to Bolshevik MRCs, the SR leaders Chernov, Gots and Avksentiev appealed to their followers to start forming Committees for the Salvation of the Motherland and the Revolution, as an effective counter-government. To everyone's surprise, salvation committees began cropping up all over the country, formed or supported by Mensheviks and other socialist factions. However,

from the very beginning of their existence, their chief weakness was that they had no military teeth. Thus, in Petrograd Gots and Braun, two leading SRs decided to furnish their Petrograd Salvation Committee with officer-cadets under the command of Colonel Polkovnikov. The cadets were to arrest the MRC and take over Petrograd, where the Salvation Committee would then become an SR government. Detailed orders were issued, and telegrams were ready for dispatch all round the country in case of success. On 11 November, on Polkovnikov's orders, the Petrograd cadets marched out of their academies, only to be shot at by Bolshevik artillery. The Bolsheviks had known about the planned SR uprising all along. They had intercepted an SR courier, Bruderer, who betrayed the conspiracy to them. On the following day, when the cadet uprising was over, the SR leaders had to run for safety: Gots and Avksentiev were arrested, while Chernov succeeded in slipping

away. He and other anti-Bolsheviks were converging on *Stavka* at Mogilëv.

Their idea for a counter-coup was simple: SR and other politicians wanted troops from *Stavka* to take them to Petrograd, and Allied recognition (Allied military missions were still in Mogilëv) for an SR government. The army would take over power and Chernov would become prime minister. *Stavka* was asked to inform various front committees about this plan. But they were soon disappointed: the replies were confused and no front had troops to take over power. *Stavka* generals became worried about their own safety since their own troops refused to protect them against Krylenko's approaching force. Allied military personnel, admittedly not the most politically sophisticated, thought that the plan was mad. Disappointed in Mogilëv, the SR leaders, without followers and armed forces, now pinned all their hopes on the Constituent Assembly, whose election took place on 12 November 1917. If the Bolsheviks permitted the assembly to meet, SRs were sure to 'come to power peacefully' through the ballot boxes. The Bolsheviks had always claimed that they would convoke the historic assembly to resolve all Russian problems, while asserting the contrary intention of the Provisional Government. However, when the results became known, Lenin began to postpone the convocation. By now he had plenty of political trouble in his own ranks stemming from this 'lost election.'

His first political clash on this subject with Kamenev and Zinoviev ended inconclusively. Many Bolsheviks still thought that even the victorious coup should be legitimized by an election. This was probably the reason for Lenin's demand for Commissar for Enlightenment Lunachardky's expulsion from the Central Committee. However, anti-Lenin 'opposition' wanted even more. They were not only pressing for a coalition government, but also for the freedom of the press, which Lenin had abolished – although he continued to pay it lip service. On 4 November the five dissident Central Committee members, four people's commissars, two other leaders and five military commissars (including Shlyapnikov) resigned. The Left SRs of the MRC resigned as well, thus really forcing what they considered the real issue: 'the preservation in power of a purely Bolshevik government by means of terror.' By this show of force Lenin was obliged to seek a compromise to reestablish party unity.

Between 18 November and 12 December agreement was reached with the Left SRs, whose seven representatives joined Lenin's *Sovnarkom*. They were all wildly romantic figures, politically inexperienced, and used by Lenin to calm his own followers. The resignations were withdrawn and the leading Bolsheviks closed ranks until the next crisis over the separate peace with Germany and Austria-Hungary. Similarly, Lenin was forced to compromise on the Constituent Assembly. In the election 41,000,000 votes were recorded: the Bolsheviks did well in industrial centers and in the northern and western armies. All the same, they only polled one quarter of the vote. Of the 707 elected members they had 175 and the Left SR coalition partners, 40. The SR party had an absolute majority with 360 elected members. The Liberals gained 17 members and the Mensheviks 16. At first, Lenin attempted to intimidate the elected majority leaders, as they emerged from their hiding places or from *Stavka*, into taking part in the proposed opening session on 28 November. Many Liberals were arrested and condemned as 'enemies of the people' to imprisonment; the rest of them were lynched or assassinated by, as Lenin claimed, Anarchist sailors. SR members of the Electoral College were also arrested and the opening was postponed until 5 January 1918. During the month of December demonstrations were organized all over Russia in favor of the Constituent Assembly. Surprised by the scale of these demonstrations, Lenin convinced his Central Committee that the assembly would become a focus of counter-revolution. He knew that two guard regiments offered to demonstrate with the SRs in Petrograd on condition they retained their arms. The SR Central Committee refused this offer and unknowingly sealed the fate of the assembly. When it finally met, the Bolsheviks submitted to the vote a long declaration which in fact recognized their seizure of power. The assembly rejected it by 237 votes to 146, elected its own speaker, Chernov, and subsequently adjourned to prepare its own agenda. During the adjournment the Bolsheviks took the decision to dissolve it, despite some opposition in their own ranks. Left SRs wanted a revolutionary convention or another election, but they were not heeded; neither was a workers' demonstration on the same day. It was dispersed by Red Guards, who killed four workmen. Next day the Constituent Assembly was also dissolved without any bloodshed. The opposition was left with no other option but war.

Peace negotiations, started on 2 December 1917 at Brest-Litovsk, were another cause for political and military polarization in Russia. German and Austrian foreign ministers talked to the Bolshevik representative, A A Ioffe, but real negotiations were conducted by General M Hoffmann. He, for example, explained to Ioffe that both ministers recognized the right of national self-determination: since occupied Poland, Lithuania, the Baltic provinces and other territories wanted to join Germany, they were free to do so. This was not an act of annexation, but self-determination. Ioffe did not like this German interpretation of events, and rejected the proposed peace terms, but he had no army to uphold his own proposals. Lenin sent Trotsky to Brest-Litovsk with instructions to delay the peace treaty as long as possible. He suspected that the German Army would resume hostilities if their terms were not accepted. At the same time there was no end to the flow of resolutions passed by all sorts of bodies, both Bolshevik and non-Bolshevik, appealing to proletarian solidarity, even to the 'imperialist' Allies who opposed the peace negotiations, to save Bolshevik Russia from the Germans. Lenin argued for the acceptance of the 'annexationist' peace terms, since he knew full well that even the few army units capable of fighting were anti-Bolshevik. There was a public outcry against German terms, especially among the Left SRs. However, extreme solutions were disregarded. The Bolshevik Central Committee passed Trotsky's futile resolution, 'Neither war nor peace,' while the resolution for a 'revolutionary war' against Germany attracted only two votes. The adoption of Trotsky's resolution became public on 10 February 1918 and the German Army resumed hostilities on the 18th.

In the end an onerous peace was signed on 3 March, but only after Lenin threatened to resign with the German advance continuing. The Bolsheviks recovered from this setback, but the Left SRs did not. They wished for a 'revolutionary war' and, in any case, suspected the Bolsheviks of granting the Germans even greater concessions than those contained in the treaty. The Germans were able to transfer some 70 divisions to the Western Front which was the main point of this treaty. In addition, they got food supplies from the Ukraine which they occupied. When the new German ambassador, Mirbach, arrived in Moscow, which became the Bolshevik capital (Petrograd was too near the German front line to feel safe), they assassinated him. After a series of revolts, the Left SRs were ejected from the coalition, but not really chastised. Most of them were allowed to rejoin the Bolsheviks and Mirbach's assassin ended up as a Soviet general during World War II. Lenin learned a bitter lesson from these events, namely that a country could not exist without an armed force. Immediately after the signature of the Treaty of Brest-Litovsk, he moved Trotsky to a commissariat of war, to build up a new Red Army. Bolshevik humiliation at the hands of the German Army also stirred up considerable internal dissent.

Below: An assembly of one of the many impromptu soviets formed after the revolution.

ASSAULT FROM THE EAST

The Bolsheviks had been grappling with the problem of creating the Red Army since seizing power. Initially they thought that they could salvage the old imperial force, but too many units proved anti-Bolshevik. Colonel Daller proposed to split the old army into two: border guards and internal militia forces. Kedrov, an old Bolshevik, had other proposals, but in the end Lenin accepted Krylenko's propositions. On 28 December 1917 Lenin attended a demobilization congress and became convinced that Krylenko's solution was right. All imperial units were demobilized and dissolved, while Krylenko's *Stavka* and the All-Russian College for the Formation of the Red Army became responsible for the reconstruction of the armed forces. Lenin appealed to the 'revolutionary units' and the sailors to hold the front line against the Central Powers and set up the Supreme Military Soviet to help with the reorganization in the rear. On 14 February Lenin drafted a decree on the establishment of the Red Army which was approved by the Executive Committee of the All-Russian Soviet and became immediately effective. K S Yeremeyev, a member of the College for the Red Army, was charged with organizing I Red Army Corps in Petrograd; another college member, L I Ulyantsov, began to organize the Red Fleet. The Red Army benefited from the imperial military establishment and many existing units were incorporated in the new army *en masse*: the 5th Zaamur Division, the 12th Finnish Rifle Division, the Latvian Division and the 45th Infantry Division. However, when the Germans resumed hostilities in February, the reorganization was not advanced enough to produce anysignificant resistance on such an immense front. Red Army units, in the face of the disciplined German Army, could only imitate irregular partisan formations. Lenin and Sverdlov then formed another body, the Committee of Revolutionary Defense, to speed up the formation of new units.

On 28 March Lenin personally supervised the 'encadrement' of the Red Army. Officers were no longer elected, but czarist officers were recruited as 'military specialists' (*voyenspets*) and given full operational powers. To make sure of their loyalty, Lenin imposed dual command on the army: all order had to be countersigned by the *politruks (politicheskie rukovideteli)*, who later became known as commissars. Political control was applied on all levels. At the top it was exercised by Lenin, Trotsky, Stalin, Sverdlov or Ordjonikidze. Throughout the ensuing civil war, political leaders were in overall control of the Red Army not only strategically, but also operationally, always endorsing final decisions, sometimes acting as arbiters. This contrasted sharply with the White arrangement in which generals (or an admiral) were in absolute control of politicians. On becoming war minister, Trotsky abolished a number of the political bodies, such as the Committee of Revolutionary Defense, and came out strongly in favor of reestablishing the old military network. The Imperial War Ministry was replaced by the Supreme Military Soviet, whose chairman became Trotsky. His deputies were an enthusiastic army doctor, E Skylansky, Podvoysky and Danishevsky. A large group of *'spets'* worked there under Major General Bonch-Bruyevish, Lenin's friend and brother of a Bol-

Previous page: A heap of dead Bolsheviks surrounded by Germans in early 1918.

Right: The first mobilization of workers in Moscow during the spring of 1918.

Left: A political meeting at the front.

shevik leader. On 8 May Trotsky created a sort of army general staff whose chief was an ex-imperial officer, Colonel I I Vatsetis; chief of staff was F V Kostyayev; General Suleym was quartermaster general. Five fronts were set up: Northern (Samoilo), Western (A I Yegorev), Ukrainian (Antonov-Ovseyenko), Southern (Don) (Sytin) and Eastern (Muravëv). Though some armies had only 3000 men in their ranks, there were numerous partisan units in existence fighting under such Bolsheviks as Voroshilov (an imperial NCO decorated with a St George's Cross), Kikvidze, Rudnak, Blyukher, Sievers, Frunze, Timoshenko, Kotovsky and Primakov, who all fought brilliantly during the civil war. The Imperial Army never commissioned these men, who were more or less forced to divert their energy and prove their valor in the Bolshevik ranks.

Historians still squabble about the dating of the Russian Civil War. Emigré historians tend to regard the Bolshevik *coup d'état* as the beginning; Soviet historians advance all sorts of dates. It is plausible to argue that the civil war was launched in February 1918 by the advancing German Army, while the Czechoslovakian Legion's revolt in May 1918 finally polarized the internecine conflict. Thus the Germans occupied the entire Ukraine and installed their own puppet régime in Kiev under Hetman (Imperial General) Skoropadsky. The Donets coal basin was under their occupation and they were aid-

ing General Krasnov's Don Cossacks. On the invitation of Georgian nationalists, they occupied Tiflis, and Georgia was proclaimed independent. The Crimea was occupied, too, though the Russian Black Sea Fleet scuttled rather than surrender to the Germans. In Finland, German intervention decided the civil war between Red and Whites in favor of the latter. The Czech Legion, consisting of some 50,000 officers and men, rebelled against the Bolsheviks and

Below: N I Podvoysky addressing a meeting in Tver in 1918 to honor the first graduate of the Red Commanders' Training Course.

Above: Lenin reviews the troops who responded to the Universal Military Training drive on Red Square in 1919.

took huge chunks of territory out of their immediate political control.

During World War I, the Imperial Government had formed an ethnic regiment from the Czechs and Slovaks settled in Russia in order that they might administer the conquered territories of Austria-Hungary. If these Russian Czechs never exercised this function, it was not their fault: Czech provinces were never occupied by the Imperial Army. However, the legion's 1st Regiment became the nucleus of a Czechoslovak National Army which fought alongside the Russian armies on the South Western Front. During 1915-16 another regiment was formed, largely from prisoner-volunteers of Czech origin, but in 1917 the Provisional Government gave permission to form three divisions of all sorts of volunteers. The Czechoslovak Legion (as it became known) distinguished itself during the June 1917 offensive, though it had to hastily withdraw after its collapse. During the revolutionary chaos, Czech

leaders in Paris succeeded in having the legion incorporated into the French Army, and Czech units started their transfer to France through Murmansk in December 1917. When the Germans invaded the Ukraine a number of Czech legionnaires were caught by the German and Austrian military authorities and treated as deserters: they were publicly hanged. This unfortunate incident made the legion's withdrawal from Russia imperative and the only way open to it was through distant Vladivostok, since Murmansk, with the Germans in Finland, was insecure. From March 1918, the 50,000 Czechoslovakians were entrained moving eastward from the Ukraine. By May 1918 the trains were strung out between Kursk and Vladivostok.

These soldier-volunteers started their journey fully armed, but as they passed through Bolshevik-held territory, they were asked to donate their arms to their Bolshevik comrades-in-arms so that they could fight the advancing Germans. Bolshevik demands continued even

after the German advance had stopped which made the Czechoslovaks suspicious of the Bolsheviks' real intentions: perhaps they wanted to disarm them and hand them over to the Germans? Coming from Siberia, in the opposite direction, they saw trains loaded with prisoners returning home which further strengthened their suspicions. Late in May 1918 a banal incident in Chelyabinsk between a Czech patrol and Hungarian prisoners sparked off the revolt. The Chelyabinsk Soviet intervened militarily to protect Hungarian prisoners whom the Czechs wanted to shoot, alleging that they had attacked them. The legionnaires made short shrift of the amateur soviet guards and took over the city, dispersing the soviet. In retaliation Trotsky ordered that 'all Czechs found with arms be shot.' This was really a declaration of war. In response, the legion executed an improvised military operation which within the space of two months destroyed soviet rule from Kazan to Vladivostock. Lenin accused the Czechoslovak Legion of being bought by the Western imperialists to suppress the Russian revolution. In reality the legion acted as it did because of its fear of German armies in Russia, its suspicion of the Bolsheviks and because of Allied promises to help it, first to get out of Russia and then make it the nucleus of an Allied military interventionary force.

The diplomatic aspects of Allied intervention will be discussed subsequently: here we shall be concerned with its military aspects. Up to the armistice in the West, Allied intervention in Russia consisted of financial aid to the Czechoslovak Legion (that point of Lenin's declaration was correct) and to the Bolsheviks' adversaries, the Whites. The financial aid to the legion was clearly insufficient, though all three Allies, France, Britain and the United States, contributed. The legion continued to depend on the Reds' goodwill and its own initiative in procuring foodstuffs. The Whites received nothing as the aid emissaries were on the whole captured by the Reds or diverted the funds for other purposes. Thus during the summer of 1918 the Allies, while fighting the war in the West, were

Left: On the eve of the October Revolution, Russian soldiers declare their support for the Bolshevik cause.

Above: Czech troops pose for the camera. Signs of battle can be seen on the building in the background.

preparing a military intervention against Germany in Russia. The legion was 'intervening' on their behalf as a vanguard. Inevitably the legion became involved in the internal Russian conflict and, since its support went exclusively to the Whites, it was this foreign force which sparked off the hot civil war.

The legion's revolt was unplanned, improvised, and spontaneous, the result of a trivial incident. Nonetheless the evacuation of the legion to France via Vladivostok was well-prepared and initiated by the Czechoslovakian exile leader, Professor Masaryk. He arrived in Russia in early 1917 to take over the political leadership of the legion and give it the objective of national independence. On the one hand, the change of the legion's mission confused the Russians who still saw it as a unit of the Russian Imperial Army. On the other hand it finally justified the recruitment of the prisoners, who were no longer mercenaries, but fighters for independence. Seeing the revolutionary chaos, Professors Masaryk and Benes negotiated the legion's incorporation in the French Army and its evacuation from Russia in February 1918. On 7 March 1918 Masaryk left Russia for a political mission to the United States and the legion followed him: he also traveled to Washington via Vladivostok. For the evacuation period Masaryk wanted to keep the legion neutral, but advised the 'legionnaires' to defend themselves energetically if attacked. The political leadership left behind by Masaryk was feeble, but within the legion itself young Czech officers were burning for action, particularly against the Bolsheviks, whom they saw as German allies. The most enthusiastic

was the commanding officer of the 7th Regiment, 'Captain' Gajda (Heidl). After the Chelyabinsk incident and Trotsky's threats, he led his men into immediate action against the Bolsheviks in Novonikolayevsk (now Novosibirsk). Lieutenant Cecek and Lieutenant Colonel Voyteskhovsky, in charge of trains stretching from Penza to Novonikolayevsk, joined Gajda without hesitation as they were even more exposed to Bolshevik threats and pressures. All three were backed by junior Czech officers and their men. Russian officers commanding the legion at the time of the revolt either resigned, ran off or were arrested by their own men. Thus the monotonous evacuation of the legion from Russia was turned into a great adventure of 'shooting one's way to Vladivostok,' which of necessity appealed to the young officers and their bored and frightened men.

Gajda, 26 years old, was a typical example. He deserted the Austrian forces in which he had served as a stretcher bearer on the Serbian Front in 1915. He joined the Serbs, who made him a captain – everybody who could read and write was a *kapetan* in the Serbian forces. Gajda joined the legion after Serbia's defeat and became the driving force behind the revolt. He hated the Bolsheviks because they seemed pro-German and was so obsessed with the Germans that he saw them everywhere. Bolshevik forces in Novonikolayevsk, where his 7th Regiment was stuck, consisted largely of German and Hungarian prisoners – seen as more evidence of the German-Bolshevik plot. He was therefore 'very energetic' in dealing with the Bolsheviks. His tactical mission was to drive westward from Novonikolayevsk to join forces with Colonel

Voytsekhovsky's group. At the same time he had to thrust eastward to contact the Czech forces in Vladivostock, which, after some delay, were driving back to Russia to meet him. It seemed an impossible task for the 1500 men he commanded, but Gajda proved to be a great improviser. He immediately enrolled White Russians as auxiliaries and they soon outnumbered his Czechs. His battlefield friends, Colonels Pepelyayev and Grivin, built up their Siberian armed forces from these auxiliaries and performed tasks, such as the seizure of Tomsk and Tayga, for which Gajda had no men available. Of course, these towns fell to the Whites because the Bolsheviks panicked under the impact of Czech victories; they could not have been taken otherwise. In return the Siberian Whites kept them under their own administration. Thus Czech-White friendship and co-operation were really forged on the battlefields of Siberia.

With substantial Russian support, Gajda made contact with Voytsekhovsky's units on 9 June and finally met the Vladivostok Czechs on 31 August. Cecek's group, the most westward, took Penza from the Bolsheviks on 28 May. Paradoxically, this was a fratricidal engagement: Penza was defended by Czech Internationalists (Bolsheviks) and they were massacred by the excited legionnaires. Cecek handed Penza over to the pre-Bolshevik administration which was Socialist Revolutionary and then immediately ordered the continuation of the evacuation to contact with Voytsekhovsky. On the way eastward, he took Samar on the Volga (now Kuybyshev), a provincial metropolis, and handed it in turn to the Russian auxili-

aries who had helped him in beating the Bolshevik forces *en route*. Though he continued his drive toward Boguruslan and Ufa to join Voytsekhovsky, he had left a small Czech garrison in Samara to help out the Whites. Curiously it was at Samara that the legionnaires finally found out that there were no Allied ships waiting for them in Vladivostok to take them to France. By 24 June 1918 the entire legion knew that its mission had been changed: instead of sailing for France, they were going to fight Germany on the Volga. The Allies were launching an intervention against the Germans/Bolsheviks and the legion was the advance guard. The anti-German front was to be reconstituted on the

Above: Kursk, summer 1918. Podvoysky sees I I Azarkh's brigade off to the front.

Below: Czech troops with the bodies of Bolsheviks killed in a bout of fighting.

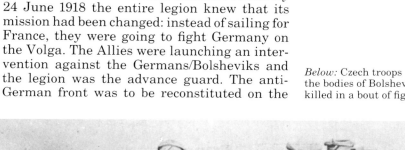

Above: Czech soldiers remove weapons discovered in a building.

Top right: Vladivostock, 1918. An illustration of the numerous countries that participated in the civil war. In all 14 countries sent troops, including over 60,000 from Japan.

Right: A mass funeral of Bolsheviks killed fighting the Czechs in Vladivostok.

Volga and Allied forces were going to join the legion from Vladivostok and from Vyatka in the north. All this was to come in the future: in the meantime, on the spot, the legion was in the thick of the Russian Civil War.

The taking of Samara was indeed a turning point. Up to then Russian combatants were used by the legion to ease its way from the Volga to Vladivostok. Since the Volga was going to be the base for an Allied offensive against Germany, the Czechs halted their movements and took stock of the situation. All the Whites who were helping them were also most enthusiastic about the Allied intervention and the planned offensive against Germany. This offensive inevitably implied the destruction of Bolshevik power; how else could it be achieved? They were, therefore, natural friends of the legion and the Allies. Another Russo-Czech alliance was forged, similar to that of Gajda in Siberia. Samara was previously under Socialist Revolutionary administration – in fact it was an SR stronghold. Its handover back to the SR forces under Colonel Kappel by the legion attracted to it the Socialist Revolutionary deputies of the extinct Constituent Assembly. The city contained a large number of officers who immediately began to recruit local men for White forces. The SR politicians persuaded Cecek, who was still in charge of the sector, to allow them to build up a Volga republic as a preliminary to the conquest of Bolshevik Russia. After all, this Samara regime, named *Komuch* after the Constitutent Assembly and presided over by Avksentiyev, was backed by the majority of the Russian nation. SR politicians were quite prepared to accept power from a foreign legion and with its help defeat the Bolsheviks. A ministry of war was set up headed by General Galkin; his chief of staff was a general, Petrov, whose task was to build a genuine Russian National Army. Since this was clearly above the capacity of the two generals, they contented themselves with confirming Colonels Kappel and Makhin as commanders of the *Komuch* armed forces and devoted themselves to political intrigue to which they owed their own appointments in the first instance. Thus the armed struggle against the Bolsheviks was still left to the foreign Czechoslovak Legion. The latter, therefore, con-

tinued its haphazard operations. With *Komuch* forces they carried out raids into the Bolshevik-held territory in the upper Volga. By chance they captured the large Volga towns of Simbirsk (now Ulyanovsk-Lenin's birthplace) and Kazan. In Kazan the Czech unit, without authorization, accompanied the *Komuch* irregulars and seized the Russian gold reserves just before the town fell back to the Bolsheviks. The legion soldiers brought the reserves to Samara, where Cecek, promoted general, promised to hand it over to the White government which was to be formed in a short time. The *Komuch* Russians, among whom was the speaker of the Constituent Assembly, Chernov, were told by Cecek to establish links with the Urals Cossacks, Bashkirs, Urals Russians, Western Siberians, Siberian autonomists and the varied Far Eastern regimes which had come into exis-

tence in the aftermath of the legion's revolt. They should even establish contact with the Don Cossacks and the Volunteer Army in the south. The Russian Socialist Revolutionaries of Samara were not interested in the latter in the slightest, considering them too 'reactionary.' However, they were most interested in extending their political power into the Urals and Siberia – provided that Cecek's legion allowed them to maintain themselves on the Volga. The idea of a conference of all these White movements and their forces was broached. It would appoint an All-Russian Government which would ultimately take over power from the Bolsheviks. The rest they left to Cecek who took himself very seriously, sending the 4th Czech Regiment down the Volga to Nikolavesk. If possible they would march onto Tsaritsyn and Saratov, to join the White armies of the south.

Above: The inside of a shed used for executions. Even the ceiling is splattered with blood.

Thus, under the legion's protection, Russian politicians became extremely busy. The most important question for them was who would govern the huge territory that was under their control? The overwhelmingly Socialist Revolutionary leaders of Samara wanted to dominate the All-Russian Government, to be called the Directorate, particularly since the Siberians and Far Eastern Russians were also predominantly SR. However, to be genuinely all-Russian, the Directory had to include representatives of Liberals (Kadets) and even of the reactionary Cossacks. They were all convoked to the Urals town of Chelyabinsk. The first meeting of the territorial representatives was scheduled for 15 July, but had to be postponed as the Siberians had no time to arrive. The next meeting, scheduled for Ufa on 1 September, had to be postponed as well. While all these politicians temporarily forgot about Bolshevik armies, they were rudely reminded of this vulgar reality by a Red partisan force led by Revkom Blücher which threatened to capture the whole assembly together with the future Russian government. The delays and divisions threatened White political unity.

When the Ufa conference finally met, it was the most representative assembly of White Russians, including minority nationalities (Bashkirs, Kazakhs and so on), that ever met and reached an agreement. Thus, the *Komuch* government was joined by the Far Eastern, Siberian and West Siberian delegates; political

parties participating were the Mensheviks, Socialist Revolutionaries, Trudoviks (Labor), Yedinstvo (Unity) and National Freedom (Liberals). Among the 200 delegates gathered in Ufa to discuss the future of Russia were even those of the legion: Generals Syrovy and Cecek, both Russian citizens. Discussions were serious and concluded with a vote of thanks to the legion whose revolt made this assembly possible. Still the final agreement did not really stem from the assembly. It was forced on it by B Pavlu, the Czech political representative, and Major Guinet, who fancied himself as the supreme Allied representative. The All-Russian Directorate was, contrary to everyone's wishes, a broad coalition, but an artificial body without political or military support. Thus, there were four prime ministers: Avksentiev (Samara SR), Vologodsky (Siberian SR), Chaykovsky (independent SR, represented by Zenzinov, since he was in Archangel), and Astrov (Liberal, represented by Vinogradov, since he was in the south). There were numerous ministers in charge of all sorts of non-existent ministries, and generals in command of non-existent armies. It became immediately apparent that the chief weakness of the Directory was the lack of military forces. The legion, the driving force behind this artificial conference and agreement, was collapsing and was no longer able to protect the assembly nor the Directory.

As the Ufa conference was dispersing, the Red Army captured Samara on 8 October. Thus the capital fell to the Bolsheviks even before the All-Russian Directorate could take up its residence in it. The military reverses were entirely due to the collapse of the legion and the absence of alternative Russian forces. Since 20 October 1918 Cecek had had to face mutinies in the three regiments, now designated as the 1st Division, under his command. He was relieved of duty and replaced by Colonel Svec, who committed suicide when the mutinies continued. Without the legion, the *Komuch* forces, which were really private armies, could not stop the Red Army's advance. Kappel's force was enlarged with the workers (and their families) of Izhevsk, a small industrial town, who resisted the Red advance with arms *en masse*. They all withdrew beyond the Volga into the Urals. The 2nd Czech Division under General Gajda, which was rushed back from Vladivostok to stop the Red advance, also mutinied. Exhaustion, lack of supplies, the Siberian winter, no Allied armies' support and the armistice in the West were blamed for its collapse. The All-Russian Directorate had to abandon European Russia and retire to the safe Urals capital, Yekaterinburg (now Sverdlovsk). From there it reorganized the war ministry and appointed the experienced General Boldyrev its chief. The unfortunate general soon discovered that compared to his predecessor he was even poorer: not only did he have no armies, he had no buildings either. He was an optimist (he ended his days as professor of tactics in the Red Army) and a skillful negotiator: he hoped that in time he would take overall command of all the private armies, Cossack formations and even the legion. In the mean-

Left: A civil war propaganda poster calling 'Everyone into the Red Army.'

time the Red advance was stopped by 'General Winter,' a Russian description of winter breaks in campaigns. Still he had no time to realize (negotiate) his plans. Though General Syrovy, commander of the legion, finally agreed to place himself under Boldyrev's command, this subordination was useless, for the legion was no longer a fighting force. He and the Directory

Below: Young recruits of the White Army advance along a city street.

were swept out of power by Admiral Kolchak in November 1918.

The advance of winter saved the Directory from the Red Army. However, it was a phantom government, which flitted from Yekaterinburg to Omsk, able only to watch its forces become demoralized and the legion collapse. Omsk, the seat of the West Siberian government, had not only ministries with buildings and officials, but also a motley collection of armed units which were certainly less demoralized and more

powerful than those of the Directory. Initially, the West Siberian government lacked general officers and solid administrators, but now it could pick and choose from the refugees flowing from Russia. One of these was Admiral Kolchak, who arrived at Omsk from the Far East and was promptly made war minister. Admiral Kolchak (a Crimean Tartar) had had a distinguished career in the Imperial Navy and left Russia disgusted by the revolution in 1917. He applied for service in the British Navy and was accepted when the legion's revolt made Siberia go White. As he was at this stage in Japan, the admiralty posted him to Vladivostok, and then on to Omsk. He was of upright character and observed the confusion, if not corruption, of West Siberian politics with disgust. He was completely absorbed in the struggle against the Reds so he accepted the post of war minister, but he proved politicially naive. He was easily persuaded by Atamans Volkov and Krasilnikov, whose Cossack detachments were supreme at Omsk, to seize power. He was convinced that this would do the White cause a lot of good. The Cossacks captured the Directory and wanted to massacre it. Uncomprehending, Kolchak forbade it and sent the Directorate into exile, thus unwittingly saving their lives for the second time. Then he proclaimed himself the Supreme Ruler of Russia and Supreme Commander of the Russian National Army. Politically, he went on pretending that he headed an all-Russian government. For this purpose he even set up a ministry of foreign affairs, and like the emperor before him, maintained close contacts with Allied representatives, who, in the meantime, had arrived at Omsk. He did all this despite himself; for he was really interested only in the pursuit of the war against the Red Army. From

Above: A Red Army
armored train on the
Southern Front in 1919.

his predecessors he inherited peculiar armies in the field: General Gajda's mutinous 2nd Czech Division; General Pepelyayev's Tomsk Corps; General Grivin's Irkutsk Corps; General Verzhbitsky's special units, including Kappel's, and a few other Cossack formations. Altogether they amounted to 19,600 men and 2300 horsemen. In addition there were, in the Western Urals, the motley force of 9000 men under General Lyupov; and 14,500 men on foot and 5000 men on horse under General Voytsekhovsky. In the south Ataman Dutov commanded 10,500 rifles and 5000 sabers of Orenburg Cossacks. All these forces existed largely on paper as they were highly volatile on the battlefield and often could not be located.

Kolchak saw as his foremost task the halting of the Red Army's advance. To achieve this he intended to launch his armies against the Reds in a limited tactical offensive. Then he intended to raise new armies in Siberia and launch them in a large strategic offensive in spring 1919. To accomplish such tremendous ambitions he set up a supreme military HQ, called *Stavka* after its imperial predecessor, and staffed it (some said overstaffed) with all the available Russian officers. As his chief of staff he appointed Colonel Lebedev. Young and inexperienced in staff work, Lebedev was politically very active in the Officers' Association, whose political opinions Kolchak did not share, but whose rights of representation in his *Stavka* he recognized. Personally Kolchak avoided interfering with the front commanders but, by making the fronts subordinate to *Stavka* for co-ordination purposes, he made quite sure that front command was interfered with by all and sundry (some alleged by himself). Early in December 1918 Kolchak decided to put the new establishment through its paces and test the front commanders in a limited offensive. He ordered the Northern Army Group, consisting of Pepelyayev's and Grivin's Siberian Corps, under overall command of Gajda, to prepare jointly with *Stavka* (Lebedev) a winter offensive against the First (Revkom Tukhachevsky) and Third Red Army (Revkom M M Lashevich).

Acquainted with the low morale of his forces, Gajda wanted the offensive in the south. When overruled by Lebedev he worked out an offensive in the direction of Perm. General Pepelyayev's Siberian Army, though badly equipped and obviously suffering from the cold weather, carried it out to perfection. It defeated the Red Armies decisively, taking advantage of surprise and faulty co-ordination among Red commanders, and took the city of Perm on 24 December 1918. Pepelyayev captured large stores in Perm, as well as numerous prisoners, but lost 5000 men including 494 officers. Still,

the first Kolchak offensive was a great victory and a veritable disaster for the Reds. It raised Kolchak's political prestige, particularly with the Allies who were sending him supplies. However, the unexpected victory enabled him to cherish an illusion of grandeur, which was subsequently responsible for the failure of his big offensive. Lenin instituted a Investigation Commission into this terrible defeat; subsequently the Red armies in the East were reorganized and resupplied, and the commanding teams reshuffled (Frunze became front commander). Kolchak rested on his laurels, he did not even replace Pepelyayev's casualties, though a recruitment drive was going on in all Siberia. At this time he also settled the fate of the legion. Since its collapse late in 1918 the Czechoslovak Legion ceased to be a military formation and, though it remained in Siberia and the Russian Far East until late 1920, its demoralized units never again took part in civil war operations. They were instead engaged in auxiliary capacities, guarding the Trans-Siberian Railway throughout 1919-20. The Russian supreme commander, Kolchak, unnecessarily humiliated the legion's officers and men, threatening, like the Bolsheviks before him, to disarm them if they did not accept this humble task. The recruitment of Siberian peasants into Kolchak's armies soon produced a rebellion in Kolchak's rear, which the disillusioned legion was asked to suppress. While Siberian partisan activity grew, the legion, increasingly reluctant to repress them, insisted on its evacuation from Siberia to independent Czechoslovakia. Kolchak's rear was completely insecure, even his

supplies from Vladivostok were interrupted, but he chose to ignore this disquieting situation and ordered the preparation of the strategic spring offensive, with the aim of taking him and his armies to Moscow.

As with the wasteful December offensive, Kolchak left Gajda in charge of the Northern (Siberian) Group. He put General Khandzhin, a regular officer previously in charge of various irregulars, in command of the Western Group. The Southern Group commander, General Belov, was widely seen as a nonentity. Further south the volatile Cossack armies were commanded by Ataman Dutov who did not even bother to come to Omsk to co-ordinate the offensive. All he wanted from Kolchak was Allied supplies, now arriving with interruptions, but in abundance. In consequence Kolchak's troops were reasonably well equipped but untrained. Kolchak wanted to exploit the element of surprise, for he knew full well from the interrogation of deserters that the Red Army was not quite ready. The real question was whether the White armies themselves were ready for such an offensive. On the eve of the March offensive General Janin, the French supreme commander of the legion, sent a report to Paris on the situation in the territory controlled by Kolchak. His report was from from flattering.

After the withdrawal of the legion and the fall of Orenburg Kolchak was in no position to launch an offensive. Not even a *coup de force* at Omsk and troubles at Krasnoyarsk succeeded in diverting his attention from the offensive, but demonstrated the weakness of his rear. He simply blamed internal troubles on Allied mud-

dleheadedness and claimed that he could suppress them ruthlessly, which he did. Politically the regime was a disaster: both reactionaries (Cossacks, officers) and progressives (SRs, Mensheviks) suffered from inertia and were capable of enthusiasm and spirit only when fighting each other. The military matters were equally depressing; he no longer attended *Stavka* meetings, as they were purely ceremonial. Basic ignorance and muddle reigned everywhere: officers were incapable of reorganizing units nor of forming a regiment. General Dieterichs was the only experienced officer at *Stavka*; he, however, lacked the strength of character to impose himself. Military incompetence extended from the top to the bottom. Frontline troops were uncontrollable and both officers and men behaved like rabble. Janin's report continued: 'Kolchak does not even try to improve the working of *Stavka*, or enforce discipline . . . he relies blindly on his officers' advice and issues nonsensical orders from Omsk, which will have a disastrous effect on his prestige. Moreover the regime is completely blind: it has no intelligence service whatsoever.'

It was true that Janin and Kolchak had quarreled bitterly during the winter months of 1918-19, and that the report was not flattering vis-à-vis Kolchak. However, within a month the pessimistic report proved to be accurate.

Early in March 1919 the Bashkir troops of the Western Army Group deserted *en masse* to the Red Army. This desertion apparently forced

Kolchak to launch his offensive on all the three fronts. In the north Gajda advanced toward Vyatka without meeting heavy resistance, and ultimately linked up with the Allied troops locked up in the Archangel area. Gajda's Siberians moved forward rapidly but soon overextended themselves, running out of supplies and ammunition. Dutov's unreliable Cossacks surprisingly advanced and took the huge territory of Orsk, Orenburg and Uralsk, which they had conquered in the autumn of 1918, from the Red Army. General Khandzhin punched his way through the Red lines, advancing over 250

Above: Kuban Cossacks, former soldiers of the Czarist First Cavalry Army, who fought with the Red Army in the defeat of interventionist troops near Rostov.

Far left: A Bolshevik commando surrounded by a group of his officers.

Below: The Volga River flotilla, organized on Lenin's initiative during the defense of Tsaritsyn.

miles, taking Ufa and moving into a position to take Samara. However, it was on his front that the first reversal occurred. The Red Army under Khandzhin's pressure withdrew in good order, but the partial defeat produced a crisis: both Trotsky and Vatsetis were accused of incompetence. In the end the Eastern Front was split into two: the Second and Third Red Armies faced Gajda, while the First, Fourth, Fifth and Turkestan Armies were concentrated against Khandzhin. They launched a counteroffensive in 28 April. Khandzhin's Bashkir cavalry deserted and Ukrainian units went over to the Reds during the decisive battle with their Allied equipment and British battledress uniforms. By the end of June the Red Army occupied all the territory conquered by Khandzhin, who found himself cut off. Gajda's Siberians also had to beat a hasty retreat which soon turned into rout. The towns of Perm and Ekaterinburg and their stores were abandoned to the Reds. In the south Dutov's defeat was comprehensive: the Reds retook Orenburg and Uralsk and struck deeply into Turkestan, driving the Cossacks before them into this inhospitable region. Kolchak felt obliged to dismiss Khandzhin, whose place was taken by Gajda. Gajda's northern command went to General Bogoslavsky, a Russian, instead of the Siberian General Pepelyayev. Dutov could not be reached and therefore remained in command until his assassination by his own troops. The reshuffle of generals did not improve the situation. Fresh reserves might have helped but there were

none. Soon Gajda quarreled with Lebedev and they were both dismissed, General Dieterichs replacing Lebedev to reorganize the defeated White armies. Kolchak was fortunate that the Red Army's offensive was suddenly halted. Commander in Chief Vatsetis, going against Lenin's views, perceived that the greatest danger to the Bolsheviks was in the south, where General Denikin's armies were advancing in an orderly fashion. While the Reds quarreled (Vatsetis lost his command and was replaced by S S Kamenev), Kolchak and Dieterichs were given breathing space to prepare their armies for the next Red offensive.

As predicted by Janin, Kolchak's rear became unsafe as soon as his defeats became known. The Siberian peasants were not very enthusiastic about the Supreme Ruler of All Russia from the beginning, but then they were not exactly consulted. However, when conscription became compulsory and food requisition rife, Siberian peasants formed partisan units consisting of both deserters and political opponents, including the Bolsheviks, which harassed the Whites in garrison towns. With increasing frequency these partisan bands also attacked the Trans-Siberian Railway which was under the protection of the legion, still waiting to be evacuated back to Europe. The legion was being dragged into the civil war, particularly in the messy partisan fighting. Exasperated Czechs committed as many atrocities against 'peasant bandits' as their Cossack and Russian allies. In the end they once again collapsed and refused to fight

Below: This group of Russian soldiers in World War I reflects the mix of nationalities inherited by the Bolsheviks in 1917.

any more, even against the partisans who
threatened their lifeline to Europe. Mutinies
were suppressed without bloodshed, though the
legion was given a fixed date, October 1919, for
its withdrawal from Siberia. Unfortunately for
them Kolchak's armies collapsed at the same
time and they were caught up in the unimagin-
able chaos of the retreat along the Trans-Siberian to the Far East.

Kolchak's 'purges' in July 1919 and Dieterichs' reorganization brought the Whites some
relief and consolidation, though the Red Army's
penetration of the Urals was substantial (some
600 miles). In September Dieterichs was able to
launch a counteroffensive which drove the Reds
back some 100 miles, from Ishim to the Tobol
River. However, both sides practiced mobile
warfare and there were no front lines in the
classic sense. In mid-October 1919 the Fifth Red
Army's counterattack, coupled with West
Siberian partisan offensive, forced Dieterichs to
withdraw his three armies, or what was left of
them, to the Irtysh River. This move entailed
the evacuation of Omsk, Kolchak's capital. The
supreme ruler was busy negotiating the re-
engagement with the Allied and Czech representatives and paid no attention to the military
situation. He also tried to force his general to
make a stand before Omsk, pointing out to him
its political importance. However, by then, Dieterichs' tactical withdrawal had turned into a
rout. Dieterichs ceased to control the armies
and wisely retreated beyond the Irtysh. Kolchak, therefore, dismissed him and replaced
him with another general, Zakharov, whom he
appointed on the discredited Lebedev's suggestion. Within 48 hours Zakharov's decision was
the same as Dieterichs': it was impossible to
save Omsk. He therefore transferred his troops
to the other side of the Irtysh, leaving the city

undefended. At the last minute, Kolchak, his
government and *Stavka* abandoned Omsk in
seven trains, taking with them the Russian gold
reserve captured by the Czechs in Kazan, to the
most uncertain destination. On 15 November
the 5th Red Army appeared from Petropavlovsk
and captured the city with its enormous stores,
artillery and transport.

All Siberia lapsed into chaos and everybody,
soldiers and civilians alike, tried to run away
from the advancing Reds. To compound the
problem the legion began its withdrawal from
Siberia. It was most important for the legion to
control the railway line and the movements
thereon, since it led finally home. The legion's
morale had been miraculously re-established
and the Czech troops were more than willing to
fight their way through the partisan-held terri-

Above: Advancing German troops come across abandoned Russian equipment in February 1918.

Opposite page, top: A Cossack wearing the uniform of the Women's Army fighting against the Reds.

Right: Refugees from the revolution. Wholesale destruction of villages and property led to a mass exodus from the civil war battle zones.

tory right up to Vladivostok, where Allied ships were waiting to embark them for their voyage to Europe. However, to reach Vladivostok, the legion had to pass through such important centers as Krasnoyarsk, Irkutsk and Chita, which had risen in rebellion against Kolchak. These rebels were officers belonging to the SR party. Even Vladivostok was organized and ready to strike at Kolchak. Unfortunately for the rebels, Gajda organized the rebellion on their behalf, but General Rozanov, with Japanese help, suppressed it ruthlessly. After this failure the SR rebels decided to strike at Kolchak more directly. They attempted to block the Trans-Siberian to Kolchak's trains. The legion had to negotiate its own free passage with them and as a result deprived the White trains of locomotives. They were obliged to march away from the advancing Reds on foot, together with the flood of refugees. In these dire straits the White generals' nerves snapped completely, and they began to quarrel among themselves. General Voytsekhovsky shot dead General Grivin for insubordination; General Pepelyayev forced the resignation of Zakharov with a pistol; General Kappel, who succeeded Zakharov, was soon dead of frostbite, advancing with his men on foot. Voytsekhovsky became commander of the reduced White armies. Kolchak resigned and placed himself under the protection of the Allies which, in effect, meant that he was under Czech protection. However, the legion, when threatened with obstruction in Irkutsk, handed Kolchak and some of his ministers over to the SR authorities who had requested his 'extradition.' The legion kept the

gold reserve to bargain with the Red Army which was catching up with the retreating Whites.

The end of White Siberia was desperately sad. Early in February 1920 the Reds seized power from the SRs in Irkutsk, and after interrogating Kolchak, who behaved courageously, executed him. General Pepelyayev's brother was also executed. When Voytsekhovsky arrived with his forces at Irkutsk, he wanted to avenge the death of his political leader but was dissuaded by the legion from doing so. His armies continued their terrible march to the Far East, where they attempted to defy the Bolsheviks until 1924 when their Japanese protectors deserted them. Voytsekhovsky ended his life in Czechoslovakia, a general of the Czechoslovak Army. On 7 February 1920 the legion concluded an armistice with the Red Army. In return the legion ceded the Reds the gold reserve confiscated from Kolchak. Henceforth, the legion could continue its evacuation unhindered. However, across Lake Baykal, particularly at Chita, there was more trouble awaiting the legion – how to deal with the remaining pro-Kolchak forces. Ataman Semenov threatened to blow up the tunnels and the Trans-Siberian line in revenge for Kolchak's death. In the end, the Ataman was bribed with arms and ammunition and the last legion train left Irkutsk on 1 March. The maritime province was under the protection of Japanese and American troops, originally landed there in the summer of 1918

Right: Refugees wait alongside the Trans-Siberian Railway in the hope of evacuation.

'to rescue the legion.' The legion's evacuation was finally completed in November 1920; the American troops left with it, but the Japanese remained, looking after their own, chiefly economic, interests. The Russian Whites continued their internecine struggles and only retired from the province in 1924, some going to Mongolia, China, Japan or the western coast of America.

The White adventure in Siberia which started with so much promise ended in total disaster. Despite the fact that this huge territory was solidly anti-Bolshevik, the Russians, whether Siberian or metropolitan, together with minority nationalities, proved incapable of achieving political unity to beat off the Bolshevik challenge. The co-existence of majority SRs and conservatives-monarchists was impossible. Perhaps European Russians should have permitted real Siberian autonomy as the Siberians wanted, but the circumstances of civil war did not favor it. The prosperous Siberian peasants wanted to be left as much alone as possible. In the end they found the Kolchak authorities even more oppressive than the Bolsheviks. It was part of the tragedy that they found out too late that the Reds were no better. By then the Red Army occupied the populated parts and the partisan movements had been dissolved. The other aspect of this tragedy was the presence of

Below: American troops at the scene of a train crash caused by the Bolsheviks.

numerous Russian officers who behaved badly, and the activity of the Cossacks, who became their willing instruments. They not only interfered by force in Siberian politics, but also suppressed peasant rebellions with great brutality. At the same time, the officers were willing to sacrifice their Siberian recruits for their grandiose schemes, offering them nothing in return. Of the personalities engaged in the civil war on the White side, their fortunes were varied. Kolchak's end was tragic and undeserved. General Dieterichs died in the United States, leaving his papers from Siberia to the Hoover Institution.

Ataman Semenov was captured in China by the Red Army and was hanged in 1946. Colonel Lebedev disappeared in the anonymous sea of refugees, while General Pepelyayev joined the Red Army. General Janin retired after his return to France and wrote detailed memoirs. General Graves, who led the US expeditionary force in Vladivostok, also wrote a book of memoirs. General Gajda became leader of the Czech Fascists, but proved too nationalistic for the Nazis who imprisoned him. He died in a communist jail in 1948. Many other White leaders met a similar fate.

WAR ON ALL FRONTS

As elsewhere in Russia, the situation in the south was also dominated by the peasant question. Like Admiral Kolchak in Siberia, the eventual leader in the region, General Denikin, also preferred war to politics. Denikin was more liberal than his reactionary officers but he was still far from 'progressive' or, to put it in non-ideological terms, realistic. He had learned no lessons from 1917. His attempts at agrarian reform were half-hearted and the slogan of 'one-indivisible Russia,' however justified, roused all the nationalities of Russia who clamored for autonomy or independence against him and his movement. Thus from the beginning of his struggle against the Bolsheviks, Denikin had against him the peasantry, though he was himself a son of a serf, and those clamoring for autonomy. Both groups were indispensable for victory. The peasants did not trust his regime as they identified his officers with their former landlords – which they were. Paradoxically, the Bolsheviks granted them more land than Denikin's Whites. Why should the peasants support the latter? Because of his alleged Great Russian chauvinism, the Don, Kuban and Terek Cossacks, not to mention the Finns, Estonians, Georgians and Ukrainians, were up in arms against Denikin.

In the south, the challenge to the northern Reds was first picked up by the elected Ataman of the Don Cossacks, General Kaledin. Throughout November 1917 his public disputes with *Sovnarkom* attracted increasing numbers of imperial officers, who thought that the south would in time become the center of anti-Bolshevik struggle, to the Don territory. Generals Alexeyev, Kornilov, Markov, Denikin and many others made their 'pilgrimage' to Novo-cherkassk, where Kaledin told them bluntly to organize their struggle against the Bolsheviks on Russian territory and not in the Don Cossack autonomous area. The generals and their officers, therefore, seized the neighboring city of Rostov and established their base there. Thus, from the start, the Volunteer Army developed separately. It consisted largely of former imperial general officers, who were often obliged to serve as private soldiers. However, by December 1917, a motley collection of Bolshevik units descended on the Don to chastize the rebellious Cossacks. They also captured Rostov. Kaledin committed suicide when his troops refused to fight the advancing Reds, while the Volunteer Army retreated into the inhospitable regions of the Northern Caucasus. During the ensuing fighting, the Volunteers suffered heavy casualties, and both Kornilov and Alexeyev were dead well before they were able to leave for Russia. By May 1918 soviet rule over the Don had collapsed and the newly elected Ataman, General Krasnov, requested and received military aid from the German command, now installed in the Ukraine. The Volunteers, known for their Allied sympathy, were deliberately kept in the 'wilderness' of the northern Caucasus. However, the tables were turned in November 1918 with the armistice in the West. The Allies were now in control and the Volunteer Army was going to be built up with their support. Despite German aid, Krasnov's Cossacks were not a magnificent force. They seemed only good in advancing historical claims. Thus, they claimed the city of Voronezh for themselves, but their expedition sent to annex it was a hopeless flop. Then, almost by chance, they took Tsaritsyn (later Stalingrad) while foraging for food.

However, they could not hold the city for long. Red troops, returning home, drove them out. Curiously, the Cossacks blamed the Volunteers for their Tsaritsyn defeat and let the Reds through from the Caucasus.

On 16 August 1918 the Volunteers captured the sizeable city of Ekaterinodar (now Krasnodar) in the northern Caucasus and instantly ran into another group demanding autonomy, the Kuban Cossacks. To avoid facing the problem head on, General Denikin set up a commission to draft a constitution to be applied in the Volunteer-controlled territories and, ultimately, in the whole of Russia. The constitution turned out to be a somewhat liberal document, but it, nonetheless, made General Denikin both commander in chief and a civilian dictator. It was vague about land distribution, insisting on the inviolability of private property and on the enforcement of 'existing laws.' In the conditions of civil war, these two constitutional clauses were absurd. Denikin was assisted in his tasks as dictator by a Special Council, a sort of government, but, since the general disliked politics and feared political interference from the Special Council in army matters, he suitably neutralized the body by appointing General Dragomirov as its chairman. Dragomirov controlled the Special Council from inside and Denikin from outside by vetoing all the practical proposals passed on by the council's chairman. The constitution and its institutions seemed like a paper exercise and both were violated by right and left. General Denikin himself issued several unconstitutional orders; one demanded that all Red Army officers caught fighting against the Volunteers were to be executed. In consequence, Denikin's administration was soon in disarray. In theory, autonomous Cossacks were left to administer themselves, though Volunteer officers always

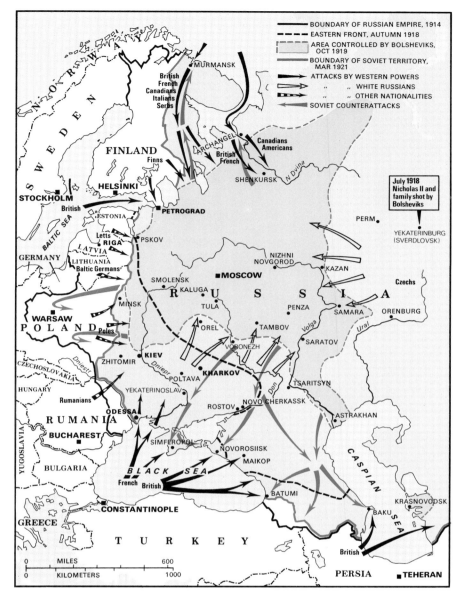

BOUNDARY OF RUSSIAN EMPIRE, 1914
EASTERN FRONT, AUTUMN 1918
AREA CONTROLLED BY BOLSHEVIKS, OCT 1919
BOUNDARY OF SOVIET TERRITORY, MAR 1921
ATTACKS BY WESTERN POWERS
" " WHITE RUSSIANS
" " OTHER NATIONALITIES
SOVIET COUNTERATTACKS

July 1918
Nicholas II and family shot by Bolsheviks

had a final say. In purely Russian provinces, Denikin appointed governor officers with monarchist views, who thought their present duties included the return of seized land to landlords. They also considered it part of their duties to persecute 'progressives' as if they were Bolsheviks themselves. These governors even resumed discrimination against local ethnic groups. General Uvarov, who applied all these measures in the province of Stavropol, had to be dismissed for provoking local revolts. Denikin did not dismiss more than a few governors, though the administrative practices of many were not so different from Uvarov's. The alienation of the local population was completed in relatively short time. But this practice became Denikin's hallmark: he delegated his political responsibilities to his subordinates and focused his attention exclusively on the armed forces.

Shortly after the armistice in the West, the French General Berthelot convoked a Russian conference at Iassi, after Romania had switched sides once more. The real purpose of this conference was, however, to gain Russian approval for a projected French military landing in the Ukraine. French Premier Clemenceau insisted on this Russian 'invitation' to intervene directly in the civil war without consulting his US or British allies. The conference at Iassi approved the French landing unanimously. In addition, it also voted for, without being asked, General Denikin as supreme commander and dictator, and expressed a desire to see liberated Russia restored to its pre-1914 frontiers (with the exception of Poland). Unfortunately, the Iassi conference completely misled the Whites as they believed that the French were intervening on their behalf to 'restore Russia' and not to safeguard their own interests. Denikin, pleased with being 'approved' by the Allies, immediately exploited his seemingly strengthened position. He brought the 'rebellious' Krasnov to heel; General Poole ordered the fusion of the Don Cossack Army (100,000 men) with the Volunteer Army (10,000 men). The Kuban Cossack Army (60,000 men) was added by negotiation, and the resulting force became the Armed Forces of Southern Russia, commanded by Denikin. Still the general was hurt when General Franchet D'Esperey, after landing in Odessa, ignored him. Moreover, he failed to hand over the occupied territory of the Ukraine to Denikin's representatives. The French would not hear of letting Denikin's troops occupy the cities of Odessa and Sebastopol, and even began to negotiate with Ukrainian nationalists about their presence on territory which Denikin claimed for himself and Russia. Clearly Deni-

Below: 'Death of the Commissar' by K Petrov Vodkin.

kin knew nothing about the French-British agreement on zones of interest in Russia.

The puzzled and disappointed Denikin nevertheless took advantage of British aid which arrived in late November 1918 after some ships forced their way through the Dardanelles. They brought in immense war stores to equip a real army. However, Denikin wanted to launch an immediate offensive with the three armed groups (the Volunteer Corps, the United Corps, and the United Cavalry Corps) under his command. The British made it clear to him that he had to train and re-organize his armies before carrying out an orderly mobilization, and only then would he be able to launch his offensive. Before he could argue out his case, a disaster struck the southern Ukraine. The French and Greek forces recently transferred from the Thessalonika front and deployed in the region suddenly mutinied and had to be withdrawn. The territory they controlled was seized by armed bands under Ataman Grigoriev and Anarchist Makhno. To avoid similar disasters in the future, Denikin, with British aid, re-organized his armies effectively: the enlarged Volunteer Army remained under General May-Mayevsky; General Sidorin, a Cossack officer, took the command of the Don Army; while General Wrangel took over the Caucasian Army which consisted of Kuban, Terek and Caspian units. The forces he mustered were not very strong, but were reinforced by well-equipped National and Crimean Army units which found refuge in his territory after the French abandoned Odessa and the Crimea. The arrival of the latest British aid, including tanks and aircraft, seems to have turned the general's head. He decided on an immediate offensive on the broadest front possible, stretching from Astrakhan to Odessa and culminating in a drive to Moscow. In his GHQ in Ekaterinodar, he conceived a strategic plan which was to take

Above: General Anton Denikin. Following the collapse of his counter-revolutionary force he fled Russia in 1920.

Left: German troops execute two Bolsheviks.

Right: Denikin's troops executing Bolsheviks.

Below: Stalin's plan for the destruction of Denikin's armies, 1919-20.

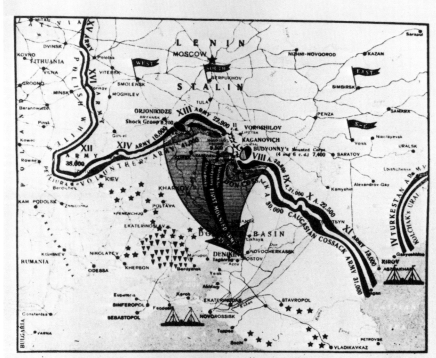

STALIN'S PLAN FOR THE DESTRUCTION OF DENIKIN'S ARMIES
1919-1920

the Volunteer Army to central Russia via Kharkov and the Caucasian Army to central Volga via Tsaritsyn in order to establish contact with anti-Bolshevik forces in Siberia. A special Volunteer group was sent on a subsidiary strike against the Bolshevik-held parts of the Caspian region. In May 1919 Denikin's armies, well equipped with British equipment but poorly trained, moved to achieve their objectives.

In the last there was immediate disappointment. The vital city of Astrakhan at the mouth of the Volga was never reached because of numerous tactical errors. The Caspian flotilla, well trained by the British, was brought into the fighting too late. Nationalist uprisings in Dagestan and the Terek territory tied up too many troops and the important port at the mouth of the Volga remained in Bolshevik hands. Moreover, the initial failures made the objective of Central Volga unattainable, as only the combined forces of the Caucasian Army were capable of effecting contact with Kolchak's armies beyond Tsaritsyn. Furthermore, the operation could not be completed after Kolchak's armies were pushed back into Siberia. Denikin, who loathed alterations to his plans should, nevertheless, have listened to General Wrangel's strategic retargeting. But as his attacks elsewhere had met with great success, particularly in the sectors of the Volunteer and Don Armies, he insisted on maintaining his original objectives. The Volunteers reached Kharkov. Kiev fell after the Ukrainian nationalists and Bolsheviks had fought themselves to a standstill, leaving the Volunteers to collect trophies of victory. However, the chief factor behind these victories was the new force employed by the Whites: the Don Cavalry Army under General Mamontov.

Mamontov, formerly in command of the Czech Legion, deployed his horsemen in deep drives into the Bolshevik rear, cutting off their communications and sowing panic among the raw recruits of the Red Army. However, by September 1919, Mamontov's cavalry had withdrawn from the front after carrying out another terrifying raid deep into Tambov province. Rumors suggested that the Cossacks went back to the Don to re-form because of the booty they had collected in Tambov. Whatever the case, Mamontov fell ill with typhoid fever and was temporarily replaced by General Shkuro and his Caucasian horsemen. They were considerably smaller in numbers and less disciplined than the Don horsemen. At the same time, the White advance continued and May-Mayevsky took Orel, only some 100 miles away from Moscow, and Sidorin's Don Cossacks finally captured Voronezh. General Kutepov prepared the next operation with the objective of Tula, the last town before Moscow, in mind. The operation began well but came to a halt after the Red Army counterattacked. Faced with defeat, the Red Army suddenly changed tactics. Unlike the Whites, they had never before employed their cavalry in massive raids. S Budyonny, a Don Cossack and czarist soldier decorated with the St George's Cross, was in charge of the Bolshevik cavalry throughout 1919 and had requested this tactical change. By October, he had Trotsky's permission and was ready for action. The Red commander in chief, Colonel Kamenev, ordered Budyonny to attack at the junction between the Volunteers and the Don Cossacks. His Red cavalry defeated Shkuro's wild horsemen and cut a gaping hole in the White front, swinging round to cut off White communications as Mamontov had done before. Early in November Kamenev launched his foot soldiers against the Whites on both fronts, and began to push them back. At first the White withdrawal was orderly. However, after November it turned into a rout because of the skill of the Bolshevik pursuers.

Since June the supreme White commander had been stationed in an armored train following the advances of his armies. He hardly interfered with operations but tried hard to co-ordinate the offensive. All this time Denikin had to listen to a constant barrage of criticism from Wrangel, who tried to explain the lack of progress on his Tsaritsyn front by Kuban Cossack 'sabotage.' Denikin tried several times to pacify Wrangel by sending him reinforcements in penny packets but, in November, he ceded to his repeated demands and permitted him to 'sort out the Kuban problem' once and for all. General Pokrovsky was detailed to Ekaterinodar, where in a *coup de force* he captured the Kuban Cossack Council, publicly hanging one of its leaders. The rest were sent into exile, while new men replaced them. Pokrovsky then returned to the Tsaritsyn front to fight against the Reds. Pokrovsky's operation was another example of paper success. In fact, it cut off the retreating White armies from their Kuban rear base. After the first reverses, Denikin decided to reshuffle the front command: Wrangel replaced May-Mayevsky; Pokrovsky replaced Wrangel;

Mamontov was replaced by Ulagay. The reshuffle was carried out at lower levels as well, but with disastrous consequences. General Ulagay was in command of the Don cavalry, but could not find Cossack horsemen. Newly arriving generals found their men dispirited and unwilling to fight with the same enthusiasm under strange commanders. The rout and panic of the White armies was on.

Early in December the Red Army drove Pokrovsky from Tsaritsyn; he hastened to the Don region with the depleted Caucasian Army. Even before they reached the northern Caucasus, the Caucasian soldiers melted away, leaving General Pokrovsky without a command. On 2 December General Dragomirov abandoned Kiev; General Schilling retreated in panic to Odessa and then to the Crimea, abandoning his men and their families to the pursuing Reds, Greens (Makhno) and Blacks (Anarchists). On 10 December Wrangel asked the Volunteers to stand and fight but was largely ignored. General Yuzefovich's V Cavalry Corps left the front without informing anyone. General Kalnitsky's Reserve Corps disintegrated under very slight Red pressure. Only Kutepov's I

Below: French Marshal Franchet D'Esperey was an adviser to the White forces during the civil war.

Above: A contemporary caricature of Denikin, depicting him with symbols of terror nd execution.

Below: Kotovsky's Bolshevik cavalry brigade entering Odessa in February 1920.

Volunteer Corps (2500 men) fought on: the wily general outmaneuvered the Red Army commanders by using the railway to full advantage. However, when Budyonny again threatened to cut him off from the south, he too was forced to retreat, but in good order. The Don Army, disillusioned, retreated sullenly, without the slightest regard for the friendly forces. Despite this rebuff, Denikin decided to defend the Don territory instead of withdrawing in good order to the Crimea. Since the beginning of the White retreat, Generals Denikin and Wran-

gel had been quarreling. The Don defense decision sparked off a first-class row between them. Wrangel even went to the British Mission and told them frankly the whole story of his objections and reservations. This move was perhaps none too loyal, but he wanted desperately to save the Volunteer armies before it was too late.

The British seemed fully aware of Denikin's military shortcomings but could do nothing about them. They did increase their criticism of Denikin's GHQ, and informed the general of Wrangel's complaints. Ironically, Denikin transferred Wrangel to Ekaterinodar to reorganize the Kuban base which he had only just repressed with force. Next, he discovered a conspiracy against himself on his train but only halfheartedly dealt with the officers involved as he was not sure of Wrangel's involvement. Later, in Istanbul, the officer-conspirators cowardly assassinated Denikin's chief of staff, General Romanovsky, whom they held responsible for their discovery. Wrangel, who found it impossible to take up the command in the Kuban, went off to the Crimea, only to be exiled to Turkey. The retreating White forces were melting away at an alarming rate and, under pressure from the British Mission, Denikin desperately tried to salvage his political influence in southern Russia. First, he tried to cobble together a military and political agreement with Makhno and his Greens. Since Ulagay's cavalry had only just scattered Makhno's forces, negotiations came to nothing, and the White negotiators were assassinated by Makhno's hench-

men. The British took over the task, but also failed. Then, out of the blue, though under British pressure, Denikin sacked his Special Council and appointed a federal Russian government headed by General Bogayevsky. The Don, Kuban and Terek Cossack *krugs* (parliaments) were convoked and elected new leaders, and southern Russia seemed to be politically united. The paradox was that Denikin's federal Russia consisted largely of separatist elements. The other paradox emerged with Denikin's veto on the formation of any major federal arrangements, but the administration was the Cossacks' precondition to co-operation. The veto was the final blow to the political reforms brought about because of British pressure in the face of defeat.

Miraculously, a glint of hope appeared in this political debacle. Hope arose from a most unexpected direction: the Don cavalry under General Pavlov checked the Red cavalry force under Dumenko's command south of Rostov, at the Bataisk Heights. But the miracle was short-lived. In turn, reorganized, Dumenko was shot for indiscipline after his horsemen had plundered Rostov, and Pavlov was decisively beaten in another battle on 25 February 1920. The Don forces became a rabble, retreating at great speed along the Black Sea coast to Tuapse in Georgia. Don political leaders attached themselves to Denikin, who was now forced to accept British mediation with the Reds. As a condition of a proposed armistice, he had to resign and he was evacuated, together with his officers, to the Greek island of Lemnos. His men were to be

amnestied, and the Don, Kuban and Terek Cossacks could retain their autonomy. Fortunately for Denikin, the Bolsheviks rejected the British proposals and the retreat continued, though it was Makhno's Greens who proved to be a greater danger to the Whites than the Red Army. By then Denikin had ceased to command and preceded the retreating forces in his train under a strong British security force. Ekaterinodar was not defended; instead, the Kuban forces (30,000 men) followed the Don rabble to Tuapse. The remaining Volunteers were

Above: The Paris Peace Conference was held from January 1919 to january 1920. (L to R) Lloyd George, Orland, Clemenceau, Woodrow Wilson.

Below: German officers pose for the camera. Active in the Baltic states their renegade forces caused problems for both sides during the civil war.

Above: Men of the Finnish Legion on the Murmansk Front in April 1919.

ordered to march to Novorossiisk, the main British naval base, to be evacuated to the Crimea. Denikin, who seemed to lapse into deep fatalism, and the despondent Whites did nothing to facilitate a smooth execution of the evacuation plans. Despite the chaos, British and French ships under Admiral Seymour succeeded in transferring most of the men and some of the British stores to the Crimea. By 28 March 1920 20,000 Volunteers had been left behind and stores to the tune of £1,000,000 too. The port fell to the Greens first but was later taken by the Red Army.

After this disaster, Denikin resigned his empty command and, on 4 April, the war council of the White movement elected Wrangel as his successor. In fact, Wrangel's election was forced on the Whites by Generals Holman and Keyes, who also delivered a British government ultimatum to the war council: negotiations with the Bolsheviks had to be resumed, else the mission would withdraw to Britain taking all the remaining stores. The newly elected Wrangel was in no position to object to British terms, but he could procrastinate. Wrangel, originally a

mining engineer, was politically much more of a realist than Denikin and he soon proved it. However, his ancient title, which he used, was exploited by Bolshevik propaganda to portray him as a reactionary ogre. He was more efficient in handling foreigners, particularly the British. Above all, he was not simply a military man as was his predecessor. To start with, he concentrated on his armed forces. He had only General Slashchev's corps (3500 men and 2000 horsemen) to protect the peninsula from the Red Army. In fact the Reds, advised by the British, were so sure that he would surrender peacefully that they went on with their operations in the Northern Caucasus, Caspian and Trans-Caspian areas. They also became preoccupied with the situation in the Ukraine and began to contemplate a war with Poland. All these diversions gave the Whites in the Crimea a much-needed breathing space. Wrangel immediately took advantage of it. First of all, he purged all the commanders appointed by Denikin, and sent into exile Generals Sidorin, Kelchevsky, Pokrovsky, Borovsky, Postovsky and many others. Then he subdued the Don and Kuban

Right: Troops of the German Freikorps take a break during their march on Riga in May 1919.

Left: Artillerymen prepare
their howitzer for action
against Polish troops near
the Western Bug River in
1920.

political leaders who were in a position to resist him. Next, since he was unwilling to conduct direct negotiations with the Bolsheviks, he affected an open rupture with the British Mission: General Percy, Holman's successor, was going to carry out British threats. In turn, Wrangel scored a diplomatic success: his Paris representative, Maklakov, negotiated with the French government an aid program to replace the British effort. France was anxious about the war between Poland and Soviet Russia and was interested in replacing Britain's influence in the Crimea, and making use of this potentially dangerous force in the Red rear. In the meantime, Wrangel reorganized his forces, placing I Corps under the capable Kutepov, II Corps was under Slashchev, who was a cocaine addict and a poor choice; the Don Cossack Corps was under colorless General Abramov; and the Special Corps was under the equally undistinguished Pisarev. In June 1920 these scratch forces defeated the Thirteenth Red Army and Zhloba's cavalry, and broke out of the Crimea into northern Tauride. However, Wrangel's intention to

occupy as much of the Ukraine as possible and even break through to the Don territory came to nothing and his small forces became dangerously overextended. Colonel Nazarov's small unit, sent to the Don to stir up the region against the Bolsheviks, ran into a large Red force and was scattered. Nazarov escaped from captivity to tell the story in person. Similarly, a larger force under General Ulagay was sent to the Kuban region to seize Ekaterinodar.

On landing, Ulagay found out that the Red forces were superior to his own and, instead of trying a raid, retreated swiftly to the coast. Neither the Don nor Kuban Cossacks responded to these landings by rising against the Bolsheviks. Their passivity demonstrated clearly that not even these relatively prosperous Russian Cossacks were prepared to fight for White Russia. Both actions were evident political and military miscalculations which condemned Wrangel's depleted forces in northern Tauride to sit and wait. After its return, the Kuban expedition was reorganized into II Corps and renamed, to boost up morale, as the First and

Second Armies. In September, when it was far too late, Wrangel tried to break through to the Don, via Bulay Pole, Makhno's capital, with a much stronger force. However, the combined Green and Red forces easily beat off this attempt. In October his Trans-Dniepr operation into the Ukraine met the same fate. He was realistic enough to see his end approaching. From the beginning he knew that he could not defeat the Reds alone, but was determined to try everything to the bitter end.

As Denikin before him, Wrangel also dabbled in political reform once he recognized his military position as hopeless. Despite his 'reactionary' reputation and title, he was a moderate liberal. He made good use of the former czarist minister of agriculture, Krivoshein, who became his prime minister. The land decree, signed by Krivoshein after his arrival in the Crimea from France, was the greatest political success achieved by the Whites in Russia. It recognized the facts and legitimized the land-grabbing of the peasants. Military and civilian justice were separated and the counterespionage department's power curtailed. Thus, as if by miracle, Wrangel avoided the terrible political conflicts which disrupted the Denikin regime. Again this commonsense measure came too late. In October Wrangel convened a conference to sort out his finances. To his amazement he found out that he had financial surpluses in

hand, even if he refused a French loan. Unlike Denikin, he started granting arms and ammunition to all the partisan forces, whether allied or not, fighting against the Reds. The conference's proposals for a real re-establishment of finances, however, remained on paper. They were too late to implement as the Wrangel regime was swept away by the Red Army.

On 26 October 1920 the Red Army suddenly crossed the Dniepr in force and four days later, with skillful flank movements, forced the two White armies to run back to the Crimean Peninsula, where a prepared defensive line was awaiting them. On 3 November a Red probing raid practically wiped out the Drozdovsky Division. On Kutepov's advice Wrangel set into motion the final evacuation of his forces. Kutepov beat off Red attacks for the next three days, but on 8 November a risky flanking move, which involved the Red force marching across the freshly frozen sea, forced him to retreat. Unlike in Novorossiisk or Odessa, there was no panic and White units with their officers reported at embarkation points in an orderly fashion. General May-Mayevsky suffered a heart attack and died before embarkation. Wrangel inspected his troops and firmly refused the Red offer of surrender, though Slashchev did accept it. By 14 November 1920 146,693 soldiers and dependents were on French and Russian ships sailing into exile.

Below: Wounded Polish prisoners being transported by way of the River Dvina to Vitebsk in May 1920.

Left: Bolshevik troops interned in East Prussia, September 1920.

Another sizeable Red-White conflict in the civil war developed in northwestern Russia, particularly in the Baltic provinces of Estonia, Latvia and Lithuania. Right up to November 1918 these provinces were occupied by German armies which after the armistice in the West withdrew, leaving the nationalists and Reds to fight over the countries. On 11 November a nationalist, Poska (Ptas), proclaimed himself prime minister of Estonia, Ulmanis did the same in Latvia and Professor Waldemar in Lithuania. Since there were still some German troops left in the provinces, the Western Allies insisted on their evacuation to Germany. To supervise the evacuation as well as help the newly independent nations to defend themselves against Bolshevism, the British Admiralty sent a squadron to Reval. In addition to the Balts, the British also promised to support any Russian individual or movement willing to fight the Bolsheviks. In a sense the Baltic provinces became a major theater of the civil war because of this British decision.

After the German withdrawal, the Bolsheviks laid claim to the Latvian province, first by sending 'home' the Latvian Rifle Division. As this was the only organized armed force in the region, Premier Ulmanis and his government were put on British ships, while Riga and almost the whole of Latvia came under a Red regime. The Estonians, who were short of ammunition and oil, were also about to surrender to the Reds. Since the Paris peace conference was unable to deal with the problems in the Baltic states, the British decided to resolve the crisis by sending in another squadron under the command of Admiral Sir Walter Cowan. On arrival the squadron joined in the fighting, sup-

porting the hardpressed Latvians and Estonians with gunfire. In March 1919 the Allied Supreme Council decided on a naval blockade of these provinces to last until such time as German troops were fully evacuated. French ships now joined the British for this purpose which, in reality, made little sense. The German troops were propping up the feeble nationalists against the Reds. Their departure would mean the Bolshevik conquest of the provinces. Whatever the Allied decision might be in Paris, the British on the spot decided to ignore it. They not

Below: Two leading Bolshevik commanders on the Polish Front in 1920.

Above: Red soldiers leaving Poltara for the Southern Front display their aims on banners: (L to R) 'Proletarians of All Countries Unite – Long Live the Communist International,' 'Death to Baron Wrangel,' 'The Barons and the Generals should Perish Once and for All,' 'The Crimea Must be Liberated Come What May.'

only tolerated the delays in German evacuation, but also, especially in Latvia where they held two vital ports, positively encouraged the Germans to continue excluding the Latvian Reds from them. However, the German command wished to back up their own political allies in the provinces, who had been building up their movements from scratch, and not the British ones. At this point the British also decided to build their own White Russian movement with an army.

The newly arrived German commander, General von der Goltz, instead of evacuating his demoralized forces, began to interfere in Baltic affairs. He even dreamt of re-establishing German influence in the provinces, seeing the weakness of the Western Allies and local nationalists. The British were training Ulmanis's Latvians and were equipping them with British arms. However, even the local Baltic Germans (*Baltisches Landwehr*) who listened to Goltz were stronger and could, with Goltz's

Right: Red Army troops beside the train captured from Kaledin. M N Tukhachevsky and G K Ordjonikidze can be seen (third and fourth from left).

help, oust the Reds not only from Riga but possibly from Latvia. The British on the spot were perfectly aware of this depressing situation and, to enable Goltz to hold off the Reds, the Allies in Paris decided to lift the blockade and even allow him reinforcements. Goltz then forced an agreement on the Baltic Germans with Colonel Balodis's White Latvians and local Russians led by Prince Lieven. This German-inspired coalition overthrew the British-protected Ulmanis, replacing him with Pastor Niedra. Only then did coalitionists set out to take Riga, but without German aid. Despite the success of the new coalition, the Allies in Paris reversed their decision on the German presence in the provinces. They forced the new German government to recall Goltz and evacuate the remaining German forces, which was easier said than done. Goltz even had time to build up a Russian force consisting of prisoners arriving from Germany. He also handed over his stores and arms to the Baltic forces of his choice before withdrawing his forces altogether. Goltz's final act made sure that the British and their nationalist allies would have to compromise with the German-sponsored Baltic forces and Russians to safeguard the provinces against a Red invasion.

The Russian forces in the Baltic provinces were small and varied. General Lieven was in command of I Russian Corps, which was in fact a battalion. Colonel Bulak-Balakhovich, who had deserted from the Red Army, organized a partisan unit which conducted raids into Soviet Russia and lived on the booty. In Finland, General Yudenich finally proclaimed himself the commander in chief of these scattered forces. He called them the North Western Army, and attempted to co-ordinate their fighting, but his command was too distant to be effective. Since the Finns, Latvians and, above all, Estonians had to defend themselves against the Red Army, Yudenich, firmly backed by the British, proposed to aid the nationalists in driving the Red forces out of their countries. They were in turn going to help him drive to Petrograd, the practically undefended former capital. British naval guns were engaged in support of this combined offensive which was launched on 13 May 1919. However, this first combined offensive was anything but combined. When Yudenich arrived from Helsinki to take over overall command, the Estonians protested loudly against this Russian interference in their war operations. The British ships refused bluntly to serve in an auxiliary capacity. General Sir Hubert Gough, head of the newly arrived Allied Mission, sent the poor Yudenich packing back to Helsinki, leaving General Rodzianko in command. Encouraged by initial success, Rodzianko pushed forward to Petrograd, telling the Estonians on his left flank to mop up the coastal fortresses which had mutinied against the Reds. The Estonian Army, without British naval guns, advanced very slowly and reached the mutineers too late. The Reds, who were led by the vigorous Stalin, were shocked by the White advance and transferred the crack 2nd Division and stabilized the front. Fortress mutineers, most of them Balts, were massacred by

Stalin's order. Rodzianko had to halt his advance and retreat to avoid being cut off from Estonia.

Immediately after this abortive offensive, Yudenich, encouraged by the ease of this uncoordinated effort, began to prepare the next one. Again the objective was Petrograd, whose fall, coupled with Denikin's capture of Moscow, would certainly topple the Red regime. He concentrated on the military planning exclusively and left the political negotiations with the Finnish and Estonian governments to his subordinates and Allied representatives. In the meantime Colonel Bermont, General Biskupsky and Colonel Durnovo were successfully proceeding with the formation of the Russian Corps in Latvia based around a nucleus of prisoners from Germany. They were so evidently financed by the Germans that Gough decided to put a stop to their effort. In his opinion these Russian military organizations needed an overall political authority, the North Western government, which, with his help, would sort out the problems of the Balts and Germans alike. By now the Baltic nationalists were refusing to help the

Above: Ordjonikidze (1880-1937), an important Red Army political leader of the civil war.

Right: Red Army scouts
with a snow-transportable
machine gun, December
1920.

Below: V I Chapaev, a
famous hero of the civil
war (right), with K P
Zakharov, chief of the 22nd
Division, at Nikolaevsk-
Uralsky station.

White Russian armies unless they promised them independence. But the Whites were not interested in such abstract promises. They were happy with their presence in the provinces, particularly in Latvia, demanding only a greater say in local politics and official Allied recognition. Early in August 1919, General Marsh suddenly rounded up all the available Russian politicians in the Baltic provinces, brought them to Reval and gave them 40 minutes to decide if they wanted to be ministers of the North Western government or not. Only S G Lianozov agreed to the British proposal and became both prime minister and finance minister. His war minister and commander in chief was General Yudenich, still in Helsinki. The government's first declaration was the recognition of Estonian independence. However, no one seemed to take the declaration by this unrepresentative body seriously and, if anything, this political initiative further complicated the situation. It appeared that the British military representatives acted without authorization. Gough, the real culprit, was recalled. However, the Lieven Corps, now under Colonel Bermont's command, refused to recognize the North Western government; above all it refused to be subordinated to Yudenich's command. It became obvious that the planned combined operation was once again a haphazard White effort.

On 10 October 1919 Yudenich launched the second offensive against Petrograd despite the bad omens. Again it went well. I Russian Corps, still under Rodzianko, took Pskov, and Gatchina and Tsarskoe Selo were occupied a week later. For the final triumphant march into Petrograd the White armies only needed an Estonian victory along the coast, a Finnish diversionary drive north of the city and reinforcements from the Bermont Corps. None of these three conditions was realized as Rodzianko waited on the southern heights surveying Petrograd. The Finns had their independence and cautiously refused to honor their agreement with the Whites; the Estonians proved quite incapable of reducing such formidable obstacles as the coastal fortresses, now held by elite Red forces, even with the support of the British monitors and their huge guns. In any case, during the intense fighting the British had to withdraw several ships and rush them down to Riga which had been seized by the Bermont Corps, supposedly reinforcing Rodzianko's weak advance unit near Petrograd. On 3 November 1919 the Red Army counterattacked, after Trotsky in person took the defense of the city in hand. The thrust pushed the Estonians and the Whites back into Estonia in one mighty stroke, only halting at the border. The White forces were dissolved on 12 December and General Rodzianko took up a successful circus career. The Latvian and Estonian armies combined to disperse the Bermont Corps, still in occupation of Riga. Its remnants retreated with the German Iron Division into East Prussia. On 2 February 1920 independent Estonia signed a peace treaty with Soviet Russia, to be followed by Latvia on 11 August. Lithuania had to wait for the end of the Polish-Soviet conflict to do the same.

The last Allied campaign against Soviet Russia, as Soviet historians term the Soviet-Polish war, was nothing of the sort. Poland became independent after Germany's surrender in November 1918. General Pilsudski, initially a socialist, became the virtual leader of Poland, though he had a nominal president, a concert pianist, over him. At first he was not interested in Russia at all, only in its western provinces which once belonged to Poland. The incredible chaos in the former empire inspired him to formulate his own solutions: he wanted to re-create the Great Federal Poland of the distant past, including Lithuania, Byelorussia and the Ukraine. Throughout 1919-20 Pilsudski was organizing his armed forces to realize his ideas. It was not an easy task. He himself fought with the Germany Army; many others, among them General Sikorski, in the Austrian armies; and still others fought in the French Army. Their equipment and command methods were as diverse as their uniforms. The power vacuum in the Ukraine attracted Pilsudski from the very beginning and enabled him to occupy part of Volhynia and Byelorussia. After November 1918 Ukrainian nationalists proved much more tactful toward Pilsudski; instead of reclaiming territories they rather sought alliance with the Poles. Soviet Russia finally offered peace to Poland in the spring of 1920, but Pilsudski rejected this Soviet offer and allied himself with the Ukrainian Ataman, Petlyura. With his agreement, Polish forces launched a sudden offensive against the weak Red armies in the west and took Kiev on 6 May. There followed a patriotic outcry in Soviet Russia, joined by such non-Bolshevik personalities as General Brusilov, and war was declared on Poland. Within a month the Poles were driven out of the Ukraine and Poland itself was under threat.

Lenin braced himself for a war against Poland after it had rejected his rather generous territorial settlement in March 1920. In fact the Soviet high command had had a plan of operation against Poland ready since February. The Fifteenth and Sixteenth Red Armies, forming the northern part of the Polish Front, were placed under Revkom Tukhachevsky and advanced onto Warsaw. The southern group under Revkom Yegerov, consisting of the Twelfth and Fourteenth Red Armies together with the First Cavalry Army under Revkom Budyonny, but politically controlled by Stalin,

was converging on the Polish capital from the south. With these offensive moves proceeding, Lenin and other Bolshevik leaders were seized by incredible euphoria. After their disappointment with the lack of a world communist revolution in the autumn of 1918 and again in 1919, they became convinced that if they conquered Poland and turned it into a communist state, then communism would triumphantly progress into Germany and the capitalist West. The usually realistic Lenin regarded this sequence of events as quite plausible. He was aware of the erroneous strategic assumption made in November 1917, when he thought that his successful revolution would be followed by similar events in Germany, France and possibly Britain. This time it was different and everyone agreed with him. He even asked his friend Dzerzhinsky to form a Polish government in anticipation of Pilsudski's downfall. This time Lenin's anticipation went too far. Pilsudski's -etreat from the Ukraine, though swift, was orderly, and once in Poland, Polish units formed defensive rings, particularly round Warsaw. Moreover, advised by the French General Weygand, Pilsudski began to plan a counteroffensive. *En route* to Warsaw Red commanders began to quarrel among themselves. Operations were unco-ordinated and out of step. As the northern group struck against Warsaw itself, the southern group was still far away, engaged in mopping-up operations around Lvov. Pilsudski exploited the quarrels and the lack of frontal cohesion by launching his counteroffensive at the paper-thin junction of the two Red groups. The breakthrough proved successful beyond hope and the enveloping movements of the Polish armies cut off the already overextended Reds from their rear and supply bases. Ultimately the Russian Reds were cut to ribbons by the despised Poles for the first time since the seventeenth century. An armistice was signed on 16 October 1920 and a formal peace treaty in Riga on 18 March 1921. Lenin had given up the idea of a revolution in capitalist countries and pinned his faith on revolution in the underdeveloped world.

Below: The office of a Bolshevik commissar with the Red Army in Poland during August 1920.

TROTSKY'S RED ARMY

Previous page: Troops gathering in Moscow's Red Square on the occasion of the Communist Congress in September 1921.

Opposite page, top: 'Proletarians of All Countries Unite!' A poster issued by the Red Baltic Fleet in honor of the second anniversary of the revolution.

Opposite page, bottom: A Red Army field kitchen at Louza in Poland, 1920.

Below: An appeal for support issued by the young Soviet republic to the workers of France, England, America, Italy and Japan.

On the Bolshevik side Leon Trotsky, a civilian, was the moving force behind the formation of the Red Army. On 22 April 1918, with compulsory military service already in force, he launched the massive effort to rebuild a centrally controlled 400,000-strong army. By July the mediocre Colonel Vatsetis had been installed as commander in chief and with the help of a field staff began to conduct offensive operations. In September a War Revolutionary Council was set up. By the end of 1918 the Red Army consisted of 3,000,000 *revkoms*-commanders, a new term for Bolshevik officers, and men. By the end of 1920 there were 5,500,000 men in the Red Army. Backed by this military might, the Bolsheviks were able to impose Soviet rule over all of the old Russian Empire. The election of officers was abolished and discipline, including the death penalty, was rigorously enforced. Imperial officers were forcibly enrolled in the Red Army: out of 446,729 serving officers, they amounted to 314,180. They were called *voyenspets* (military specialists); their families were held as hostages against their desertion, a policy introduced by Trotsky himself. The specialists were also under the strictest political control and even their operational orders had to be countersigned by *poli-*

truk-commissars. Many units were stiffened by contingents of communist workers and, on the whole, these units fought well when compared with the Whites, though desertions were rife even among the communist elites. The combination of well-used tactics such as hostage taking, combined with newer methods, such as posting security detachments behind the front and the application of systematic terror against White sympathizers and deserters, made the Red Army a more efficient war machine than its rivals and ultimately led to a Bolshevik victory in the civil war.

The outcome of the struggle was influenced by several unique factors which favored the Bolsheviks. The first was Lenin's seizure of the central government in Petrograd and the subsequent consolidation of Bolshevik power in central Russia. Second, the geographical distribution of nationalist movements was also to their advantage. In theory, Lenin acknowledged national self-determination for the ethnic minorities of the former Russian Empire, but was fortunate that the most significant movements were in the borderlands which also became centers of White opposition. The minorities trusted the Bolsheviks more than the Whites: the Finns and Estonians deserted the north-western White Russians; while the Ukrainian Brigade, Bashkir troops and Kirghiz cavalry, all of which deserted at the height of Admiral Kolchak's offensive, fought well for the Reds until 1920: General Denikin had endless trouble with the Cossacks, not to mention Adzerbeijanis, Georgians and Armenians.

Still, Lenin and the Bolsheviks were the same Great Russians as the Whites, they only differed in their tactics. Thus, on 7 May 1920 Soviet Russia signed a treaty of friendship with the Menshevik Georgian Republic, to the great dismay of the local Communist Party. On 11 February 1921, a communist uprising in Georgia petitioned Soviet Russia for help; as a consequence the Red Army occupied the country and annexed it. Lenin, who harbored an element of doubt in this case, was disturbed, but did nothing. In the matters of non-Russian nationalism, the Reds were tactically superior to the Whites. Controlling the central government also gave Lenin additional advantages in the civil war. Though he did not interfere directly with military operations, he set their political objectives and acted as final arbiter in military disputes. At the beginning of the civil war, in July 1918, it was he who ordered the assassination of the Romanovs. His reasons were to prevent the Whites from exploiting politically the imperial family; to make it clear to his fellow Bolsheviks that the revolution had to continue; and, possibly, to avenge his brother's death. It was also Lenin's decision to designate the Eastern Front as the chief center of operations. In May 1919 he ordered the operational planning in support of the Hungarian Soviet Republic and it was his decision to continue the offensive in the East, which was the cause of Vatsetis's downfall, in the following summer. The change in tactics on the Southern Front was also his decision. Again, in March 1920, he ordered the ending of military operations else-

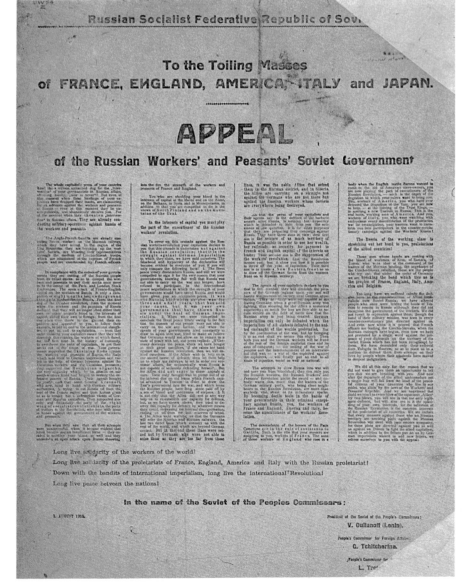

Russian Socialist Federative Republic of Sov...

To the Toiling Masses of FRANCE, ENGLAND, AMERICA, ITALY and JAPAN.

APPEAL

of the Russian Workers' and Peasants' Soviet Government

Long live solidarity of the workers of the world!

Long live solidarity of the proletariats of France, England, America and Italy with the Russian proletariat!

Down with the bandits of international imperialism, long live the international Revolution!

Long live peace between the nations!

In the name of the Soviet of the Peoples Commissars:

President of the Soviet of the People's Commissars:
V. Oulianoff (Lenin).

People's Commissar for Foreign Affairs:
G. Tchitcherine.

People's Commissar for
L. Tr...

where in Russia and the Red Army's preparation for the invasion of Poland. Last but not least, in March 1921, he ordered the storming of the rebellious Kronstadt naval base, symbolically the last operation of the civil war. In comparison, there was no one in a dominant position on the White side: no one to co-ordinate political and military objectives; and no one to exercise absolute authority over the military high command.

Lenin was also fortunate to have Trotsky, a senior member of the party's leadership, as his minister of war. Both men trusted each other, and worked well together. Lenin occasionally protected Trotsky, who as a Jew was disliked by Russian military men and intensely hated by his political rivals, particularly Stalin. In return, Trotsky proved a ruthless organizer with unshakeable determination, personal traits which no other Russian, on either side, exhibited so effectively during the conflict. Even Lenin was depressed by Kolchak's offensive in early 1919, and after the defeat in Poland late in 1920, was struck by apathy. Throughout the civil war, however, Trotsky was unaffected by either victory or defeat. As Denikin was approaching Moscow from the south, he single-handedly organized and galvanized Petrograd's defenses aginst Yudenich. From the start, Trotsky chose to stand for military orthodoxy in army matters, rejecting the theories of Frunze and Voroshilov on partisan warfare. Right up to 1920 his orthodox approach served him well: it enabled him to reshuffle the Red Army's command structure when it proved unsuccessful; to control the progress of the war by frequent reorganization and the armies by frequent changes of command. However, his insistence on following Russian military orthodoxy blew up in his

Above: White Russian officers present a captured Bolshevik standard to Commander R T Down RN. The cooperation between White and interventionist forces was extremely limited, however.

Below: Lenin addresses students taking courses for Red Army heavy artillery commanders during the ceremony at which they were presented with their colors by the Rogozhsky District Party Committee.

commander in chief, though subsequently replaced by Colonel Kamenev. The Latvian Vatsetis performed an excellent job until the summer of 1919 when his strategic views clashed with those of Lenin and he was dismissed. Trotsky surrounded himself with a group of able *voyenspets*, who included Colonel (future Marshal) B M Shaposhnikov, Colonel P P Lebedev and Colonel (future General) A A Svechin and many others. The 16 Red armies which Trotsky put in the field invariably contained a cadre of up to 18 percent industrial workers-communists. These 760,000 industrial workers had a strong sense of purpose and generally fought well. Trotsky also transformed such partisan leaders as Frunze and Blücher into outstanding orthodox commanders. Moroever, he opened the way to the top for many ex-imperial subalterns: Tukhachevsky (future Marshal), Yakir, Primakov, Putna, Zhukov (future Marshal), Budyonny (future Marshal) and many others. Future political leaders earned their spurs in the civil war armies as super-commissars: Ordjonikidze, Kuybyshev, Kirov, Gusev, Shvernik, Mekhlis and Stalin himself. Under Trotsky's leadership the combined command worked so well that in 1919 Smilga, the chief *politruk*, abolished the dual operational command.

From the very beginning of the 'hot' civil war in the summer of 1918 until the autumn of 1919, the chief battlefield was in the east. Trotsky personally supervised the establishment of the front, and did not hesitate to execute with his own hand political commissars who were retreating in panic from Kazan after a raid by Czech forces. In the initial emergency, Vatsetis took the front command in person. The Fifth

face in 1920: the perfectly planned Polish campaign ended in disaster, perhaps because Polish military doctrine was at that stage superior. He was also wrong to oppose partisan warfare in principle. The technique proved useful against Kolchak's rear and in certain parts of the Ukraine.

Nevertheless, the Supreme Military Council (*Revvoyensoviet*) enabled Trotsky to run the Red Army efficiently. He was its chairman and had Skylansky, Podvoysky and Danishevsky, all experienced soldiers, as his deputies. Strategic coordination was carried out by himself, Aralov and Vatsetis, whom he appointed as his first

Red Army (Lashevich) and the First (Tukhachevsky) went into action immediately, encountering little resistance. Subsequently, three more Red armies, the Second (V I Shorin), Third (R I Berzin) and Fifth (Z K Blumberg) were concentrated in the region under the overall command of S S Kamenev. The senior command comprised the best available staff officers, such as Belitsky, Gay and Novitsky, and was supervised by able *politruks*, of whom S I Gusev proved the most outstanding. They planned the first counteroffensive in the autumn of 1918, in which pride of place belonged to the First Red Army. A youthful imperial subaltern, Mikhail Tukhachevsky, was in command. Scion of an improverished noble family from Penza, he became a Bolshevik in April 1918, and was appointed to succeed the Left SR traitor Colonel Muravëv by Trotsky in the face of much criticism. But Tukhachevsky soon displayed strategic talents and tactical abilities of the highest order, on several occasions saving the Eastern Front from disaster.

However, fortunes on the front fluctuated wildly, and sudden disaster struck the Third Red Army when Perm fell to the Siberian White Army in December 1918. Stalin and Dzerzhinsky were sent by Lenin to inquire into the events, and were indirectly critical of Trotsky and Vatsetis. In the consequent reshuffle another outstanding military leader, M V Frunze, arrived to take over command of the Fourth Army. Frunze, a veteran Bolshevik intellectual, displayed outstanding administrative ability well before assuming active command. He found the Fourth Army in a parlous condition; he quickly reimposed discipline and positioned himself in the southern sector of the planned offensive. His army had some 20,000 men, while the Red Army in the east fielded 76,400 men, 8570 cavalry, 1471 machine guns and 372 guns in total.

The Whites managed to stage their offensive before the Reds were ready for action. The White breakthrough precipitated another crisis for Trotsky, who hurriedly left Moscow for the front. The command was completely reorganized: Frunze took command of the Turkestan Army as well as the Fourth Army; G D Gay took charge of the First; Tukhachevsky the Fifth, V I Shorin the Second; and S A Mezheninov the Third. The front was split into northern and southern groups. Frunze was in charge of the southern group, helped by General Novitsky and politically backed by Kuybyshev. The trio masterminded the Urals operations and completely routed the White forces under General Belov and Ataman Dutov in a series of pitched battles. Tukhachevsky's Fifth Army operated independently and was responsible for the capture of Ufa. The triumphant progress of the Fifth Army was only halted after contradictory orders, issued by changing front commanders, made any further action difficult. The crisis on the Eastern Front attracted Lenin's attention. Against strong military opposition, he wanted to continue the offensive deep into the Urals, a region Trotsky himself considered a White power base. This led to the greatest upheaval of the civil war; Trotsky offered to resign as mini-

Above: A Royal Naval vessel on the Murmansk-Archangel Front in 1919.

Left: Grigory Kotovsky (1881-1925), commander of a cavalry brigade, a division and eventually a corps, and a Bolshevik hero of the civil war.

ИДИ НА КОМАНДНЫЕ КУРСЫ,-

ster of war. His offer was not accepted, but Vat-setis was replaced by Kamenev, who immediately approved further attacks in the east. Tukhachevsky split his Fifth Army into three groups which, supported on the flanks by the Second and Third Armies, captured Zlatousk, the key to Western Siberia. Blücher's 51st Division distinguished itself in the fighting, as it was to in subsequent battles.

By this stage, the center of gravity had shifted from the Eastern to the Southern Front. G K Eikhe took over Tukhachevsky's command; Tukhachevsky was also sent to the south. By September 1919 only the Fifth Army continued the pursuit of Kolchak and his armies, the others were either moving on Turkestan or against Denikin.

The Southern Front had been long neglected by both Lenin and Trotsky. They disliked it largely because of the partisan-type of operations that were conducted in the region despite their objections. This relative neglect enabled the infamous triumvirate, Stalin, Voroshilov and Budyonny, to establish their sway there. Thus the *partizanshchina* continued despite the presence of the Ninth and Tenth Armies. In May 1919, when Denikin began his long march on Moscow, only the Ninth Army was shattered, its commander, Vsevolod, deserting to the Whites. The Whites occupied the Donets basin, taking Kharkov. In July 1919 the Red front commander, Gittis, was replaced by V N Yegorev, who took over responsibility for a gradual build-up of Bolshevik forces for a counteroffensive. The Eighth, Tenth, Eleventh, Twelfth,

Thirteenth and Fourteenth Red Armies were added to the Ninth, which was reorganized. Revkom Kamenev planned the counteroffensive in the eastern part of the front; its objectives were the Don and Kuban bases. Trotsky and Yegorev opposed this counteroffensive deep into enemy territory and favored a major thrust toward Kharkov, which contained a pro-Bolshevik population. They were overruled by Lenin himself. Shorin and Selivachev launched their Red armies against the White Caucasian Army but soon got stuck, suggesting that Trotsky's strategic assessment was correct.

The White successes forced the Red high command to carry out several agonizing strategic and tactical reappraisals. Despite the devastating White cavalry raids in the past it was only now decided to create the First and Second Cavalry Armies to be deployed in a similar fashion. Trotsky was backed in this decision by Lenin and Stalin. Budyonny, a former imperial NCO whom Trotsky considered a bandit, became commander of the cavalry corps, after its initial commander, Dumenko, fell ill of typhoid. Voroshilov became *politruk*, and the formations produced such outstanding officers as Timoshenko, Zhukov and Rokosovsky. Trot-

sky reorganized the front once again, splitting it into two, with Budyonny's First Cavalry Army being sent to the southeast. In late October 1919 Budyonny, disregarding his orders, broke through the White front near Voronezk. The breakthrough caused Denikin's drive to Moscow to collapse and successful strikes by the Eighth, Thirteenth and Fourteenth Armies turned the whole White offensive into a rout. In the resulting pursuit operations, the Red Cavalry Corps, now upgraded to the First Cavalry Army, acted independently and played havoc with the White rear. Only in January 1920, with Dumenko in charge, were the Red horsemen finally checked by General Pavlov's cavalry on the Bataysk Heights, south of Rostov. Dumenko, innocent of disobedience according to Budyonny, paid with his life for this blunder. The severe reverse was put right a week later, however, and the pursuit of the White forces continued. Apart from Trotsky, Tukhachevsky and Ordjonikidze, who were in command in the North Caucasus, also quarrelled with Budyonny, but they were reconciled by the scale of their victories. Kuybyshev went on to Trans-Caspia and Frunze subdued Turkestan. As Tukhachevsky's Eleventh Army

Left: A Red Army poster of 1920 urging men to join command courses in order to learn how to lead the defense of the workers' and peasants' republic. The implied progress this can lead to is illustrated in the bottom corners: on the left is the sleeve-patch of a platoon commander, on the right that of an army commander.

Below left: P Dybenko and I Fedko, leaders of the suppression of the Kronstadt uprising.

Below: The Red Army enters Odessa in 1919. Note once again the mix of nationalities.

Above: A Red Army conference in Petrograd's Uritsky Hall during March 1921.

Opposite page, top: American troops of the interventionist forces landing in Vladivostok in 1918.

Right: A group of Red Army soldiers on the South Eastern Front reading a news bulletin in 1919.

which contributed largely to the Red victory in the war: the use of security detachments.

On 7 December 1917 Lenin formed, on Dzerzhinsky's recommendation, a governmental committee, known as *Cheka*, to combat the counterrevolution. Though *Cheka*'s original function was investigative, in a short time it took on board extensive judicial and executive powers. By the end of the civil war there were 250,000 *chekists*: 30,000 investigators, 137,000 internal guards and 94,000 border guards. Their chief task was the application of terror. In response to the assassination of Bolshevik leaders, including an attempt on Lenin's life, *Cheka* was given sweeping powers to combat White terror. A September 1918 decree publicly made *Cheka* the dominant internal security organization. From late 1918 to the end of the civil war in 1920, *Cheka* played a decisive role in national security, including within the army. Its record was unparalleled. In July 1918 *Cheka* detachments, mainly consisting of Chinese coolies brought to Russia during World War I to work on road and railway construction, shot 407

moved against Adzerbeijan, operations in the area were disrupted when many armies were shifted to the west to comply with Lenin's strategic decision to invade Poland.

Tukhachevsky was put in overall command and started his operations on 14 May 1920. The Fifteenth and Sixteenth Armies under Kork and Sollogub broke through Polish defenses in Byelorussia and moved in the direction of the Polish capital. Tukhachevsky moved the Third, Fourth and Fourteenth Armies, with Gay's 3rd Cavalry Corps acting as reinforcement, into the northern sector and waited for Yegorev's southern group – the Twelfth, Fourteenth and First Cavalry Armies – to complete an encircling movement of the Polish capital from the south. The southern maneuver was never executed. Budyonny's horsemen scattered Makhno's Green troops but then they became involved in mopping-up operations around Lvov. Yegorev was not sent any reinforcements. On 16 August the Polish counterattack destroyed both flanking movements by outflanking them in turn. Trotsky had his opinion of the Red Army confirmed: it was superior to any enemy in defensive fighting and was reasonably efficient in offensive fighting at home, but it could not be sent on foreign expeditions against regular armies, even those of Poland or Romania. He told Lenin the conclusions he had drawn from the fiasco and both revised their revolutionary strategy. As Lenin put it, 'the way to Paris and London went via Kabul and Bombay, and not through Poland and Romania.'

All the other Red operations, though successful, were of little military significance, since they were fought against White partisan units. In Outer Mongolia the mentally deranged White general, Baron von Ungern, was defeated in 1922. Ataman Semenov, a sadistic killer, escaped to China. Partisan fighting on a small scale, however, continued until the late 1930s, and until 1947 in parts of the Ukraine. These battles were fought by special anti-insurgency troops. They represented another factor

captive SR rebels in Yaroslavl. Before the September decree was published, 500 hostages in Petrograd were also executed. During the civil war *Cheka* agents executed 140,000 hostages and a further 140,000 'rebels.' Lenin and Trotsky commonly sanctioned the placement of these security detachments immediately behind the front line to prevent units from deserting and to pre-empt attempted mutinies. Dzerzhinsky, who was chairman of *Cheka* throughout, was also given full powers over the transport system in order to suppress any rebellion in the Bolshevik-held territory as well as to requisition foodstuffs from the countryside. In 1919 the army's security departments were transferred to *Cheka* which became the most powerful body in Lenin's Russia. It did not disappoint Lenin's expectations and contributed most significantly to the Bolshevik victory.

Communist historians argue that if it were not for Allied intervention, there would not have been civil war in Russia. During the war Allied diplomacy was inclined toward mutual intervention in cases of grave difficulty in the

Right: A typical example of the avant-garde art which enjoyed popularity in the early years of Soviet power. Here, a Red sailor and soldier are depicted. This form of art was, however, to be almost totally repressed as the tenets of 'socialist realism' were more strictly applied.

Right: A typical example of the avant-garde art which enjoyed popularity in the early years of Soviet power. Here, a Red sailor and soldier are depicted. This form of art was, however, to be almost totally repressed as the tenets of 'socialist realism' were more strictly applied.

Opposite page, top: Propaganda poster justifying the war against Poland in 1920. It shows the Poles destroying the towns and murdering the population of the Ukraine.

Opposite page, bottom: 'The Entry of the Red Army into Krasnoyarsk in 1920,' painted by Nikanov in 1923. A good example of 'socialist realism.'

Below: Members of the Revolutionary Soviet at the Caucasian Front in 1920. (L to R) Gusser, Ordjonikidze, Tukhachevsky and Trifonov.

war theaters. This interventionist policy was ratified under the terms of the Pact of London signed by Britain, France and Russia on 15 September 1914. Subsequently, all the other Allied nations signed it, fully aware of its implications: Serbia, Luxemburg, Belgium and Japan (October 1914), Italy and Romania (1915). In 1915 Russia concluded an agreement with France and Britain on Constantinople and the Dardanelles, and in 1916 countersigned the Sykes-Picot Agreement which further amplified Allied war aims. The terms of these latter agreements were kept secret. In all of these pacts and agreements there was one vital stipulation: the Allies pledged themselves to fight loyally side by side to final victory, and never conclude a separate peace with the enemy. Mutual help, even in military terms, was foreseen and practiced; in 1917 11 Anglo-French

divisions were rushed to Italy after the disaster at Caporetto; there were French divisions at Thessalonika in Greece; Russian armies were fighting in Romania from 1915 and even on the Western Front in France; there were small British detachments at Archangel and later in Murmansk to handle and guard war stores; Russian troops were sent to 'intervene' in Persia; and, after the American declaration of war, US soldiers were sent to Vladivostok. However, all these depositions were carried out by mutual consent and invitation. After the Bolshevik coup, an unprecedented situation arose: the Bolsheviks asked the Allies to start peace negotiations with Germany, and thus back their own peace efforts. Both France and Britain warned the Bolsheviks and refused to release them from the terms of the Pact of London. Trotsky, then foreign minister (People's Commissar), rejected these warnings, published the secret treaties and started peace negotiations which led to the signing of the separate peace treaty, the Treaty of Brest-Litovsk, in March 1918.

This unprecedented development demanded an unprecedented response. Both France and Britain, apart from the alliance, had important economic and financial interests, not to mention immense war stores, in Russia. Early in December 1917, Britain and France signed an agreement in which they pledged themselves to treat Russia in a co-ordinated way. For convenience's sake, they divided Russia into zones of influence. Later that month the Supreme Allied Council promised support to any and every force in Russia which opposed the Bolshevik's separate plans. Both agreements were vague and were never enforced to the full. In the same month the British sent a mission to the Don territory which, strictly speaking, was in the French zone. What mattered immediately was to delay the conclusion of the separate peace treaty and mitigate its effects on the war. It was obvious that the most efficient way of achieving

the delay would have been to topple Lenin's government by direct intervention, but this was impossible. At this stage of the war, the Allies did not have enough troops available for such an operation and, even if they had been available, it would have been impossible to transport them to Russia. The two Allies came to favor indirect intervention in Russia through Bolshevik opponents – the Whites, the nationalists, or any other group. At the same time, frantic attempts were made to raise interventionary forces. No one thought of the Czech Legion, which only became an Allied army with its incorporation in the French Army overseas in February 1918. Many Allied diplomats and soldiers thought that Japan, which had been a member of the alliance since 1914, should undertake the military mission.

During the first five months of 1918, Allied diplomats tried feverishly to come to an agreement which would make Japan a mandatory of the alliance in Russia. After all, Japan's contribution to the world war itself was negligible. It could intervene massively, protect the Eastern Front with its own armies and then, perhaps, satisfy it own economic ambitions in the Russian Far East and Siberia. Although communist historians decried the Anglo-French agreement as an imperialist plot to dismember Russia, it was nothing of the sort. The agreement with Japan would not have resulted in a substantial loss of Russian territory, for the other major Western ally, the United States, would not have consented to it. On the other hand its successful application would indeed have meant the destruction of Bolshevik power. Even the final, ambiguous, agreement concluded by the Allies was not the result of cynical imperialist greed, but of Allied, mainly French, despair at the course of the war. They were believed to be in such desperate straits that they were willing to grant the Japanese any territorial concession (Siberia) to encourage their intervention. The other allies, the British

Right: Kamenev studying a map of the progress of the civil war.

Below: Bolshevik troops attack Kronstadt across the ice to suppress the revolt in March 1921.

and Americans, were more cautious. At first, Japan seemed enthusiastic in the talks with the French. On 5 April 1918, however, when Admiral Kata landed a boarding party at Vladivostok and Captain Payne of HMS *Suffolk* countered with the same, the Japanese became conscious of the political realities behind the intervention. To them it appeared that the Western Allies were equally concerned with blocking Japanese intentions. Within a month, after loud Bolshevik protests, both parties of marines were back on their ships. Dismayed, the Allies put pressure on Japan to intervene in Russia on behalf of the Czech Legion which had

just rebelled against the Bolsheviks. This time it was US opposition which delayed Japanese action; only in August 1918 did the 12th Division disembark in Vladivostok. Later that month it was transferred to Manchuria, the real Japanese objective. By November 1918 there were 70,000 Japanese troops in the Russian Far Eastern provinces. They were there not to help the legion, as they initially claimed, but to safeguard Japanese interests. At the same time the US President, Woodrow Wilson, decided to send 12,000 troops to Vladivostok, to keep an eye on the Japanese and only incidentally help the legion. The British and French supported the supposed Japanese intervention on behalf of the legion by sending to Vladivostok two battalions, one from Hong Kong and the other from Indochina.

These efforts were the sum total of Allied intervention in the Far East and Siberia. It is a fact that Allied troops subsequently interfered in internal Russian affairs. However, throughout their occupation of Siberia and the Far Eastern provinces from 1918 to 1924, Allied troops remained inactive and were only infrequently involved in fighting the Red Army. The Czech Legion, on whose behalf they were all 'intervening,' was not fighting the Red Army as a result of any Allied decision. In spite of Allied intentions, the legion was fighting the Bolsheviks because they prevented it from leaving Russia, even if it was via Vladivostok. The Czech revolt was the result of hazard, a fluke of war, not design or contingency planning. It surprised everyone, especially the Allies. The legion's subsequent fate illustrates this view. The initial fighting involved the legion in the civil war. Its interference in internal Russian affairs demoralized it to such an extent that the legion was unusable as an Allied force from December 1918. In 1920, the legion concluded an armistice with the victorious Red Army, and had to withdraw from Russia and be eventually repatriated to Czechoslovakia.

The only direct Allied intervention in Russia

was Premier Clemenceau's idea to replace the German and Austrian troops evacuating territories as the result of the armistice in the west with French troops. Since southern Russia was a French area of responsibility and there were French forces in Thessalonika, he was led by his military advisers to ship them to Odessa. In turn, the French Military Mission in Russia led General Franchet d'Esperey to believe that any operations would be unopposed. There seemed no armies capable of opposing the French once they were ashore. However, the reports did not mention the armed irregulars who were capable of stopping any French advance from the landing bases. Furthermore, French morale was at a low ebb. French and Greek troops landed expecting a 'joyride to Kiev' or even Moscow; instead they had to fight against savage bands of partisans in harsh winter conditions. Senega-lese soldiers, who had fought well in France, panicked in the frozen conditions and the Bolshevik partisans captured their first tanks from them. When the French ships anchored in Odessa mutinied, the expedition collapsed, and General Franchet withdrew ignominiously from Odessa and Russia, without getting to grips with the Red Army. This early failure ruled out any further direct Allied intervention. The French communists, who inspired the naval mutinies off Odessa, frightened Clemenceau sufficiently for him not to have another try. The British prime minister, Lloyd George, was opposed in principle to direct intervention in Russia, even before the French disaster. He also suspected that the Labour opposition would make life difficult for his government if it tried to intervene. Only Winston Churchill, his war minister, was an enthusiastic supporter of

Below: Senior Bolshevik officers confer on the Polish Front in 1920.

Above: Infantry of the Red Army on parade in April 1922. Organized by Trotsky, the army proved more than a match for the White forces during the civil war.

Below: American artilleryman deploy their light guns in the open during a training exercise.

intervention, but he was checked by his cabinet colleagues. Direct Allied intervention on a large scale was impossible.

The other two areas of direct Allied intervention were in the north, around the ports of Murmansk and Archangel, and largely concerned the British. In March 1918 the Murmansk Soviet asked for British protection and a small force of 500 marines was landed in the city. The marines stayed until the general Allied withdrawal from northern Russia in 1919. A larger Allied force, consisting of British, American and Canadian troops, disembarked at Archangel in August 1918, a vanguard of the proposed 'massive' Allied intervention. Some 13,000 soldiers were stuck in the northern cities for no

other reason than to guard the stores accumulating in them. They were too weak to break through the thin defensive lines of the Red Army; they, therefore, had to wait for the White forces to break through to them. Their presence needlessly complicated Admiral Kolchak's 1919 spring offensive: his northern wing was given the impossible task of reaching the Allied troops. The overall casualties were 178 killed and 401 wounded. Apart from its strategic nuisance value, the small-scale British intervention achieved nothing.

The supply of arms and equipment to the White forces was equally unco-ordinated, unplanned and badly executed. General Denikin was the chief beneficiary of British aid: he received 1200 guns, almost 2,000,000 shells, 200,000 rifles and 500,000,000 rounds of ammunition. There was a British tank battalion and two squadrons of the Royal Air Force available for training purposes but they often took part in the fighting. Altogether Britain spent over £100,000,000 in Russia; France, the United States and Japan much less. Admiral Kolchak received most of his aid from the United States and Japan, and paid for it himself. The supply system was chaotic – Japanese ammunition did not fit American rifles or guns. Finally the British sent two battalions to support Kolchak's armies, but they did not do much fighting as they were used for security duties. They were withdrawn in September 1919. As can be seen, Allied intervention was a chaotic affair which achieved little. Perhaps it prolonged White resistance but, because the aid came in penny packets, and was handed over to the Whites with the minimum of control, it did little harm to the Reds. This material aid was to have been paid for out of the Russian gold reserve which

PROCLAMATION.

There seems to be among the troops a very indistinct idea of what we are fighting for here in North Russia. This can be explained in a few words. We are up against Bolshevism, which means anarchy pure and simple. Any one of you can understand that no State can possibly exist when its own internal affairs such as labour, railways, relations with Foreign Powers etc are so disorganised as to make life impossible for everybody. Look at Russia at the present moment. The power is in the hands of a few men, mostly Jews, who have succeeded in bringing the country to such a state that order is non-existent, the posts and railways do not run properly, every man who wants something that somebody else has got just kills his opponent, only to be killed himself when the next man comes along. Human life is not safe, you can buy justice at so much for each object. Prices of necessities have so risen that nothing is procurable. In fact the man with a gun is „cock of the walk" provided that he does not meet another man who is a better shot. The result is that the country as a whole suffers and becomes liable to be the prey of any adventurers who happen along. Bolshevism is a disease which, like consumption kills its victim and brings no good to anybody. Undoubtedly things will be changed after the war, but not by anarchy and wholesale murder. Bolshevism to start with was only commenced with the sanction of Germany to rid the latter of a dangerous enemy, Russia. Now Bolshevism has grown upon the uneducated masses to such an extent that Russia is disintegrated and helpless and therefore we have come to help her to get rid of the disease that is eating her up. We are not here to conquer Russia, and none of us want to stay here, but we want to help her and see her a great power, as at present she is lying helpless in the hands of the adventurers who are simply exploiting her for their own ends, and who, in order to attain their ends, kill off their opponents from the highest to the lowest, including those who have the best brains in the country, whose powers could be utilised to restore her prestige and place among the nations. When order is restored here we shall clear out, but only when we have attained our object, and that is, the restoration of Russia.

Арх. Губ. Тип.

Left: A propaganda leaflet distributed to British interventionist troops. Despite the efforts of senior officers, their morale declined due to harsh conditions and lack of action.

Below: Trotsky (right) and Muralov at a Red Army sports meeting in October 1923.

the legion had handed over to the Bolsheviks in Irkutsk in 1920!

The Whites, in return for the aid, had to suffer the constant political interference of Allied representatives on the spot. Denikin was not allowed to do anything about the Caucasus where a string of newly independent countries had British political and military support. In northwestern Russia, British policy was the reverse of that in the Caucasus: Churchill insisted on a United Russia and would not back Baltic independence. Confusion and troubles between the Baltic nationals and the Whites were the results of this policy and no aid could put them right. In his Siberian redoubt, Kolchak had to perform political and military somersaults to obtain Allied aid: he promised independence to Finland, concessions to Japan and gold to the legion. His unreasonable reliance on the Allies cost him his life. On top of all this the Allies, particularly the British, but

Left: British bluejackets on the Murmansk Front guarding locomotives damaged by the Bolsheviks at Saroka on 12 April 1919.

Right: American prisoners being released from Soviet Russia in August 1921.

Below right: American soldiers of the North Russian Expeditionary Force take cover behind a snowdrift.

Below: Russian prisoners captured on the Murmansk-Archangel Front held in a camp in Troitsa.

also the French, took it upon themselves to negotiate with the Bolsheviks over the heads of the Whites. President Wilson publicly offered the Bolsheviks a compromise solution to the Russian problem at the Prinkipo Conference. The Bolsheviks rejected this solution which the Whites would have had to accept. Still the Western Allies realized some of their political aims: there was no declaration of war between Bolshevik Russia and the Western Allies and unofficial peace negotiations resulted in a sort of settlement after the civil war. The Bolsheviks also profited from the Allied intervention: sometimes fully equipped units deserted to them and White supplies were often captured by them, including tanks and aircraft. But, above all, the botched Allied effort strengthened their resolve and they could appeal to Russian patriotism to fight against the foreigners. In 1920 General Brusilov and many other imperial commanders responded to Bolshevik calls to resist foreign intervention. Finally, it furnished the Bolshevik propaganda machine with a powerful weapon: it pictured the Bolshevik triumph as a victory over the combined might of the White and Allied forces.

The Bolsheviks proved victorious in the economic field as well. While economic activity in the White-controlled territories collapsed, the Bolsheviks kept their economy more or less running. Subsequently this relative economic success was labelled as 'war communism.' The free market disappeared and 'goods were distributed according to people's need'; this period of transition to full communism seemed to be accelerated by the civil war.

It is also true that the Bolsheviks nationalized banking and credit but, with the exception of the Putilov Works, which were semi-nationalized because of their involvement in state defense and armament, industry was untouched. However, at the outbreak of the civil war Russian industry was in a poor condition: some plants were nationalized by local soviets; some were abandoned by owners or managers; while others were taken over by the workers who often drove away their owners and managers. A government decree introduced large-scale nationalizations and 80 percent of industry was run by the Supreme Economic Council by the autumn of 1919. In practice, the plants were managed by the workers themselves. They had to obtain supplies for production and then had to sell their products as well. If they did not succeed in running the factory, the plants had to close – this was one of the main reasons for the large number of industrial workers in the Red Army. In 1920 small-scale industries were nationalized. In theory, all Russian industrial production was nationalized and part of the centrally directed economy. Circumstances also forced the Bolsheviks to abolish free trade and, by the end of the civil war, a barter economy was operating. The Bolsheviks inherited food rationing and a state monopoly of grain from the Provisional Government. The peasants, who refused to sell their grain for

worthless money, were offered industrial products in exchange after the Bolshevik coup. However, with the outbreak of the civil war wholesale and retail operations involved with basic foodstuffs and manufactured goods were nationalized. Consumer co-operatives were turned into state distributive agencies. All these actions were emergency measures to guarantee supplies of food to the industrial workers and army, and were justified ideologically. Only the working population had the right to food rations; the bourgeoisie and capitalists had no such rights and could die of hunger, which many did, unless they were able to barter their possessions for food. In time barter trading became the norm as money lost its value. By 1920 wages and salaries were paid partly in kind. The Red government made an effort to base its budget on commodities rather than money.

In contrast to the Whites, the Bolsheviks succeeded in keeping most of their industrial plants, particularly armament works, going. Some were run by workers' committees and continued to be so even after nationalization; others were run by state-appointed managers, who were sometimes former managers or owners. However, they were always supervised by works committees. Though the economic situation was difficult, activity never ceased entirely, as was the case in White-controlled territory. Both sides shared a common policy as far as the gathering of foodstuffs was concerned. The Reds sent workers and soldiers into the countryside to obtain hoarded grain from peasants, either voluntarily or by force. This was accepted by the peasants, though resented. To facilitate food gathering the Bolsheviks formed Committees of Poor and Landless Peasants which were supposed to denounce richer peasants and co-operate with Soviet power. The committees were a dismal failure. After the land redistribution of 1917-18, there

were hardly any landless peasants left, even the poor peasants benefited from the land distribution. The Bolsheviks appeared as meddlers in village affairs, though they were not treated with the same hostility as former landlords or White officers. The greatest conflict between the peasants and the Bolsheviks arose at the end of the civil war when returning Red Army soldiers were encouraged to establish collective farms (*kolkhozy*). Members of the traditional peasant communities (*mirs*) felt threatened because the *kolkhozy* appeared more efficient than the old *mirs* and were subsidized by the state. In addition, the Bolsheviks established state farms (*sovkhozy*) on former crown land which were capitalist enterprises paying their laborers wages for their work. Both forms of agricultural activity preferred by the Bolsheviks gradually alienated the peasantry – but not before the victorious conclusion of the civil war. After the war, the struggle in the countryside continued with renewed vigor.

Below: British sailors and marines from HMS *Ceres* in Odem. The Hotel London (left) may have helped to make them feel more at home.

LENIN TRIUMPHANT

The Bolsheviks (henceforth known as communists) won the civil war largely because of Lenin's political skills, Trotsky's Red Army and Dzerzhinsky's security police. By November 1920 the civil war was over and the communists found the country in an appalling state. The survival of the economy depended on the black market, where peasants bartered foodstuffs for what was on offer. Workers bartered industrial products for commodities to keep the wheels of their plants rolling as often as possible to obtain food from the black market. The towns were hungry and half empty; Petrograd had lost more than a half of its population. Coal production was only slowly picking up; the transport system was largely disrupted and industry hardly ticking over. Peasants had resented the food confiscations during the civil war and now resorted to guerrilla tactics to avoid further requisitions. The rich Tambov province had to be subdued by 50,000 Red Army troops. Industrial workers, the proletariat on whose behalf Lenin had seized power, were no better off. Because of plant closures, military conscription, administrative promotions and, above all, hunger in the towns, the numbers of workers dropped from 3,600,000 to 1,500,000. The numbers of deaths from hunger and epidemics in the first two years of peace (1921-22) were more than the combined total of deaths in World War

I and the civil war (over 7,000,000). Over 2,000,000 educated Russians emigrated between 1917 and 1920.

The greatest problem the communists had to face was the demobilization of the Red Army. This was the largest 'proletarian' body in the country, some 5,000,000 men, and had the best revolutionary fighters. Some 2,000,000 of these soldiers and sailors had to be found some sort of employment to prevent them from becoming dangerous to the very regime they had fought for. Hungry, stranded, without houses and families, but armed, they were causing trouble all over Russia. Before the veteran problem emerged, Lenin became convinced that 'war communism' had to be abolished and replaced by something better. In consultation with his ex-imperial '*spets*,' N N Kutler, he was preparing a set of measures to restore monetary order. But he was doing so in secret, without the knowledge of his party colleagues, for he was convinced that his new economic policies (they became known by the acronym NEP) would, at best, displease many party leaders and possibly anger the rank and file. The latter seemed to have become proud of 'war communism' and many leading party intellectuals favored the retention of the chaotic system. Lenin prepared his measures for approval at the Tenth Congress scheduled for March 1921.

Previous page: Lenin addressing a meeting in Petrograd's Palace Square to mark the opening of the Second Congress of the Communist International on 19 July 1920.

Below: Women marching to Lenin's mausoleum on Red Square in Moscow on the occassion of International Women's Day, 8 March 1925. The banner proclaims: 'In the Soviet Country the Woman-Slave Has Become the Creator of a New Life.'

Two events saved him from the embarassment of telling his fellow communists to approve 'a tactical return to capitalism' which they thought they had destroyed. Late in February 1921 large-scale industrial unrest occurred in Petrograd because of food and fuel shortages, and also because the *Cheka*, acting on Zinoviev's orders, was effecting numerous arrests. Simultaneously, Mensheviks and SRs were making their influence in the trade unions felt by opposing Trotsky's proposal to 'militarize' them. A general strike was efficiently averted by the dual measures of rushing in food and arresting the strike leaders, Mensheviks and SRs. The unrest of the revolutionary vanguard in Petrograd, however, inspired another of these original revolutionary groups to revolt against the communist 'betrayal' of the revolution in 1917.

On 28 February 1921 the crew of the battleship *Petropavlovsk* passed a resolution which became the program of action for the whole of Kronstadt. They demanded election to soviets by secret ballot; freedom of speech for workers and peasants; freedom of assembly as well as free trade unions and peasant unions; the liberation of political prisoners, be they workers, peasants or socialists; review of cases of those in concentration camps (*gulags*); abolition of the *Cheka* special departments in the army and navy; equal rations for all; freedom for peasants to do whatever they wished with their land; and freedom for small-scale business enterprises. This program was almost a copy of the measures that Lenin was preparing to force the congress to approve. The Kronstadt sailors hoped that after the Petrograd strike their example would be followed in other places and by other social groups. The Kronstadt Soviet voted for the pro

gram with one dissenting vote, that of M Kalinin who was also the chairman of the Central Executive Committee and a member of the communist Politburo. The local communist party largely supported the program, but Lenin demanded the surrender of the fortress-island. When his ultimatum was rejected Lenin ordered the army and *Cheka* detachments under Tukhachevsky's command to storm the island. Since the Tenth Congress was in session, Lenin insisted on sending a group of 200 delegates to see the action. He wanted them to be impressed by the violent action. Red troops crossed the ice-covered sea on foot and, after some tough fighting, reduced the fortress. Allegedly, some 18,000 rebels were 'liquidated.' For the first time the Soviet press made a major effort to conceal the truth about the rebellion: it was apparently inspired from abroad and led by

a mysterious White general. However, the list of captured ringleaders only contained a priest, five former officers and seven peasants. They were never tried. Under the shock of these dramatic events, Lenin's new economic policy was endorsed by the congress without very much discussion.

NEP went into force immediately. Expropriations of food were replaced by a tax in kind; when the currency stabilized the state resumed payments for grain deliveries with money. It was logical to allow the peasants to sell their surplus grain on a free market which did not exist legally. Peasants were already permitted to sell grain openly by local soviets, who preferred it to the black market. Seeing this spontaneous development, Lenin and the communist party bowed to it. Wholesale nationalization was also abandoned and the private sector was revived. Only heavy industry, foreign trade and banking remained under state control. Foreign investors were invited to apply for concessions and Dr Hammer, the US capitalist, bought his first bankrupt pencil plant, but was not followed by many Western entrepreneurs. The government budget was cut and its revenues were increased by more efficient taxation. School fees and medical care had to be paid for, and pensions, sickness and

unemployment benefits were only available to contributors and not free to all as in the past. The impact of these measures was dramatic and in a comparatively short time the Soviet Union was bustling with activity.

Not everybody was happy about this development, including Lenin. Very soon, NEP 'profiteers' made their appearance and life in many ways assumed its pre-1914 form: peasant women sold their produce in the streets; nightclubs resounded to gipsy music; restaurants were crowded with fur-clad men; opera houses overflowed with elegant women; beggars and bearded priests were seen; and even church bells could be heard. The communist elite, the party and state bureaucrats, felt uneasy looking at this turn of events but refused to assume responsibility. However, NEP was a tactical retreat and admission of partial failure.

Lenin made it rapidly clear that the tactical retreat did not apply to politics. As all non-socialist parties were suppressed at the beginning of the civil war, he turned on the Mensheviks and Left SRs, who were still exercising some political influence, particularly in trade unions. The Mensheviks even published illegal pamphlets thanks to the backing of the Printers' Union. With NEP in full swing and with Menshevik taunts of 'we told you in 1917 to retreat' in the air, Lenin ordered the dissolution of all trade unions in which there was a Menshevik majority. They were replaced by bodies with suitable communist majorities. At the same time, Menshevik Central Committee members were arrested; altogether 2000 leaders were imprisoned. The party was wiped out and in 1922, in a show of magnanimity, 10 leaders were allowed to emigrate; Zinoviev's call for their 'liquidation' was rejected. The Socialist Revolutionaries were rounded up and tried at several public trials in 1922, especially after the GPU (*Glavnoye Politicheskoye Upravleniye*), *Cheka*'s successor, enticed B Savinkov, their famous leader, back to the Soviet Union. When asked by Kursky, the justice minister, whether fellow socialists should be shot, Lenin assented,

Above: May Day celebration, Moscow 1924. The occasion was marked by a march before Lenin's tomb. The British in particular were singled out for strong criticism. The float illustrates the conflict between Russia and Britain in the years after the civil war. Note especially the gallows on which Britain has been hung (right).

Opposite page, top: Scenes of starving children were all too common in Russia during the famine of the early 1920s.

Left: The Central Committee for fighting the famine in Russia, chaired by Kalinin (seated, right of center), meeting in Moscow during June 1923.

Above: There was a
tremendous literacy drive
in the years of the first
Five Year Plans. Here, a
literacy class is being held
in the village of Algeshi in
Chuvashia during 1928.

but recommended the occasional substitution of
condemned SRs by foreign exiles. On this occasion Radek and Bukharin were against the
death sentences, but Trotsky did not oppose
them. In 1922 and 1923 the remaining SR and
Kadet leaders were forcibly deported from the
Soviet Union. Lenin's treatment of the Left SRs
was ambivalent: they were invited to join the
communist party, but those who declined were
harassed and maltreated like all the socialists.
The Anarchists were next. Right up to the end of
1920, they managed to survive, despite administrative harassment. They kept their clubs
going and even published reviews. Now they
were all rounded up and 30 were shot. In
February 1921 they were all released for one day
to attend the funeral of Prince Kropotkin, the
internationally known Anarchist leader, and
then shipped to the *gulags*. Opposition members left free were tolerated, provided they
abstained from political activity or made themselves useful to the regime. Patriarch Tikhon
joined Gorky in his appeal for international aid
to relieve a famine which broke out in parts of
the Soviet Union where the harvest failed. This
was the price that had to be paid for NEP, the
communist tactical retreat. Once their political
opponents were dealt with, Lenin and his fellow
leaders turned inward to tidy up the communist
party itself.

In the circumstances of the tactical retreat
Lenin made it clear that it had to be an orderly

process with the slightest violation of party discipline severely punished. All the communists accepted Lenin's principle of democratic centralism which helped them to seize power in 1917 and win the civil war. The principle allowed party members to discuss any policy proposed by Lenin, but once a majority had voted for it, all members had to apply it loyally, whether they agreed with it or not. This principle remained in force even now. However, other matters were undefined: how long should a debate last?; how strongly could a leader be criticized?; and should critics form pressure groups or platforms? In the past, minorities had remained in the party even after their defeat. For the Tenth Congress the factions advocating a different approach to trade unions were well organized and delegates were structured according to their platforms. Lenin permitted it but then, taking as a pretext the 'danger of present circumstances' (Kronstadt), proposed that the party should put its house in order. Lenin considered the debate on trade unions a waste of time and saw in the factions a challenge to his leadership. He therefore organized his own faction, persuaded the majority of delegates by underhand methods to back him, and then defeated both Trotsky and Shlyapnikov on the trade unions issue. He then had his factional members voted to the Central Committee, allowing each faction limited representation while retaining an overwhelming majority. This majority then voted a resolution 'On Party Unity,' which dissolved all the existing factions and forbade, under the threat of sanctions, the formation of new factions in the future. Party unity in the period of NEP was paramount and

Lenin promised that the unity resolution would remain in force for the duration of NEP.

Whatever excuses Lenin might have used for this undemocratic measure within the party, it became the basic principle of party life. The secret clause of the resolution, which enabled the party leadership to expel persistent factionalists from the party or remove elected Central Committee members from office for the same offense, were never applied in his lifetime. In a sense he had not time to benefit from the resolution, for within a year he was dangerously ill

Above: Felix Dzerzhinsky, first head of the Soviet secret police, the *Cheka,* pictured in Moscow in 1918.

Below: Collecting the bodies of famine victims, February 1922.

Right: Children of the 'Young Spartacus' movement dressed in military uniforms, December 1923.

and had ceased to participate in party politics. It was the party's secretariat which was the chief beneficiary of this resolution. Trotsky's friends were voted off the secretariat and they were 'punished' by being posted out of Moscow to distant provinces. They were replaced by Lenin's henchmen. Subsequently Stalin made use of this 'administrative measure' to ensure party unity more formally. He also invoked and applied the secret clause.

Lenin next decided to fight bureaucracy. Like all revolutionaries, the Russian communists hated bureaucracy. Once in power, however, they found it necessary and then justified it on ideological grounds: without state machinery there could be no revolutionary changes in society. Lenin was a supreme realist; he knew he needed the expert knowledge of imperial bureaucrats in administration, finance, railways, health and geological surveys, and never

hesitated to make use of them. He had hoped that in time they would be replaced by a new type of communist expert. In fact, many communist industrial workers were sent to work in administrative jobs, but Lenin soon found out that they were more bureaucratic than the imperial officials (*chinoviki*), but without their expertise. Moreover the communist party itself was rapidly becoming a bureaucratic institution, particularly after it had curtailed internal freedom of expression and assembly. In time the central secretariat came to head a massive bureaucratic structure. Party bureaucrats seemed to permeat all strata of Soviet society. On the local level soviet organization was chaotic and under little control. In contrast, party committees received policy statements from the secretariat and, in time, forced local soviets to apply them. At the district and regional levels, the situation was similar to that of the old *zemstva*, which the soviet administration also failed to control. However, the respective party committees were capable of enforcing communist policies on the *zemstva*, passed on to them by the secretariat. There was no problem in central government, because ministerial offices coincided with party offices.

Inertia, the chief disease of bureaucracies, upset Lenin so much that he wanted to make it an issue at the Eleventh Congress scheduled for March 1922. However, already ill, he rescheduled the issue for the next congress. The Eleventh Congress was his last major public appearance and his address was entirely devoted to NEP. His fight against bureaucracy was carried on by his two henchmen: Stalin, who became party general secretary, and Trotsky. The latter declined the post of political vice-premier and chief anti-bureaucrat in the government. Stalin took immediate advantage of his appointment to build up his own bureaucracy, much to Lenin's dismay.

Below: Communist Red Week in Moscow, November 1924. Trotsky (center) receives the military oath from soldiers in Red Square.

While Lenin was incapacitated by illness, Stalin took over from him. He was not a charismatic figure or an erudite theoretician like Lenin or Trotsky. Sukhanov described him as a 'grey blur.' But his political skills were as great as Lenin's who he had actively aided in 1921 in packing the Tenth Congress with his own delegates. As secretary general he controlled the appointment, promotion and posting of important party figures. Once in such a powerful position, he determined to maintain his position. To this purpose he invented the system of a 'circular flow of power.' The point of this system was for Stalin to select his own factional followers as delegates for future party congresses. He appointed all the permanent secretaries (or sacked them if they let him down) and they, as a matter of routine, headed the provincial delegations to congresses. They in turn made sure that their delegates consisted of the right followers. At the congresses Stalin's delegates always upheld his resolutions, particularly since the motions were invariably those of the Central Committee, a body also stacked with Stalin's personal followers. To remain in power Stalin had to outmaneuver the top party leadership, the members of Lenin's Politburo, before he

Left: Mikhail Kalinin (1875-1946).

Below: Komsomol (Young Communist League) members demonstrate in Red Square during May 1925 beneath a banner calling all young workers into the *Komsomol.*

Right: Peasants admire the
first tractor delivered to
their village in 1926.
Tractors became a great
sign of Soviet progress in
the countryside, even to
the extent that children
were named 'Traktor.'

could assume supreme power. The Politburo
consisted of Lenin, Stalin himself, Trotsky (war
minister), Zinoviev (Leningrad leader and President of the Comintern), Bukharin (Editor of
Pravda) and Tomsky (Chairman of the Trade
Union Council). While Lenin lay sick, the Politburo pledged itself to rule collectively; none of
its members seemed ambitious enough to aspire
to Lenin's position. However, the succession
struggle was already in progress in secret, particularly after Lenin's second stroke in March
1923. Stalin allied himself with Zinoviev and
Kamenev against Trotsky, and fought against
him with implacable energy. While Lenin was
alive, the conspirators had to watch their step
and avoid direct conflict.

Lenin himself did not think that any of them
should succeed him, and found Stalin the least
worthy of the group. Previously, as the commissar for nationalities, Stalin had behaved badly
toward minority groups. He or his emissaries
invariably bullied nationalist representatives,
especially Stalin's fellow Georgians, into following central policies which were often at variance with their own interests. When Stalin
became secretary general, he left his henchmen
behind to harass the nationalities. In December
1922 a constitutional document was signed
which eventually created a Federal Union of
Russia including the Ukraine, Byelorussia and
Transcaucasia (Georgia, Adzerbeijan, Armenia). The Georgian communists were not consulted about federation and their central committee resigned in protest. Lenin, who was
aware of Stalin's highhanded dealings with the
minorities, blamed him for this constitutional
fiasco and wrote several memoranda condemning his brand of chauvinism. Stalin, who was
informed by one of Lenin's secretaries about the
criticism, wanted to discuss the problem with

Lenin. He was, however, frustrated by Krupskaya, Lenin's wife, who would not admit him to
the sick room. He abused her in excellent
Russian; normally, he spoke with a pronounced
Georgian accent. On hearing of Stalin's outburst, Lenin demanded that he make an apology to Krupskaya and later added a footnote to
his political testament which bid the Politburo
remove the rude secretary general from office.
The pretext was to have been the Georgian
question and Lenin's notes were sent to Trotsky
to be raised at the Twelfth Party Congress in
April 1923. Fortunately for Stalin, Lenin had a
third stroke in March, and neither Krupskaya
nor Trotsky was able to carry out Lenin's political wishes.

The conflict with Lenin was the last threat to
Stalin's party position. The Twelfth Congress
was packed with his delegates and he defeated
Trotsky on all the major policy issues. As soon
as it became clear that Lenin would never be
able to resume active political life, Stalin, Zinoviev and Kamenev began to act on their own
behalf without the slightest reference to Lenin.
He had full knowledge of this exclusion and suffered agonies. Stalin even criticized Lenin,
though in veiled terms, at the Thirteenth Party
Congress in early January 1924. Trotsky was
also completely routed when the representatives of the Central Government, universities
and the Red Army sent to the conference on his
ticket went over to the Central Committee
headed by Stalin. Lenin never found out about
Stalin's triumph as he died three days after the
conference. Trotsky did not seem to realize what
was happening. He was shocked by the lack of
support for the forthcoming congress, the first
one since Lenin's death. Zinoviev and Kemenev
did not realize that the elimination of Trotsky
and the retention of his post by Stalin, was, in

reality, a victory of the party machine over the party intellectuals and its rank and file.

After this crucial battle Stalin immediately attacked his allies and easily outmaneuvered them: Zinoviev and Kamenev lost their party offices in 1926. Too late, they realized their error. They quickly turned to the defeated Trotsky, who had also lost his job at the war ministry; and formed an alliance, but they could not dislodge Stalin who had the ability to have himself and his Central Committee 'confirmed' at all succeeding congresses. The lone leaders were expelled from the party in 1927. Trotsky was subsequently deprived of his Soviet citizenship and deported to Turkey, the only country willing to have him. Even before his political victory, Stalin made sure that his party machine (*apparat*) had a complete hold over not only the party rank and file, but also the country as a whole. Whether Stalin simply appropriated the technique of keeping extensive records of all party members from the czarist secret police is not known. Whatever the truth, he set up a central archive of records which contained personal details of all party members. The possession of these records gave Stalin immense powers. He was able to give assignments to the 'right' officials, discipline individuals by dismissal or even exile and select delegates and other

officials. The establishment of Central Committee departments to work under the direction of the general secretary completed Stalin's takeover. Moreover, the departments enabled Stalin to control all aspects of Russian life: his cultural department looked after culture and his press department after the press.

Such internal party developments were not part of Lenin's plans. In 1922 he was obliged to admit that all of his 1917 and 1918 government decrees were pure propaganda and had nothing to do with communism. Just before his death, he thought that communism would flow from the Bolsheviks' revolutionary triumph. In his own words, communism in Russia would be achieved when the whole country had access to electric power. Lenin himself condemned Trotsky's sketch of communism which consisted of NEP and militarized labor as a bureacratic utopia. What he would have thought of Stalin's centralized bureaucratic system we will never know. But it seems indisputable that at the end of his life Lenin thought of NEP not as a tactical expediency, but as a permanent feature of communism. To Russians emerging from 'war communism,' Lenin's new system seemed the preferable, if not the best, system and, if given a chance, one they would choose themselves.

The abolition of food expropriations had

Below: Even more significant than the arrival of the tractor, however, was the arrival of electricity. After all, Lenin had declared that communism equalled Soviet power plus the electrification of the whole country.

Above: Soviet diplomats M Litvinov (left) and V Vorovsky at the Geneva Conference in 1922.

communists or at least collaborated with the new regime. Even Stalin thought that the communist party had to accept the collaboration of non-communist intellectuals until such time as they could be replaced by communists. While many distinguished scholars of the former Imperial Academy of Sciences, such as the psychologist Pavlov and the physicist Nesmeyanov, were winning a high reputation in science, the communist authorities were preparing for their substitution by newly trained communist scientists from the Socialist Academy. The Institute of Red Professors was set up to train a future intellectual elite. Both institutions produced scholars whose works, especially in the legal and historical fields, were highly regarded. In literature, Gorky and Mayakovsky were renowned supporters of the new regime, but many non-political poets and writers were also allowed to flourish.

Religion fared comparatively less well. Lenin was well known for his atheist militancy, but remained silent on the subject. Repression was carried out either spontaneously by various fanatically anti-religious groups, or systematically, chiefly against the Orthodox Church, by the *Cheka.* If the constitution of 1918 reflected Lenin's thought on the subject, then he was rather tolerant. The Church was separated from the state but both religious and anti-religious propaganda was permitted. This constitutionally guaranteed freedom existed largely in theory, however. Priests, if they were not shot by *Cheka* agents as counter revolutionaries, were harassed. Church property was arbitrarily seized and church marriages were not legally recognized. In 1922 Patriarch Tikhon was arrested and 54 Orthodox and Catholic churchmen were put on trial. The communist authorities also encouraged a schismatic movement, the Living Church, but it faded away after the recognition of the Patriarchal Church led by Sergey, the eventual successor of Tikhon. The Orthodox Church was consistently accused of monarchist leanings and of maintaining relations with émigré churchmen. The accusation indicated that the regime was unwilling to relent in its persecution of these potentially political bodies. Only religious Jews were not persecuted, but they were recommended for assimilation. International public opinion was heeded in this respect, especially since the communist regime needed recognition and loans.

The first opportunity for legal recognition, the conference at Genoa in April 1922, proved a disappointment. The other international outcast of the time, Weimar Germany, was also rebuffed. However, the two outcasts concluded an agreement at Rapallo which compensated the Soviet regime for the loss of Western loans. A secret agreement enabled the Germans to conduct the research and development of prohibited weapons (tanks and aircraft) in Russia.

Between 1924 and 1925 there was a sudden upsurge in Soviet industrial development. This boom could not be compared to pre-1914 growth periods, but at least the workforce and their wages returned to 1914 levels. NEP was replaced by the idea of 'building up socialism.' The concept was vague, but on the whole it

immediate and benevolent effects. As surpluses could be sold freely after the payment of taxes, the peasants began to increase their production. The leasing of land and hiring of labor were also legalized and benefited the more ambitious peasants (*kulaks*), who became quite prosperous. The monetary system was rationalized by the former liberal minister of finance and commercial practices were codified to make transactions easier and safer. The new policy even attracted limited foreign investments. However, many foreign concerns were deterred from investing in the Soviet Union because of the government's repudiation of all czarist debts. Three-quarters of retail trade was in private hands, and though industry did not react as well as agriculture to the stimuli that Lenin administered to the economy, it began to show signs of recovery. Yet workers in heavy industry between 1922 and 1923 were taking home half the wages of 1913 in real money terms. NEP seemed to confirm the widely held view in Russia and the communist party that only the peasants really prospered in the years immediately after the revolution:

The revolution also brought about a flowering of intellectual life. It is true that the majority of well-known figures in the Russian intelligentsia preferred to emigrate or join the Whites but many lesser-known artists either joined the meant further economic development and modernization. Communist Russia needed the same range of economic reforms as Imperial Russia: more factories, railways and machines. It also needed greater urbanization, the establishment of a permanent working class, a shift from the country to towns, more schools, greater literacy, and many more skilled workers and engineers. The problem was how to carry out all this development without capitalist aid.

Trotsky saw the solution to this problem in 'permanent revolution,' particularly in capitalist countries which would then help the Soviet Union to develop. Stalin had different ideas. In 1925 he launched the slogan of 'socialism in one country' by which he meant that the Soviet Union would grow without foreign aid. Debate on the subject had already been going on and practical measures were taken. Dzerzhinsky, who was one of the few efficient communist organizers, became chairman of the Supreme Economic Council (*Vesenkha*), a sort of superministry of industry. This body made strategic decisions which were strikingly similar to imperial ones. Emphasis was placed on the development of metallurgy and machine building. Stalin was attracted by Dzerzhinsky's vision and, when the latter suddenly died, he made it his own. Declaring himself the great 'industrializer,' he compared his drive to the coup of 1917. Since Lenin was responsible for the latter, Stalin's efforts to equal his triumphs represented the political exploitation of industrial development. Finding the capital for his plans remained a problem.

Lenin and the communists knew from Marx that a period of capital accumulation was necessary before launching an industrial revolution. They also knew they had no accumulated capital. The imperial bourgeoisie's capital had been used up during the civil war. The NEP bourgeoisie had had insufficient time to accumulate capital. So, as foreign capitalists refused to invest, capital had to come from domestic sources. Two party theoreticians, Preobrazhensky and Bukharin, who had previously published the utopian *ABC of Communism*, debated the political and economic aspects of the problem. Preobrazhensky argued that as the peasantry had become prosperous because of NEP, they should now contribute to the prosperity of the towns and workers. The industrialization drive should be financed through taxes imposed on the peasants. Bukharin found this unacceptable because it was bound to put strain on, if not destroy, the peasant–worker alliance which was the basis of Lenin's NEP. However, the dilemma was not resolved: Bukharin agreed that capital was vital and that it had to be found somewhere, while Preobrazhensky thought that to raise it from the peasantry was politically undesirable.

The party debated 'Thermidorian degeneration,' which equated NEP with the Thermidor (decadent) period of the French Revolution. Curiously both the Stalinists and the anti-Stalinist opposition agreed that the communist revolution was stagnating and that party members, above all young people, were becoming disillusioned with it. Workers resented the privileges

of the old '*spets*' and the new soviet officials; the high profits and the ostentatious way of life of the 'NEPmen' (private entrepreneurs); high unemployment; and the permanent inequality of opportunity and their lower standard of living. Stalin opted to win the support of the workers by attacking the more prosperous peasants. He did not advertise his decision to confront the peasantry, but hinted at it in 1927, when he wrote: 'The economic recovery of NEP, which has brought industrial output and the size of the industrial proletariat almost up to prewar levels, has changed the balance of power between town and country, in favor of the town.' If economic development meant a confrontation with the peasantry, he was ready for it and he intended to win, even if the revolution had to be relaunched. The struggle for control of the land dominated the years immediately after the civil war period.

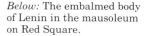

Above: Lenin and his wife at Gorky in 1922 with his nephew Viktor and the daughter of a worker.

Below: The embalmed body of Lenin in the mausoleum on Red Square.

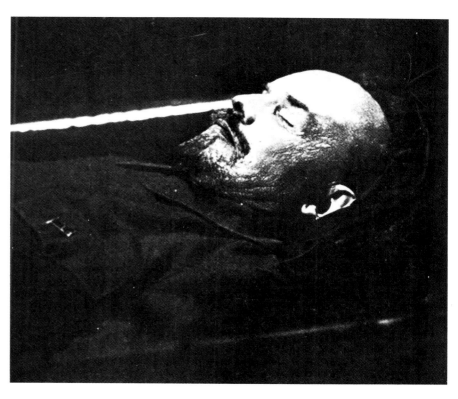

In 1927, when Stalin first announced his intention to launch an intensive industrial drive, he was an experienced and refined manipulator of the party *apparat*, though it was obeyed more by the rank and file than by intellectuals. It was also clear that the days of the firebrands Trotsky and Zinoviev, or the volatile alcoholic Bukharin, were numbered, and a new type of communist leadership was emerging, its members strikingly resembling Stalin. In private Stalin was as rude and extreme as before, but in public he spoke and acted like a great moderate. Moderation apart, he was the most methodical communist in Soviet Russia. He was also a great tactician who skillfully exploited every political opportunity. Though he liked to compare himself to Ivan the Terrible, he was more like Peter the Great, whose methodical 'revolution from above' thrust the backward and obscurantist Russia of the early eighteenth century into the forefront of world politics. Nazi Germany's invasion of 1941 thrust Stalin's Russia into the center stage of world affairs and the defeat of Germany would surpass even the military triumphs of Peter I. However, these world events occurred only after he had completed his 'revolution from above' which would transform the Soviet Union into a major industrial power.

Stalin's revolution assumed the form of a war. At the same time, a great war scare gripped the Soviet Union. Both the party and the Soviet people widely believed that the leading capitalist countries were preparing to launch another interventionary war against Russia. The British raided the Soviet Trade Mission (ARCOS) in London; the nationalist Kuomingtang in China attacked and heavily mauled the Soviet Union's ally, the Chinese communist party; Ambassador Volkov was assassinated in Warsaw. Tensions rose as the secret police began to arrest suspected enemies of the communist regime. Cases of terrorism and anti-Soviet conspiracies were widely reported. In reaction to this war scare, peasants began to hoard foodstuffs, which led to panic buying of food and other commodities in the towns and countryside. Whether party leaders believed in the possibility of war is difficult to assess. Certainly Bukharin did believe in it; however, the foreign ministry did not. Trotsky probably did not believe in the possibility either, though he used the communist defeat in China in his last attacks against Stalin, blaming him for it. Stalin remained calm and acted to stifle dissent.

First of all he turned the war issue against Trotsky and the united opposition in the communist party. Despite the supposed war dangers, Trotsky theatened to oppose Stalin and the party. This pledge smacked of treason to pro-Stalin party men and the entire opposition was expelled from the party. Pleased with this victory, Stalin used the industrial drive and the collectivization of farms against alleged internal opposition groups. The threat of war was

Previous page: The construction of the Grand Fergana Canal in Uzbekistan during 1939.

Opposite page: The Dniepr hydro-electric power station built during the first Five Year Plan (1928-32). When completed in the autumn of 1932, it was the biggest hydro power station in the world.

Below: Building the Turkestan-Siberian Railway in 1930. Here tracks are being laid by hand.

Right: The iron and steel works in Stalino (now Donetsh) in 1930. The region had seen the beginnings of heavy industry at the end of the nineteenth century. From its foundation in 1869 up to 1924, Stalino was called Yuzovka, in memory of the Welshman John Hughes who started the first factory there. It was renamed Donetsh in 1961.

illusory, but Stalin needed the threat of war to push his policies through. He mobilized communists and Soviet forces for the battle for collectivization and industrialization. The bourgeoisie and *kulaks* counterattacked, laid ambushes and otherwise fought Soviet power. Stalin, on behalf of the Russian proletariat, led the struggle against both foreign and domestic class enemies. His first attack was directed against the old bourgeois intelligentsia.

Early in March 1928, the war-scare strategy was prolonged by staging the Shakhty show trials. A group of engineers, encouraged by foreign powers, was allegedly sabotaging mining operations in the Donbas region. All the

accused confessed their guilt and gave detailed accounts of their espionage and sabotage activities. Invariably class opposition to Stalin's regime was linked with foreign enemies. At the same time, the party launched a massive propaganda campaign to convince the Russian people of the class war within and intimidate them into supporting Stalin's actions. This propaganda effort, skillfully directed by Stalin himself, even succeeded in convincing foreigners of the justice of Soviet claims and the validity of the victims' confessions. Many communist leaders were convinced by the abject confessions of their purged fellows. The liquidation of the engineers and other experts, just like the *kulaks*, could not be

Left: V M Molotov, People's Commissar for Foreign Affairs, signing the agreement of friendship, mutual assistance and postwar co-operation between the USSR and the Czechoslovak Republic.

justified in rational terms. After all, they were the only technical elite Russia had, and without them there could be no industrialization. Still, these actions were the striking hallmarks of Stalin's revolution: irrational violence, class war and confrontation.

After the expulsion of the left opposition, Stalin turned against the right. With the war scare and a food crisis to deal with, the party leadership was divided as to a solution. Right-wingers (Bukharin, Syrtsov, Rykov) wanted to avoid a confrontation with the peasantry over the procurement of grain. They suggested raising grain prices and making more consumer goods available in the countryside. Stalin went to Siberia to see the problems for himself and came back with his own solution: the *kulaks* could not be won over with concessions, they had to be fought. They had to be forced to sell grain at state prices, a solution known as the 'Urals-Siberian method of procurement.' In the long term, collectivization was the only solution, and this meant the transformation of land-owning peasants into a landless proletariat. Initially the communists considered private farming more efficient than traditional, communal methods, but now they argued that collectives, exploiting large tracts of land by modern means, would be suited to agricultural conditions in Russia. No one really imagined that Stalin was ready to launch his internal 'war' at once and on all fronts. It should be pointed out that Stalin had completed his takeover of the secret police, the army and the trade unions. With this repressive *apparat* in hand, he was certain to overcome any resistance to his policies. He forced his own wishes through the Politburo, despite Rykov's and Bukharin's opposition, and once they were approved as policies, he applied them.

Academician Strumlin, head of the State Planning Commission, had been working on the outline of the first Five Year Plan of industrial expansion and modernization since 1926. The plan was ready in August 1928 but its aims were subject to several reservations. To succeed there had to be no serious crop failure and an upswing in world trade; production costs had to decrease

while productivity increased; and defense expenditure had to be reduced. Stalin nevertheless launched the plan in spite of these reservations. In 1929 the Great Depression hit the industrial West and the Japanese invasion of Manchuria caused increased defense spending. Both events worked against any chances of the plan succeeding. To make matters worse, wages doubled but productivity remained low. As a result, more workers had to be employed than intended and consumer demand went through the roof, pushing prices up. Stalin was forced to

Below: A hoarding publicizing the development of the first Five Year Plan in the Asian part of the Soviet Union, and calling on the support of all workers.

introduce food rationing. Brute force and political fanaticism had to replace economic incentives to accomplish the plan.

The overall objectives of the plan were to increase industrial production by 250 percent; heavy industry by 330 percent; and agricultural production by 150 percent. These aims were declared impossible by Bukharin. However, the Central Committee session in the summer of 1929 revised the objectives upward, and Bukharin was removed from the Politburo. As Stalin put it: 'We are advancing full steam ahead.' In 1930 the party adopted a slogan, stating that only four rather than five years would be needed to complete the plan. The huge Ural-Kuznetsk Combine project was endorsed with full knowledge that this iron and coal development would put heavy strains on the transport system. Other signs of trouble caused by the forced pace of development appeared at the same time. Plants erected by shock brigades had no machinery; others had machines, but they were wrecked by unskilled labor. In others, skilled workers with machines lacked raw materials. In response to these difficulties Stalin proclaimed the last three months of 1930 a 'shock quarter,' and workers and technicians were bullied into even greater efforts. Early in 1932 the plan was declared accomplished, though published figures have since been questioned: machine and electrical equipment production rose by 157 percent; heavy metallurgy by 67 percent, coal output by 89 percent and consumer goods by 73 percent. However inaccurate these figures might be, the Soviet

Above: Another sign of progress in the countryside: a Soviet-made cotton-picking machine.

Left: New apartment blocks in Stalinogorsk.

Right: The defendants at the so-called 'wreckers' trial in Moscow in November 1930.

Union was a transformed country: no longer a backward agricultural economy. It was a bustling industrial giant, still expanding while the industrial West was only just getting over the Great Depression. Workers, managers, party leaders, rank and file members, however, all suffered terribly, forced to sacrifice their living standards and lives for the sake of Stalin's industrialization and modernization drives.

The effects of the plan on agriculture and agricultural society were sweeping. In 1928 Stalin declared that expropriating the *kulaks* would be an act of folly; the following year he ordered their liquidation as a class. They were not allowed to join the collective farms. The result was the devastation of the land, bloodshed and chaos. Security detachments encircled whole villages and deported inhabitants if they resisted or refused to join collectives. Early in 1930 there were slightly over 4,000,000 peasants working in collectives; by March there were 14,000,000 collective farmers, some 55 percent of the peasant class. It has been estimated that 12,000,000 *kulaks* were deported and that some 5,000,000 perished during the collectivization and in the resulting famine. Then, out of the blue, Stalin declared in *Pravda* that 'the party was dizzy with success,' which apparently meant that collectivization had to be stopped temporarily. The following year, as a result of Stalin's intervention, there were only 6,000,000 farmers in the collective farms. By 1932, according to official statements, 65 percent of peasants were collectivized, a figure which seemed to have satisfied both Stalin and the party zealots. However, the consequences were dire. Millions of animals – horses, sheep, goats and cattle – died. Horses were supposed to be replaced by tractors but the other animals were irreplaceable. Tractors and other machinery were not available in anything like the numbers required. Anyway, they were pooled at Machine-Tractor Stations (MTSs) and were not available at the collectives. The stations became the headquarters of communists who ruled over the local countryside.

There were different types of collectives. In the end Stalin accepted the *artel* type as the norm; in these the peasants retained their own livestock and small plots of land to cultivate on their own. This was the direct result of the peasants' resistance. Eventually, the *artels* ran 96 percent of Soviet agriculture. The MTSs provided their machinery and looked after maintenance. Harvests were split in three ways: compulsory deliveries to the state came first; the MTS share next; and the shares of individual members of the collective last. Politically this was a huge success, because at long last the proletariat (communist party) had squared its accounts with the agricultural 'exploiter,' the peasant. With modern means and better organization, the collectives, it was hoped, would progress economically as well. But these

Below: (L to R) Orzd, onikidze, Voroshilov, Stalin and Bulgarian Communist G Dimitrov acknowledge crowds from the top of Lenin's mausoleum.

Above: Soviet statesmen of the late 1920s: (L to R) Yaroslavich, Kaganovich, Ordjonikidze, Voroshilov. Stalin, Andreev and Molotov.

hopes were soon dashed. Pre-1928 *per capita* production was reached in 1937, but has not been surpassed since. Collectivization was the source of capital investments in industry, for the state sold off the confiscated or forcibly delivered grain at higher than average prices. Industrialization and collectivization combined to make Stalin's hold on the economy absolute. However, there was another sphere of Soviet life, the intellectual and cultural, to be 'fought and won in the class war.'

The relative moderation shown toward the old intelligentsia evaporated as Stalin launched his two-pronged attack on the workers and peasants. Culture also became a battlefield. The struggle involved fighting old bourgeois values, elitism and privileges and was called a 'cultural revolution.' It aimed at establishing absolute party control over intellectual and cultural life, and the replacement of old intellectual and professional elites by new, communist ones. This often meant that workers were pushed into professions without training, and intellectual and professional standards declined in consequence. This cultural revolution even affected the higher reaches of central administration: out of 861,000 'leading cadres' 140,000 came directly from the factory floor. Some 500,000 workers moved into clerical jobs. Altogether 1,500,000 workers were 'promoted' into the white-collar category.

The cultural revolution filled a need felt by the *Komsomol* (communist youth) and young graduates from the Socialist Academy and the Institute of Red Professors: they desperately wanted to replace the old establishment, most of them bourgeois '*spets*.' The Russian Association of Proletarian Writers (RAPP) and the League of Militant Atheists came into their own. Though Stalin unleashed the movement, it soon got out of hand and produced bizarre results. Thus *Komsomol* atheists, raiding the villages during collectivization, confiscated crosses and desecrated churches. Their raids confirmed the peasants' belief that the *kolkhoz* was the work of Antichrist. The *Komsomol* 'Light Cavalry' disrupted the functioning of government departments, and the *Komsomol* 'Cultural Army,' intended to fight illiteracy, was responsible for the abolition of local education departments on the ground that they were bureaucratic. *Komsomol* enthusiasts disrupted the performances of 'bourgeois' plays and RAPP attacked even Maxim Gorky, whom Stalin was trying to entice

back to Russia. Apocalyptic visions abounded: the state would wither away – probably; law certainly; school possibly. Stalin, whose intentions and actions were contrary to these visions, swiftly warned the *Komsomol* members to put an end to their 'hare-brained schemes.' Still plans went ahead for 'new socialist cities,' a 'new world,' even a 'new Soviet man.'

Despite the chaos and disruption, the cultural revolution did produce one concrete achievement: 150,000 specially trained workers were sent into higher education. While Stalin was too busy with his struggles to benefit from it, most of his henchmen and many future leaders did: N Khrushchev, L Brezhnev, A Kosygin and many others were trained as engineers in crash courses, but almost immediately went into political jobs. Stalin decided that he wanted to control every aspect of life in the Soviet Union. He accomplished this by removing old party members and replacing them with his 'young' men. Stalin's hold on the country was unchallenged and his state apparatus became omnipotent. Individual, political, economic and all the other freedoms vanished. All economic activity was a monopoly of the state; culture was also firmly under party-state control.

This was 'state capitalism' and a totalitarian state in action. The system looked new, it sounded modern, and Stalin was certainly its creator. However there was a precedent, Peter the Great's system. Like Stalin, Peter was an absolute monarch whose power was upheld by a secret political police. To enforce his will on the population, he used the standing army and the state bureaucracy, both of which were staffed with his supporters, the serving nobility. This elite had to spend their lives in the service of the state, else they forfeited their status and property. The state held the monopoly of commerce (internal and external), controlled newly founded industries and totally dominated agriculture. The army was used against the population whenever it dared to rebel against Peter's reforms. Peter also made the Orthodox Church a department of the state. He only failed to become Stalin's equal in power because he lacked the financial support that Stalin obtained from confiscations, and modern means of transport and communications. In many ways Stalin's power in the twentieth century was based on the same principles as Peter's in the eighteenth. In the use and abuse of power, Russian history had repeated itself.

POLITICAL GROUPINGS AND PERSONALITIES IN 1917

Revolutionary Parties

1917 was a turbulent and crucial year in Russian politics. When it began Czar Nicholas II was still on the throne; when it ended the Bolsheviks, led by Lenin, were in power and beginning to establish the world's first socialist state. In the meantime two revolutions had taken place: the February Revolution (later termed 'the Bourgeois Revolution' by the Bolsheviks) had deposed the czar; and the October Revolution ('the Great October Socialist Revolution') which had seen the seizure of power by the Bolsheviks. The period between the revolutions had been confused and unstable. Power lay in two areas: the Provisional Government which grew out of the czarist Duma, and the soviets. The soviets did not actually fit into any official system of government, and had sprung up as bodies to represent the workers in the 1905 Revolution. Of particular importance was the Petrograd Soviet. The Provisional Government and the soviets were both composed of a mixture of political groupings – a more accurate title than the formal 'party' – which fell principally into the following divisions:

The **Bolsheviks** were originally part of the Russian Social Democratic Labor Party which split in two at the Second Congress in 1903, largely over the question of membership. Lenin and his Bolshevik supporters insisted that the party must be a small collection of dedicated revolutionaries while the other faction, the Mensheviks, were keen to admit anyone to their ranks who supported their cause. The Bolsheviks were largely unprepared for the February Revolution, many of their leaders (including Lenin) being abroad. They refused to participate in the Provisional Government because of the bourgeois nature of its members and their support for Russia's continued participation in World War I. Instead they concentrated their efforts on gaining influence over the soviets, supporting Lenin's cry of 'All Power to the Soviets.' By the time of the October Revolution they had obtained a majority in the local soviets. Prominent party figures included V I Lenin, A S Bubnov, L B Kamenev, G I Sokolnikov, J V Stalin, L D Trotsky and G E Zinoviev. This group was elected as the Bureau for Political Guidance of the Insurrection (Politbu008) in October 1917. The first Politburo proper, elected in March 1919, omitted Bubnov and Sokolnikov and included N N Krestinsky. Zinoviev was made a candidate (non-voting) member and was joined by N I Bukharin and M I Kalinin. After Lenin's death in 1924 and Stalin's assumption of power, many old Bolsheviks were discredited and executed including Kamenev, Sokolnikov, Zinoviev, Krestinsky and Bukharin. Trotsky was exiled and then assassinated by one of Stalin's agents in Mexico in 1940.

Kadets were members of the Constitutional Democratic Party which was founded in October 1905 and composed largely of the bourgeois intelligentsia and liberal landowners. The Kadets originally wanted a system of constitutional monarchy modeled on the British system, but following the overthrow of the czar in February 1917, the party called for a republican system. As members and supporters of the Provisional Government they tried to secure total power for the Provisional Government with the help of the Socialist Revolutionaries and the Mensheviks. Prominent figures included A A Manuylov, P N Milyukov, N V Nekrasov, F I Rodichev, A I Shingarev (all members of the first session of the Provisional Government), A V Kartashev, N M Kishkin, A I Konovalov and S A Smirnov (members of the final session). At the time of the February Revolution Konovalov had been a member of the Progressive Party which held a position between the Kadets and the Octobrists. Shortly after the revolution, however, the party split up with some of its members going to the Kadets and others forming the Radical Democratic Party.

Top left: A S Budnov, a leading member of the Bolsheviks, was executed in 1937 – a victim of Stalin's purges.

Above left: N Bukharin, a member of the Politburo, was a victim of Stalin's regime.

Above right: Kamenev, Lenin and Trotsky in 1920.

Left: M I Kalinin, one of the candidate (non-voting) members of the first Politburo.

The **Mensheviks** were heavily criticized by the Bolsheviks for 'perverting' true Marxism after the split in 1903. They were ultimately to suffer defeat for allowing too great a divergence of opinion in the party and for participating in the Provisional Government. The party fell into two main factions: the larger Menshevik-Defenders and the smaller Menshevik-Internationalists. The Internationalists, led by Julius Martov, were critical of the Provisional Government and of the policy of continuing the war. However, they could propose no practical alternative as they believed the time was not right for the socialist revolution and that Russia should experience a period of bourgeois rule first. Wishing to avoid a split, the Internationalists remained with the Defenders and thus opposed the Bolshevik Revolution. Prominent Mensheviks included P B Akselrod, N S Chkheidze, F I Dan, L Martov, A S Martynov, G V Plekhanov and A N Potresov.

The **Octobrists,** a party of landowners and businessmen, took their name from the czarist declaration of 17 October 1905 and called for a united Russian Empire under a monarch. When Nicholas II abdicated they tried to persuade his brother, Grand Duke Michael, to take the throne. Although Guchkov, a leading Octobrist, was appointed minister of war in the first session of the Provisional Government, the Octo-

brists put their support behind the Kadets. After the October Revolution the Octobrists fought against the Bolsheviks, many of them taking up leading positions in local White Guard organizations and governments. Those who survived the civil war emigrated. Leading party figures included I V Godnev, A I Guchkov, M V Rodzianko, S P Shidlovsky and D N Shipov.

The **Socialist Revolutionaries (SRs)** were an amalgamation of various groups which came together in 1902. The SRs were outlawed before the February Revolution, largely because of their use of terrorism. After the overthrow of the czar the SRs became very active in both the soviets and the Provisional Government. By May they had over 500,000 members throughout the country including a significant representation in the army and navy. At the first All-Russian Congress of Soviets in June 1917 the SRs represented the largest single group, having 285 of the 777 delegates (the Bolsheviks had 105). Following the Bolshevik Revolution the SRs resorted to terrorism once more, assassinating several leading politicians. N D Avksentev, C Breshko-Breshkovskaya, V M Chernov and A F Kerensky (prime minister of the Provisional Government from the end of July until the October Revolution) were all leading lights of the Socialist Revolutionaries in the period before and after 19017.

INDEX

Page numbers in italics refer to illustrations

Abramov, General 137
Aehrenthal, Count 26
agrarian reforms 18, 90, 129,
   162-3
Akashev, Commissar 82
Akselrod, Paul B 20, 21
Alexander II 10, *11*, 12, 13, *13*
Alexander III 12, 13, 24
Alexandra, Czarina *14*, 42, *42,* 43,
   49
Alexey, Czarevich *14*, 42, 50, 51
Alexeyev, General M V 29, 35,
   36-7, 38, 50, 51, *54, 57,* 62,
   65, 66, 128
Allied governments 58, 62, 65
Allied intervention 109-10, 111-12,
   118-19, 123-4, 128, 130-31,
   134-6, 139-43, *153,* 153-9, 161
All-Russian Congress of Soviets
   59-60, 61, *63,* 70, 71, 72, 74,
   81, 84-6, *90*
All-Russian Directorate 114-15,
   116
Anarchists 59, 60, 61, 133, 170
Anayev, Colonel 81
Andronnikov, Prince 31
Antonov-Ovseyenko, V A 74, 76,
   79, 81, 82, 84, 91, 107
Aralov (Red Army) 148
armed forces
   Imperial 24, 25-8, *29*, 32-3, 36,
      56, 66
   Officer Corps 28-30
   in Petrograd 58, 60-61
   reconstruction of 106
   reforms in 30, 31
   Russian National Army 116-21,
      131
   Volunteer Army 128-34
   see also Imperial Army, Red
      Army
Armenia 98, 174
Armenians 146
Astrov (Socialist Revolutionary)
   114
Aurora, cruiser 77, 78, 83, 84
Austria 26, 27, 32, 95
Austria-Hungary 24-5, 26, 102
Austrian Army 34, 35, 38, 60, 65
Avksentiev (Socialist
   Revolutionary) 101, 112, 114

Bagrateni, General 76, 78
Balkans 24-5, 26, 27, 30
Balodis, Colonel (White) 141
Baltic Fleet 66
Baltic provinces 103, 139
   see also Estonia, Latvia,
      Lithuania
Belyaev, General M A 48
Balyev, General 95
Belitsky (Red Army) 149
Belov, General (White) 118, 149
Benes, Prof Eduard 110
Bermont, Colonel (White) 141,
   142-3
Berthelot, General 130
Berzin, General R I 95, 149
Bezobrazov, General 38
Biskupsky, General (White) 141
Blücher, *Revkom* 114, 148, 150

Blumberg, General Z K 149
Blyukher (Bolshevik) 107
Bogayevsky, General (White) 135
Bogoslavsky, General (Red Army)
   120
Boldyrev, General (White) 94, 115
Bolsheviks 15, 16, 21, 48, 49, 55,
   58, 59, 64, 65, 66, 67
   July coup attempt 60-62, 70
   November coup 66, 67, 70, 72-9
      passim, 82-6, 90-95, 107
   party organization 172
   political takeover by 96-103,
      106, 124, 146, 166
   Sixth Congress 70
   see also civil war
Bonch-Bruyevish, Maj Gen (Red
   Army) 106
Borisov, V 37
Borovsky, General (White) 136
Braun (Socialist Revolutionary)
   101
Brest-Litovsk 95
   Peace Conference at *102,* 103,
      154
Brezhnev, L I 187
Britain 25, 26, 32, 109, 131, 154,
   155, 159, 180
   armed forces of 134, 135, 136,
      139-42, 154, 156, 158, *160, 163*
British Mission 137
Broz-Tito, Josif 100
Bruderer (Socialist
   Revolutionary) 101
Brusilov, General A A *29,* 38, 62,
   66, 143, 161
Bublikov, A, Duma
   Commissioner 50, 54
Bubnov, A S (Bolshevik) 76, 79,
   96
Budyonny, General S M (Red
   Army) 133, 134, 143, 148, 150,
   151, 152
Bukharin, N I 170, 174, 177, 180,
   183, 185
Bulak-Balakhovich, Colonel 141
Bulgaria 27

Cecek, Lieut later General 110-13,
   114, 115
Chapaev, V I *142*
Charykov, Ambassador 27
Chaykovsky (independent SR) 114
Cheka 90, 152-3, 166, 167, 169, 176
Cheremisov, General 73, 78, 79,
   83, 93
Chernov, V 59, 61, 101-2, 103, 112
Chernyshevsky, N G 19, 21
Chkheidze, N S 56, 57, *60*
Chubar (Bolshevik) 90
Chudnovsky (Bolshevik) 79, 84,
   96
Churchill, Winston 157, 159
civil war *66,* 90, 94, 106, 107, 110,
   111-19, 112-25, *122-5,* 146-50,
   166
   maps 129, 132
   in North West 139-43
   in South 128-39, 146, 150
Clemenceau, Georges 130, *135,*
   157
Constantine Mikhaylovich,
   Grand Duke 31
Constituent Assembly *100,* 102-3
Constitutional Democrats *see*
   Kadets
constitutional reforms 10, 15-17
Cossacks *31*, 35, 48, 49, 75, *75,* 78,
   82, 84, 92, 93, 94, 97, 107,
   114, 116-19 *passim, 123,* 125,
   128, 146
   Don Cossacks 81, 96, 98, 113,
      128, 130, 132-3, 135, 137
   Kuban Cossacks 98, *119,* 128-31
      passim, 133, 135, 137

Orenburg Cossacks 99, 117
   Terek Cossacks 98, 128, 131,
      135
Cowan, Admiral Sir Walter 139
Czechoslovak National Army 108
Czechoslovakian Legion 107,
   108-15, *110-11,* 117, 118, 120-24
   passim, 133, 155, 156

Daller, Colonel (Red Army) 106
Danishevsky, General (Red
   Army) 106, 148
Davilov, General 32, 33
Denikin, General A I 29, 62, 120,
   128-31 *passim, 131,* 132, 133,
   134, 134-6, 138, 141, 146, 147,
   150, 151, 158, 159
*Development of Capitalism in
   Russia, The* (Lenin) 20
Dietrichs, General M K (White)
   119, 120, 121, 125
Down, Cdr R T, *148*
Dragomirov, General 46, 129,
   133
Dukhonin, General 79, 82, 95
Duma 12, 15, 16-17, 18, *20,* 27, 36,
   39, *43,* 43-4, 47, 48, 50, 54,
   61, 66, 81
   Provisional Committee of 54-5
Dumenko, General (Red Army)
   135, 151
Durnovo, Colonel 141
Dutov, Ataman 99, 117-20
   passim, 149
Dybenko, P (Bolshevik) 94, *150*
   Dzenis, Commissar 78
Dzerzhinsky, F E 76, 90, 143, 149,
   152, 153, 166, *171,* 177
Dzhunkovsky, General 98

East Prussia 33, 34
economy, revolutionary 161-3,
   166, 169, 175-6, 176-7
   Five Year Plan 183, 185-6
   NEP 166-7, 169-72 *passim,* 175,
      176, 177
Eikhe, General G K (Red Army)
   150
Ekaterinburg *121*
Estonia 139, 142-3
Estonians 66, 128, 141, 142-3, 146
Evert, General 38

Famine *168-9,*170, *171*
Fedko, I *150*
Feirman, Commissar 78
Finland 107, 141
Finns 128, *136,* 141, 142, 146
foreign policy, imperial 24-7, 30
France 24, 25, 26, 28, 32, 109,
   130-31, 137, 154, 157, 161
French forces 33, 108, 110, 131,
   157
Franchet d'Esperey, General 130,
   133, 157
Franz-Joseph, Emperor 24
Frunze, M V 97, 107, 118, 147,
   148, 149, 151
Fullon, Police General *17*

Gajda, Captain later General
   110-11, 112, 115, 117-20
   passim, 122, 125
Galkin, General (White) 112
Gapon, Father 15, *17*
Gay, G D (Red Army) 149, 152
Georgia 60, 90, 98, 107, 146, 174
Georgians 128, 146, 174
German Army 33, 35, 38, *59,* 60,
   65, 103, 107, *131,* 139, 140
   Freikorps *136*
Germany 24-7 *passim,* 32, 39, 42,

61, 75, 95, 102, 176, 180
Giers, N K 24
Gittis, General (Red Army) 150
Golitsyn, Prince N D 42, 50
Goltz, General von der 140-41
Gorky, Maxim 74, 170, 176, 187
Gots (SR leader) 101
Gough, General Sir Hubert 141,
   142
GPU 169
Graves, General 125
Greece 27
   Greek forces 131
Grigoriev, Ataman 131
Grigoriev, General 35
Grivin, General (White) 111, 117,
   122
Guchkov, A I 55, 59, 64, 66
Guinet, Major 114
Gusev, S I 90, 148, 149
Gutenberg (Provisional
   Government) 81

Hammer, Dr 169
Hoffman, General M 103
Holman, General 136, 137

Imperial Army *18, 23,* 35, *30-31,*
   32-5, *33-7,* 37, 38, *39,* 42,
   45-9 *passim, 58-60, 109*
   dissolution of 106
   1917 mutiny 45-6, 50, *50,* 56,
      57, 58
   Stavka 32-7 *passim,* 42, 46, 47,
      49, 50, 75, 79, 83, 95, 102
   under Provisional Government
      60, 62, 64, 65, *71,* 75
industrial development 19, 44-5,
   177, *179-81,* 180, *182,* 182-3,
   184-5, 185-7
Industrialist Union 39
Ioffe, A A *102,* 103
Iskra, journal 20, 21
Ivanov, General 38, 50
Izvolsky, Alexander 26

Janin, General 118, 119, 120, 125
Japan 15, 18, 24, 25, 27, 154, 155,
   156
   Japanese forces 122, 123-4, *162*
Jews 35, 61, 176

Kadets 16, 17, 55, 114, 170
Kaganovitch, L M *187*
Kaledin, General 128
Kalinin, M 167, *169, 173*
Kalnitsky, General (White) 133
Kamenev, L B 61, 70, *70,* 71-2, 74,
   76, 92, 102, 174-5
Kamenev, General S S 120, 133,
   148, 149, 150, 151, *156*
Kappel, Colonel (SR) 112, 115, 117,
   122
Kartashev, Minister 78
Kata, Admiral 156
Katz, Commissar 78
Kazakhstan 99
Kedrov (Bolshevik) 106
Kelchevsky, General (White) 136
Kerensky, Alexander 48, *54-5,*
   55-9 *passim,* 62, 66, 70, 74,
   75, 78, 79, 81, 84, 93, 94
Keyes, General 136
Khabalov, General S S 47-50
   passim
Khandshin, General (White) 118,
   119, 120
Khokhryakov, P D 98
Khrushchev, Nikita 187
Kikvidze (Bolshevik) 107
Kirov, Commissar 148

Kishkin, (Provisional
Government) 81
Kislyakov-Uralov, Commissar 79
Kolchak, Admiral A V *116*,
116-25, 128, 132, 146, 147, 148,
150, 158, 159
Kolotukhin, Commissar 94
Kondzerovsky, General 33
Komsomol 128, 173, 187
Kork, General (Red Army) 152
Kornilov, General L G 29, *55*, 62,
65, 66, 128
Korovichenko, General (White)
98
Kostyayev, F V 107
Kosygin, A N 187
Kotovsky, General G 107, *149*
Kotsubinsky (Bolshevik) 97
Krasilnikov, General 116
Krasnov, General P N 92, 93-4,
107, 128, 130
Krivoshein (White) 138
Kronstadt naval base 147, *156,*
167
Kronstadt sailors 61, *73,*74, 77,
81, 90, 91, 93, 99, 167
Kropotkin, Prince 170
Krupskaya, Nadezhda K 20, 93,
174, *177*
Krylenko, N V 90, 95, 102, 106
Krymov, General 62
Kuropatkin, General *27*, 28, 38
Kursky, Justice Minister 169
Kutepov, General (White) 133-4,
137, 138
Kutler, N N 166
Kuybyshev, Commissar 98, 148,
149, 151

Lambsdorff, Foreign Minister 25
Land and Liberty Society 12
land expropriation and
redistribution 90, *129*, 162-3
Lashevich, Revkom M M 117, 149
Latsis (Bolshevik) 90
Latvia 139, 140-42, 143
Latvians 66-7, 94, 140, 141
Lazimir (Socialist Revolutionary)
73
Lebedev, Colonel (White) 117,
120, 121, 125
Lebedev, Colonel P P (Red Army)
148
Left Socialist Revolutionaries 91,
92, 93, 98, 102, 103, 149, 169,
170
see also Socialist
Revolutionaries
Lenin (V I Ulyanov) *10*, 13, 16, *19,*
48, 59, 60, 67, *90, 108,* 1⁵
174, 176, *177*
background 19, 20
and Brest-Litovsk 103
in civil war 118, 120, 146-7,
149-53 *passim*
on communism 175
and Czech Legion 109
in Finland 70
illness and death 171-2, 174
NEP 166-7, 169, 171, 172, 175,
176
and October Revolution 71-2,
74, 77, 78, 79, 81, *81, 83-6
passim*, 90, 92, 94, 95
in Petrograd July '17 60-61
and Poland 143, 152
political ideology 19-20, 177
political takeover 96, 101,
102-3, 146, 166, 169-71, 172
post civil war *166*, 166-7, 169-73
and Red Army 106, *148*, 149,
152
return from Finland *56*, 59, 71
revolutionary tactics and
strategy 20, 21, 59, 70, 90,

143, 152
and Social Democratic
Party 20-21
on Stalin 174
Lianozov, S G 142
Lieven, General Prince 141
Lithuania 103, 139, 143
Litvinov, M M *176*
Lloyd George, David *135*, 157, *167*
Lunacharsky, Commissar A V
102
Lvov, Prince G Ye 12, *54*, 55, 56,
59, 62
Lvov, N V 62
Lyupov, General (White) 117

Makhin, Colonel (White) 112
Makhno (Anarchist) 131-5
passim, 138, 152
Maklakov (White Russian) 137
Malevsky, Commissar 78
Malyshev, I M 98
Mamontov, General (White) 133
Markov, General (White) 128
Marsh, General 142
Martov, Julius 20, 21
Marx, Karl *14,* 70
Marxism, Marxists 19-20, 21
Masalsky, Prince 38
Masaryk, Prof. T G 110
Masons 55, 58, 59
Mayakovsky, Vladimir 176
May-Mayevski, General (White)
131, 133, 138
Mekhlis, Commissar 148
Mensheviks 21, 48, 56, 57, 64, 70,
81, 84-5, 94, 98, 101, 102, 114,
119, 167, 169
Menzhinsky, Commissaar 93
Mezheninov, General S A 149
Michael, Grand Duke 50, 51, 54
Military Revolutionary
Committee 73-4, 75, 76, 79,
90, 91, 93, 94, 97, 101, 102
Miliutin, General 32
Milyukov, Prof. 50, 54, 55, 58-9,
65, 70
Mirbach, Wilhelm 103
Molotov, V M 48, 90, *183, 187*
Moscow 70, 90, *91-3*, 97, 103,
118, 141, 150, 151, *172, 177*
in WWI 48, *51, 106, 145,
166-7, 169*
Muravëv, Colonel (Left SR) 93,
95, 107, 149
Myasoyedov, Colonel 39

Nakhichevan, Khan of 34
Nazarov, Colonel (White) 137
Nesmeyanov, physicist 176
Nicholas I 10, 29
Nicholas II 10, 13-17, *14*, 24-32,
35, 36-9, *42*, 42-4, 49-51, *51*,
54, 55, 65, 121
Nicholas, Grand Duke 25, 28, *32*,
32-3, *35*, 36, 39, 56
Niedra, Pastor 141
Niessel, General 94
Nogin, Viktor P 97
Novitsky, General (Red Army)
149

Obruchev, General 32
October Revolution 70-77, *71,
76-9*, 78-9, 81-6, 90-95, *96*
map 73
Octobrists 16, 55
Okhrana 12, 15
Ordjonikidze, G K 96, 106, *141*,
148, 151, *154, 186-7*

Palchinsky, General 81, 82

Palitsyn, General 28
Paris Peace Conference *135*, 139
Pavlov, General (White) 135, 151
Pavlov, Ivan P 176
Pavlu, B 114
Payne, Capt, RN 156
peasantry 10, 12, 15, 18, 43, 44,
45, 176, 177
Pepelyayev, General (White) 111,
117, 118, 120, 122, 123, 125
Percy, General 137
Pestkovsky, Commissar 77
Peter I 10, 12, 180, 187
Petlyura, Ataman 143
Petrograd 103, *129*, 141-3, 147,
153, *165*, 166, 167
attempted coup in 60-61, 62, *64*,
70
Bolshevik coup in 67, 70, *71,*
72, *74-81*, 81, *82-9*, 90-91, 95
in WWI *28, 41*, 42, 44, 45, *46*,
47-50, *49-50*, 53, 54, *56-7*, 67,
72
see also St Petersburg
Petrograd Soviet 54-7, 58-61
passim, 66, 70-71, 72, 76, 77
Petrov, General 112
Pilsudski, General J 143
Pisarev, General (White) 137
Plekhanov, G V 20, 21, *21*
Podvoysky, General N I 60, 67,
74, 79, 106, *107, 111*, 148
Pokrovsky, General (White) 133,
136
Poland 33, 35, 103, 130, 136, 137,
137, 143, 147, 148, 152
Poles 12, 15, 27
Polivanov, General 36, 66
Polkovnikov, Colonel 74, 75, 76,
79, 101
Poole, General 130
Postovsky, General (White) 136
Potresov, A N 20, 21
Preobrazhensky, Evgeny 177
Primakov (Bolshevik) 107, 148
Protopopov, A D 42, 47
Provisional Government *54*, 54-6,
58-62 *passim*, 64, 65, 66, 72-9
passim, 81, 84, 94, 95
Purishkevich, Vladimir 42, 91
Pustovoytenko, General 37
Putna (Red Army) 148

Radek, Karl 170
Rakovsky (Bulgar) 95
Rasputin 42, *42*, 47, 48
Rasstovsky, General *54*, 54-6,
Red Army 90, 103, 106-7, 114, 117,
117-25 *passim*, *120, 125*,
132-9, *140*, 140-43, *142*, 146,
147, 148, *151, 152, 155, 157-8*,
166
Red Guards 76, 77, 78, *78*, 81, 84,
86-7, 91, 93, 97
Revolution of 1905 15-16, *15-18*
Rödiger, General 26, 27, 29, 30
Rodzianko, General 141, 142-3
Rodzianko, Mikhail *44*, 50-51, 54,
67, 70
Rokosovsky, General K 151
Romanov, I P 98
Romanovs, assassination of 146
Romanovsky, General (White)
134
Roshal, S G 96
Rozanov, General 122
Rudnak (Bolshevik) 107
Rudnev, Moscow mayor 97
Rumania 38, 96, 130, 154
Russo-Japnese War 15, 18, 24, *25*,
25-6, 27, *27*, 28
map 26
Ruzsky, General 48, 50-51
Ryabtsev, Colonel 97
Ryazanov (Bolshevik) 92
Rykov (Bolshevik) 183

St Peter and Paul Fortress 70, 74,
76
St Petersburg 15-16, *16-17*
see also Petrograd
Samara 111-15, 120
Samoilo, General (Red Army) 107
Samsonov, General A V 34
Savinkov, B 62, 169
Sazanov, Serge 26, 32
Schilling, General (White) 133
Selivachev, General (Red Army)
151
Semenov, Ataman 100, 123, 125,
152
Serbia 27, 32, 154
Sergey, Patriarch 176
Seymour, Admiral 136
Shaposhnikov, Colonel B M 148
Shoherbachëv, General 96
Shcherbatov, Prince 35
Shkuro, General (White) 133
Shlyapnikov, A 48, 49, 102, 171
Shorin, General V I 149, 150
Shuvayev, General 36
Shvernik (Bolshevik) 98, 148
Siberia 99-100, 111-13, 116-25, 128,
149, 155, 156
Sidorin, General (White) 131, 133,
136
Sievers (Bolshevik) 107
Sikorkski, General 143
Skobelev (socialist) 57
Skoropadsky, General 107
Skrypnyk, Commissar 97
Skylansky, General (Red Army)
106, 148
Slashchev, General (White) 136,
137, 138
Slutsky, Commissar 97
Smirnov, General 35, 38
social democrats 19, 20, 21
Socialist Revolutionaries 18, 21,
48, 56, 59, 64, 70, 73, 74, 76,
78, 84-5, 94, 98, 101, 102, 103,
111-14 *passim*, 119, 122, 123,
124, 152, 167, 170
socialists 48, 55, 61-2, 73, 74
Sokolnikov (Bolshevik) 92
Sokolov, N D 58
Sollogub, General (Red Army)
152
Solodovnikov, industrialist 39
Sovmarkom 95, 96, 98, 102,
128
Stalin, Josif 70, 94, 147, 172, *186*
character 174, 180
complete control by 187
dispute with Lenin 174
economic development by 177,
180, 182-3, 185, 186-7
in October Revolution 72, 73,
86, 90
and Red Army 106, 141, 143,
148-51 *passim*
succeeds Lenin 172-5
Stankievich, Commissar 81
Stark, Commissar 77
Stolypin, General Peter 17-18, *21*
Strumlin, planner 183
Stürmer, Boris 42, *43*
Sukhanov (Menshevik) 71, 173
Sukhomlinov, General V A *25*,
27, 31-2, 33, 35, 37, 39
Suleym, General (Red Army) 107
Surin, Colonel 78
Svec, Colonel 115
Svechin, Colonel A A 148
Sviatopolk-Mirsky, Prince 14, 15
Sverdlov (Bolshevik) 90, *90, 94*,
106
Syrovy, General 114, 115
Syrstov (Bolshevik) 183
Sytin, General (Red Army) 107

Tereshchenko, M 59

Tikhon, Patriarch 170, 176
Timoshenko, later Marshal S 107, 151
Tomsky, Politburo member 174
trade unions 92, 167, 169, 171
Trotsky, Leon 13, 21, 61, 70, 94, 167, 170, 171, 172, 172, 177, 180
    at Brest-Litovsk 102, 103
    and Czech Legion 109, 110
    fall and deportation 174-5, 180
    foreign minister 86, 92-3, 154
    leader of MRC 73, 90
    in 1905 Revolution 15, 16
    in October Revolution 71-4, 76-8, 81, 85, 94
    in Petrograd Soviet 71-3, 81
    and Red Army 103, 106-7, 120, 133, 143, 146-53, 159, 166
Trushin (Bolshevik) 94
Tsarskoye Selo 49, 50-51, 55, 121
Tsereteli (social democrat) 60
Tukhachevsky, later Marshal M 117, 143, 148-52 passim, 154, 167
Turkestan 98, 99, 100, 120, 150, 151
Turkey 25, 26, 27

Ukraine 35, 60, 95, 96, 103, 107, 108, 128, 131, 136-8, 143, 148, 152, 174

Ukrainians 66, 95, 120, 128, 130, 132, 143, 146
Ulagay, General 133, 134, 137
Ulmanis, Latvian premier 139, 140
Ulyanov, Alexander 13, 19, 146
Ulyanov, V I see Lenin
Ulyantsov, L I 106
Ungern, General Baron von 152
United States 109, 154, 156
    US forces 123-4, 124, 125, 153, 156, 158, 162-3
Uritsky (Bolshevik) 90, 94
Uvarov, General (White) 130

Vatsetis, Colonel I I 94, 107, 120, 146, 148, 149, 150
Verkhovsky, General 66, 75
Verzhbitsky, General (White) 117
Vinogradov (Socialist Revolutionary) 114
Vladivostok 108, 110-11, 113, 122, 153, 154, 156
Volkov, Ataman 116
Volkov, Ambassador 180
Volodarsky, Commissar 97
Vologodsky (Socialist Revolutionary) 114
Voroshilov, later Marshal K Y 97, 107, 147, 150, 151, 186-7
Voyeykov, General 31
Voytinsky, Commissar 93

Voytsekhovsky, General (White) 110-11, 117, 122, 123
Vsevolod, General 150

Waldemar, Professor 139
Warsaw 35, 47, 143, 180
Weygand, General M 143
What is to be Done? (Chernyshevsky) 19 (Lenin) 20-21
White Russians 109-14, 115, 116-25, 130, 132-43, 146, 148, 149-51, 155, 158-9, 161, 162, 169
William II, Emperor 25
Wilson, Woodrow 135, 156, 161
Witte, Count 15, 25
World War I 24, 32-9, 47, 66
    economic/social problems in 44-5, 45, 62, 66-7
    maps 31, 37
Wrangel, General 131-4 passim, 136-8

Yakir (Red Army) 148
Yanushkevich, General 33, 36, 46-7
Yegorev, General A I 107, 143
Yegorev, General V N 150, 152
Yelisarov, Mark 61
Yeremeyev, K S 106

Yudenich, General N N 141, 142, 147
Yurenev, I 74
Yusupov, Prince 42
Yuzefovich, General 94, 133

Zakharov, General (White) 121, 122
Zakharov, General K P 142
Zakutovsky, General 38
Zalutsky, P 48
Zasulich, Vera 20, 21
zemstva 12, 14, 39, 43, 55, 59
Zenzinov (Socialist Revolutionary) 114
Zheleznyakov, Anatoly 83
Zhilinsky, General 33
Zhloba, General 137
Zhukov, later Marshal G K 148, 151
Zinoviev, G E 61, 70, 70, 71-2, 74, 102, 167, 169, 174-5, 180
Zubatov, General 12, 15

Acknowledgments

The Publisher would like to thank Stephen Dalziel for his help in the preparation of this book and Ron Watson for compiling the index. We would also like to thank the following for supplying illustrations:

Archiv Gerstenberg: pages 1, 6, 8, 13 (bottom), 16, 17, 18 (top), 20, 21 (top & bottom), 22-3, 27, 35, 42, 43 (top), 51 (bottom), 54, 61, 63 (bottom), 64, 65, 70 (both), 71 (top), 73 (bottom), 75 (top), 84 (top), 87 (top), 107 (top), 120, 121 (top), 147 (top), 154 (top), 155 (top), 188-9 (all four).
BBC Hulton Picture Library: pages 30, 30-1, 58, 60, 67, 72, 79 (bottom), 80 (bottom), 88-9 92 (top), 96, 98, 99 (bottom), 100 (top), 102, 104-5, 109, 115

(bottom), 116 (bottom), 123 (both), 132 (bottom), 135 (bottom), 136 (top), 139 (top), 142 (top), 143, 144-5, 147 (bottom), 148 (top), 149 (top), 152 (top), 158 (top), 159 (bottom), 160 (both), 161 (top), 166, 167 (both), 168 (both), 169, 171 (bottom), 172 (both), 183 (bottom), 184 (top), 185 (bottom), 187.
Bison Picture Library: pages 43 (bottom), 45 (bottom), 64 (bottom), 66, 86 (bottom), 97, 107 (bottom), 110 (top), 111 (top), 118, 136 (bottom), 161 (bottom).
Communist Party UK Picture Library: page 159 (top).
Hoover Institute Archives: pages 14, 24 (both) (Isadore Yelsky Collection), 25, 29 (bottom), 44 (Winifred Ramplee Smith Collection), 47 (top), 57 (bottom), 57 (top) (Loehr Collection), 101 (Russian Pictorial

Collection), 111 (bottom), 112, 113 (both) (all four Eric Steinfeldt Collection), 114 (Russian Pictorial Collection), 138 (Boris Sokoloff Collection), 146, 150 (top), 158 (Marmaduke Clark Collection).
Robert Hunt Library: pages 13 (top), 25 (top), 29 (top), 33, 38, 40-1, 59, 99 (top), 122, 131 (both), 132 (top), 133, 134 (top), 162 (top), 163 (top).
Imperial War Museum, London: pages 26, 55 (bottom).
David King Collection: pages 4-5.
John Massey Stewart: pages 10, 12, 15, 18 (bottom), 48, 49, 55 (top), 77, 78 (top), 86 (top), 95, 115 (top); 163 (bottom).
Peter Newark's Historical Pictures: pages 2-3, 14, 19, 28, 32, 36, 39, 56, 103, 121 (bottom), 125, 135 (top), 177 (bottom), 184 (bottom).

Novosti Press Agency: pages 11, 37 (bottom), 46, 50, 51 (top), 52-3, 63 (top), 74 (both), 75 (bottom), 76 (top), 78 (bottom), 83 (top), 84, 91, 92 (bottom), 93, 94 (both), 100 (bottom), 117, 119 (top), 126-7, 128, 129 (bottom), 139 (bottom), 141, 142 (bottom), 149 (bottom), 150 (bottom), 151, 153 (bottom), 154 (bottom), 156 (top), 162 (bottom), 170, 171 (top), 173 (both), 174, 175, 176, 178-9, 180, 181, 182.
Photosource/Keystone Collection: pages 76 (bottom), 80 (top), 83 (bottom), 87 (bottom).
Society of Cultural Relations with the USSR: pages 7, 68-9, 81 (both), 108, 130, 155 (bottom), 157 (bottom), 164-5, 177 (top), 183, 186.
Soviet News Agency Tass: pages 71 (bottom), 79 (top), 82, 90, 106, 116 (top), 119 (bottom), 134 (bottom), 137, 140 (both), 153 (top), 156 (bottom), 157 (bottom).